BI [illegible] RAPHS

AROUND ROTHERHAM

ANTHONY P. MUNFORD

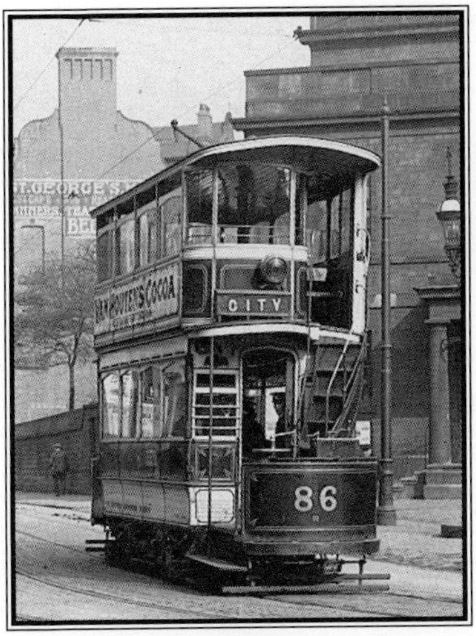

Budding BOOKS

First published in 1995 by
Sutton Publishing Limited · Phoenix Mill
Thrupp · Stroud · Gloucestershire · GL5 2BU

This edition first published in 2001 by
Budding Books, an imprint of
Sutton Publishing Limited

British Library Cataloguing in Publication Data.
A catalogue record for this book is available from
the British Library.

ISBN 11 84015 138 2

Typeset in 9/10 Sabon.
Typesetting and origination by
Sutton Publishing Limited.
Printed in Great Britain by
J.H. Haynes & Co., Sparkford.

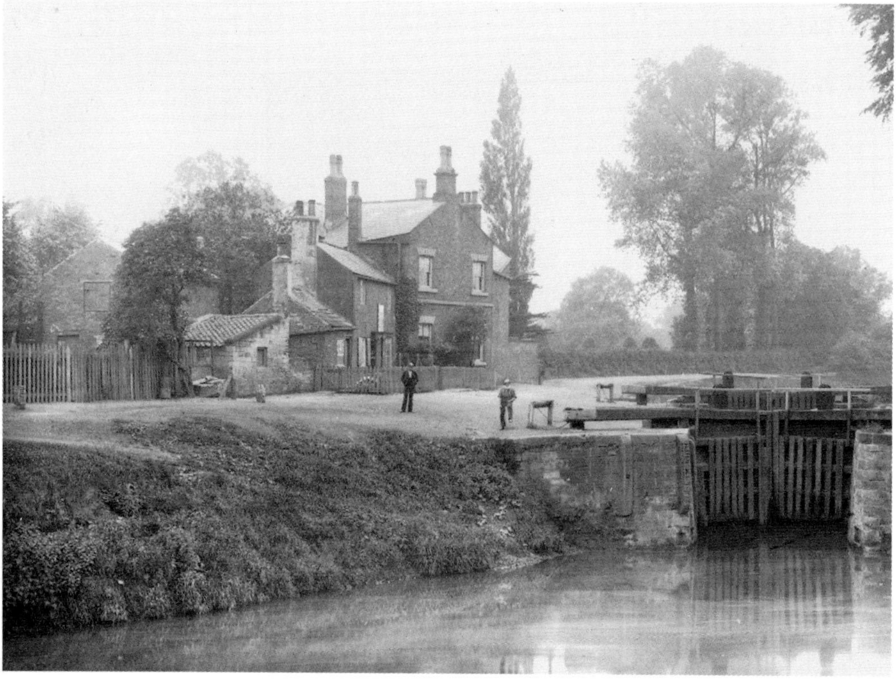

Aldwarke Lock, *c.* 1900.

Contents

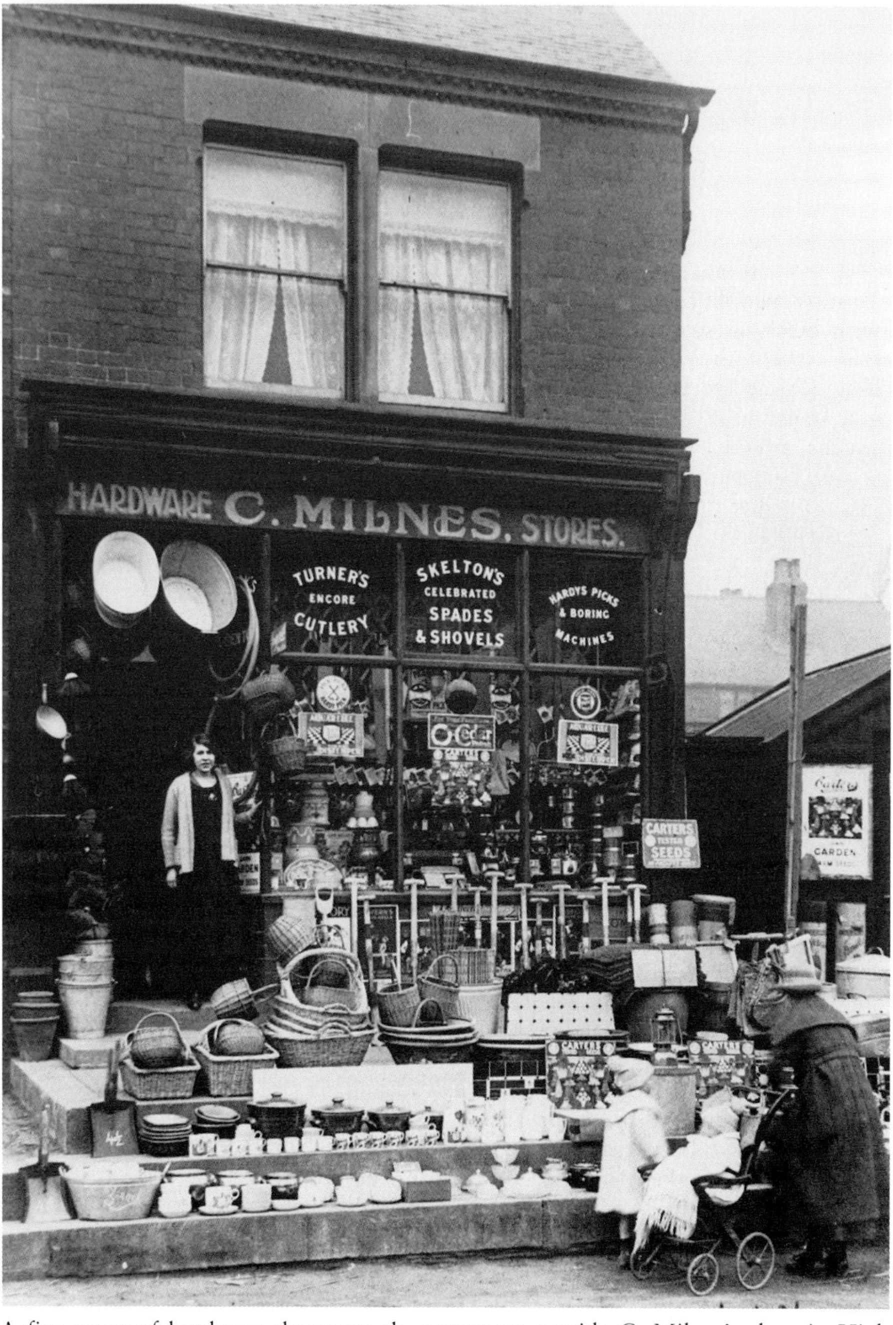

A fine array of hardware decorates the pavement outside C. Milnes's shop in High Street, Maltby, in 1930. The shop seems to be equipped to outfit everything from a private garden to a coal mine. [3536]

Introduction

To most people outside South Yorkshire, the name Rotherham is synonymous with belching steelworks, towering colliery headgear and other dark, satanic mills. The colliery headgear have all but gone and the surviving steelworks no longer belch red smoke, but even in Rotherham's industrial heyday the picture was inaccurate. Industrial towns such as Rotherham and Wath-upon-Dearne are balanced by the farming villages of Firbeck or Wentworth, ancient settlements such as Brampton-en-le-Morthen are paralleled by 20th-century creations like Thurcroft, country houses like Sandbeck or Aston Hall offset the terraces of miners' houses, while the slag heaps and pit tips must be set against the rolling countryside around Laughton.

The present Metropolitan Borough of Rotherham covers an area of 69,881 acres and has a population of around 250,000. Although the scars of industry past and present disfigure large areas, there have always been large acreages devoted to farming. Coal measures sandstone dominates the geology of the western side of the borough while the east lies on magnesian limestone. These differences are reflected in the varied building styles and history of the two areas.

The presence of seams of coal and ironstone shaped the industrial heritage of the area. These seams were first exploited in the north where they were closest to the surface. The Romans were smelting iron at their fort at Templeborough in the 1st century AD and the monks of Kirkstead Abbey exploited the iron ore near Scholes from the 12th century. The expansion of coal mining and iron and steel plants around Rotherham came in the mid-18th century, following the completion of the Don Navigation through Rotherham to Tinsley and the discovery that iron could be smelted with coke. As demand increased and deep mining techniques were perfected, new mines were sunk around Maltby, Dinnington and Wath, turning sleepy villages into colliery towns. In more recent years the mines have closed one by one, and traditional industries such as steel have contracted.

Since the mid-19th century these developments and their impact on the landscape have been recorded by photographers. Some of the photographs in this book were taken for official purposes, others where taken by amateur or professional photographers. The great majority, however, first appeared as picture postcards. The modern local historian owes a great debt to the efficiency of the Post Office in the early years of this century. A postcard could be guaranteed to arrive the next day, if not the same day. This meant that our ancestors sent a postcard where we would use the telephone. As a result, picture postcards were produced and sent in great numbers. The survivors now provide valuable evidence of a world that has long gone. Many were published by national firms such as Francis Frith's or Valentine's, but large numbers were also printed by local photographers such as Crowther Cox of Rotherham or E.L. Scrivens of Doncaster. Local photographers could react quickly to local events, rushing out views of tram and railway accidents, fires and local celebrations. As a result, many of the most interesting cards came from local publishers.

If your particular village or interest has been omitted, I can only apologise. I have tried to illustrate as many aspects of life in the Rotherham area as the available space and photographs have allowed. In a book of this size it has not proved possible to include every village and hamlet or every sport and industry.

Section One

TOWNS AND VILLAGES

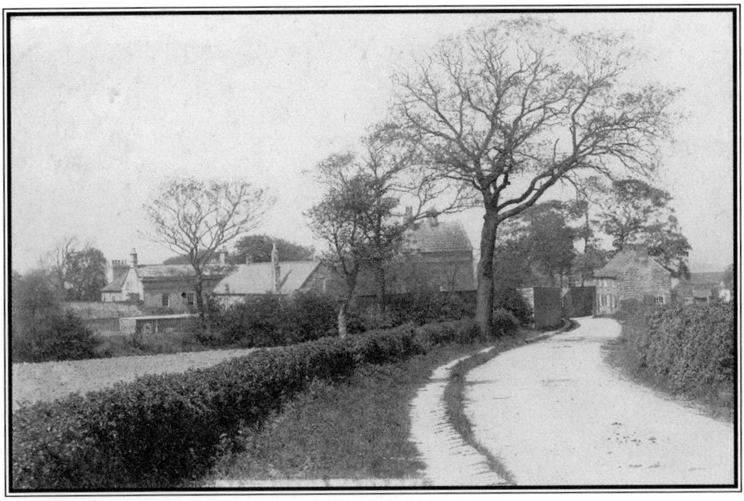

Few of the motorists speeding down Herringthorpe Valley Road will realise that Herringthorpe was a sleepy hamlet until the present dual carriageway was built in the 1930s. In this view, from a postcard postmarked 1908, Herringthorpe Hall, home of the Jubb family in the 19th century, can be seen at the left. [2706]

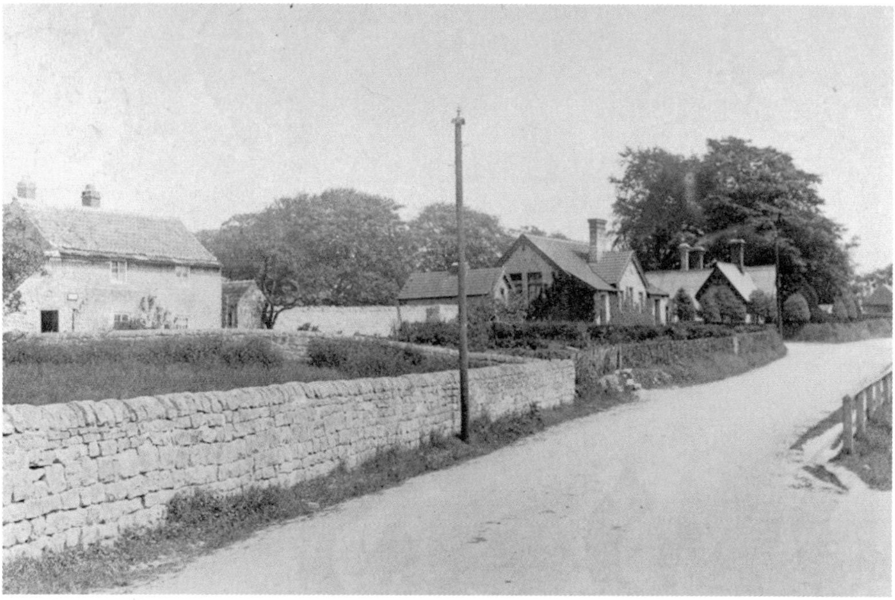

Stone is a small hamlet on the Maltby–Blyth road, on the edge of the park at Sandbeck. Most of the inhabitants worked on the Sandbeck estate, and the school, in the centre of this postcard (postmarked 1905), was supplied by the Earl of Scarbrough. Beyond the school is one of the lodges to the park. [13593]

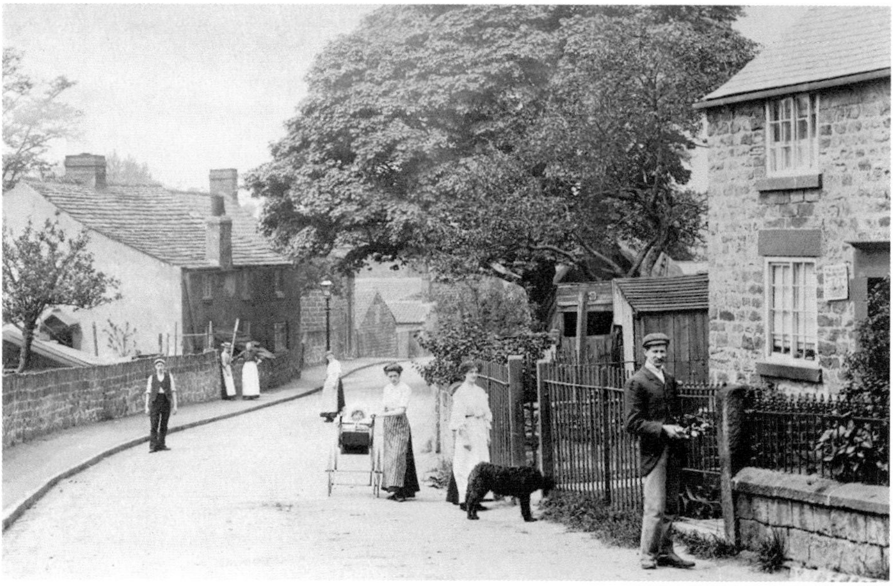

A baby takes the air in its perambulator on a sunny day in about 1905 on the Green, Whiston. [10970]

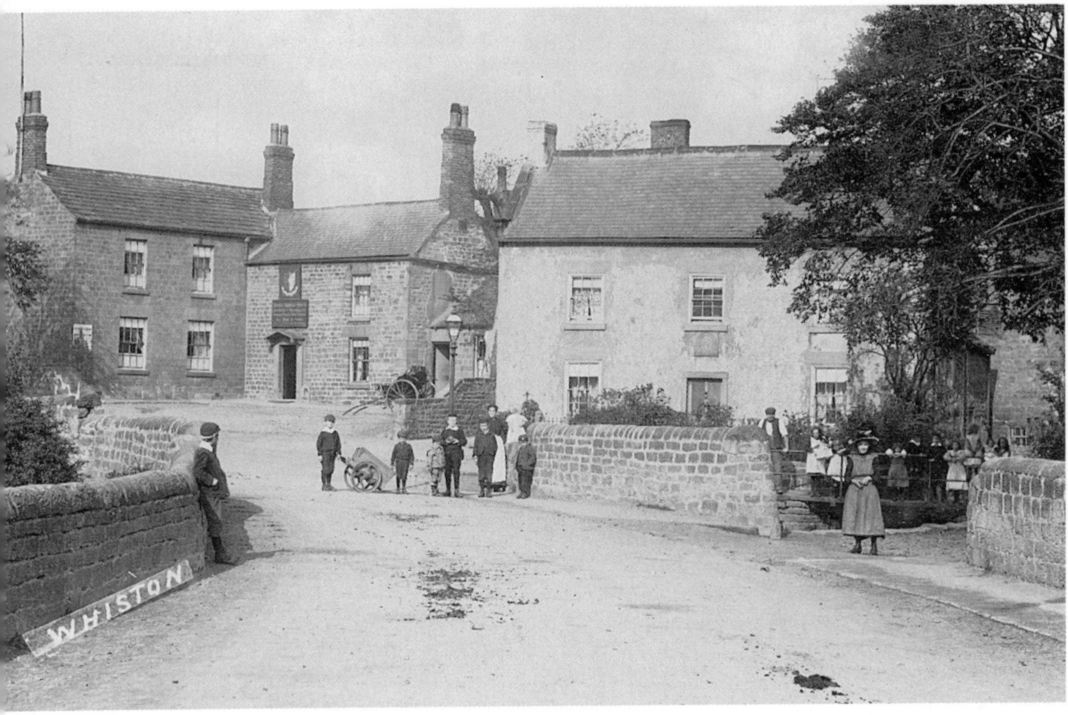

Pleasley Road, Whiston, *c.* 1903, with a collection of village children watching the photographer. In the background is the Sitwell Arms. The pub took its name from the Sitwell family of Renishaw (Derbyshire), who bought the lordship of the manor of Whiston from the Duke of Norfolk in 1823. [4419]

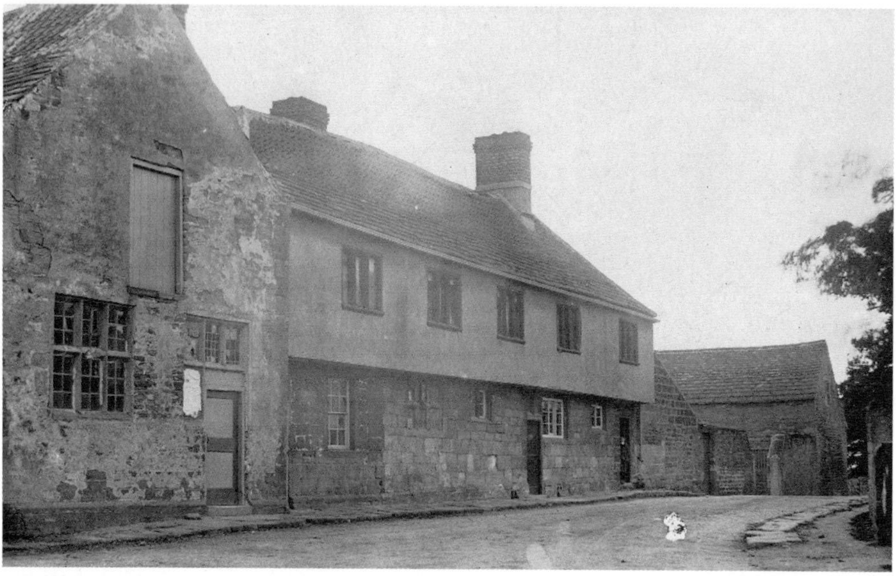

The three cottages in the centre of this view of Brampton-en-le-Morthen in about 1910 were originally the Manor farmhouse. As the projecting upper storey suggests, this is a timber-framed building dating from the 16th and 17th centuries. The wing at the left was used as a Wesleyan meeting-house. [811]

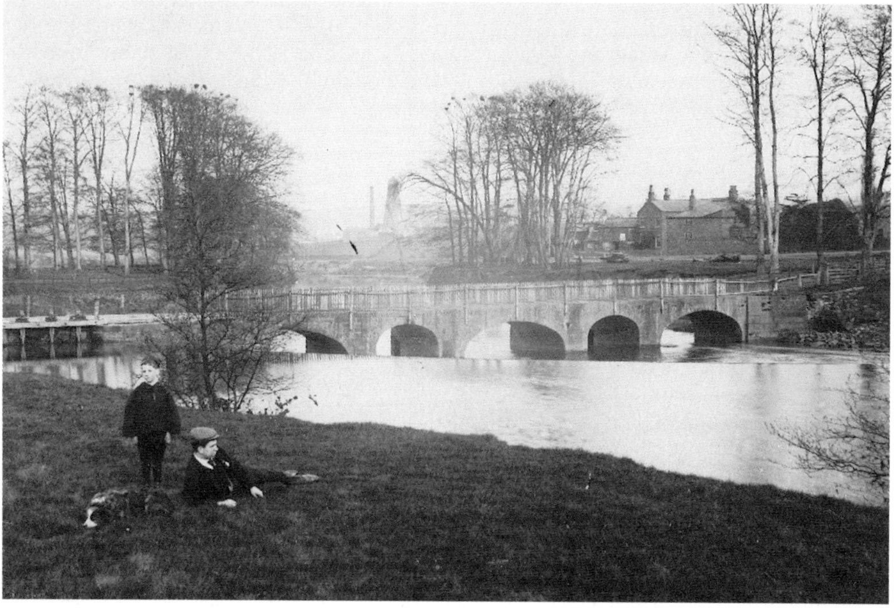

The bridge carrying Aldwarke Lane from Parkgate and Aldwarke to Dalton over the River Don, *c.* 1895. Salmon were reputedly caught at Aldwarke Weir in the 18th century. The tower of Dalton Brook windmill is visible in the distance. [6284]

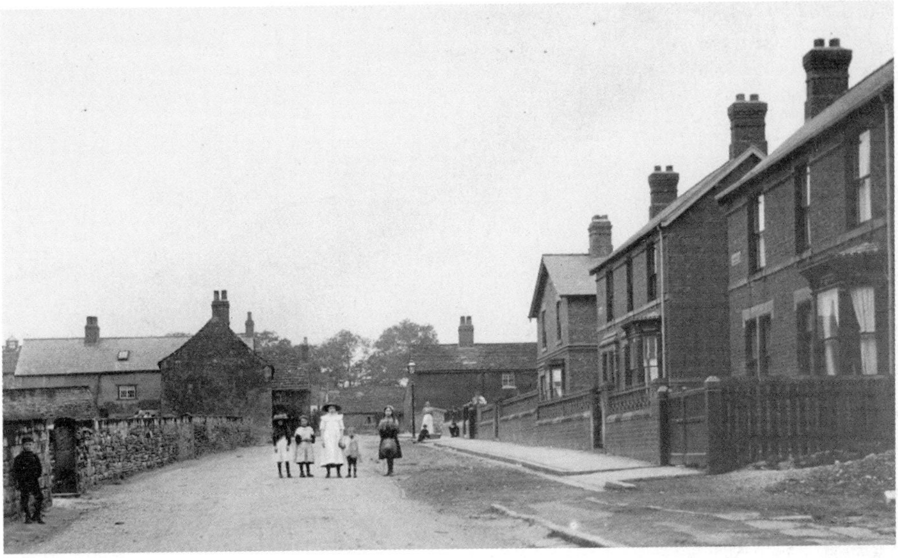

The girl at the left of the group of children in the centre of Church Street, Greasbrough, has been identified as Mabel Mercer (later Sheard), who was still alive in 1993, aged 91. To her left are Hettie Goodall and Alice May Mitchell. Alice's mother, Alice Mary Maud Mitchell, stands in the background. [5138]

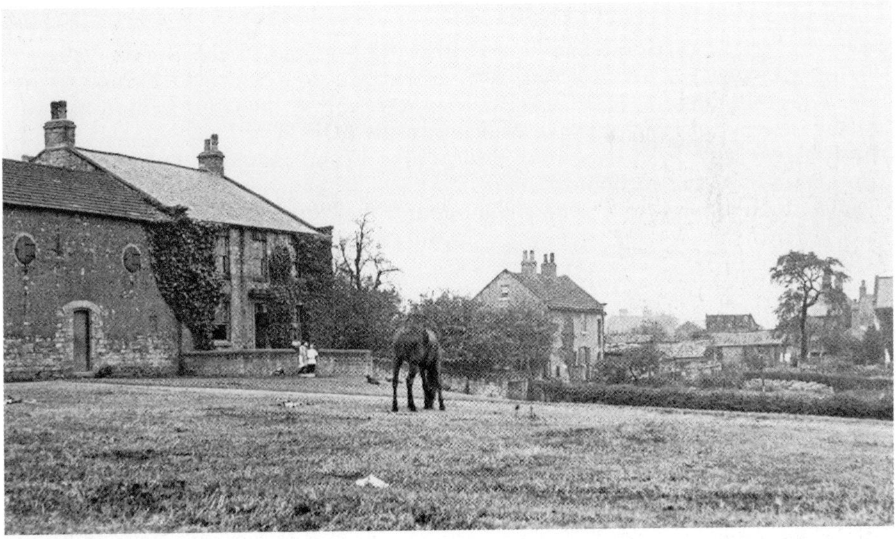

The house to the left of the horse is 1 Greenside, Greasbrough, a farmstead belonging to the Wentworth estate. Until 1883 it was the home of Edward Jackson, farmer, clerk to the Local Board and insurance agent. He was followed by Mr Cobham, head gardener at Wentworth. Some rooms in the house were used as the Parish Church Institute and were the headquarters of the local Home Guard during the Second World War. [5178]

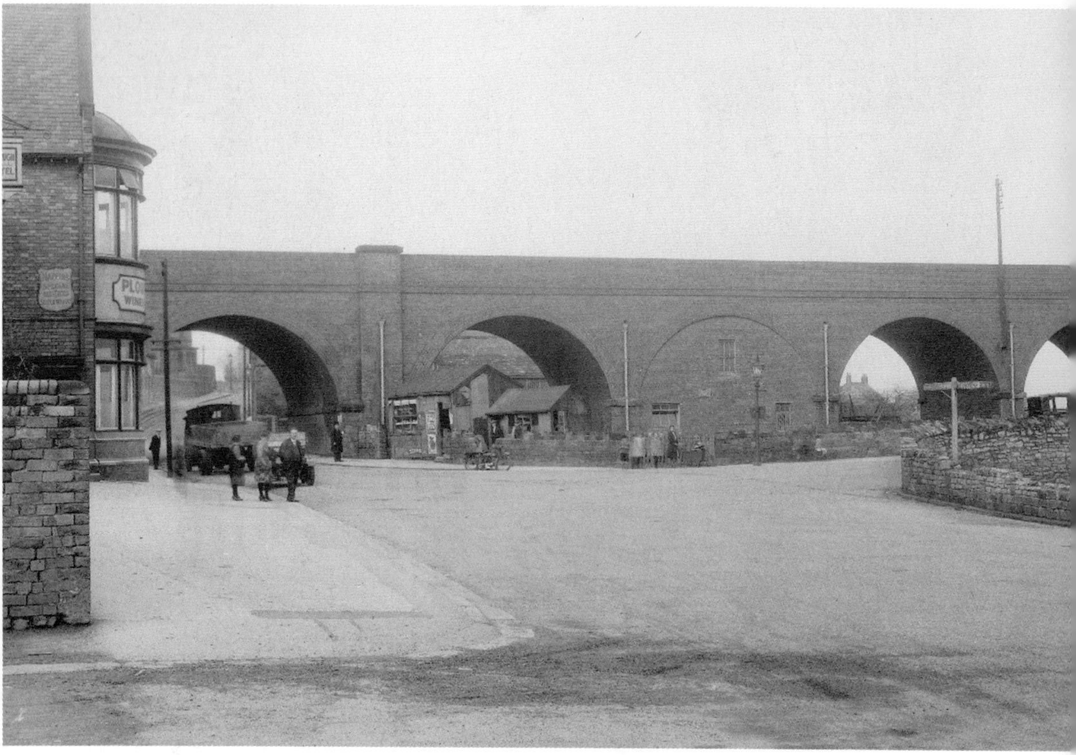

Nine brick arches carry the Sheffield District Railway across the Rother Valley at Catcliffe, 1930. Opened in 1900, the railway was the Sheffield branch of the Lancashire, Derbyshire & East Coast Railway, later part of the Great Central Railway. Passenger trains ran from Sheffield Midland to the LDECR at Langwith and later to Mansfield, but lasted only until 1939. Beneath the second arch, the two wooden sheds are occupied by J. Russell, boot repairer (right), and an anonymous grocer and fruiterer. The road to Treeton leads off to the right, opposite the Plough Hotel. [8754]

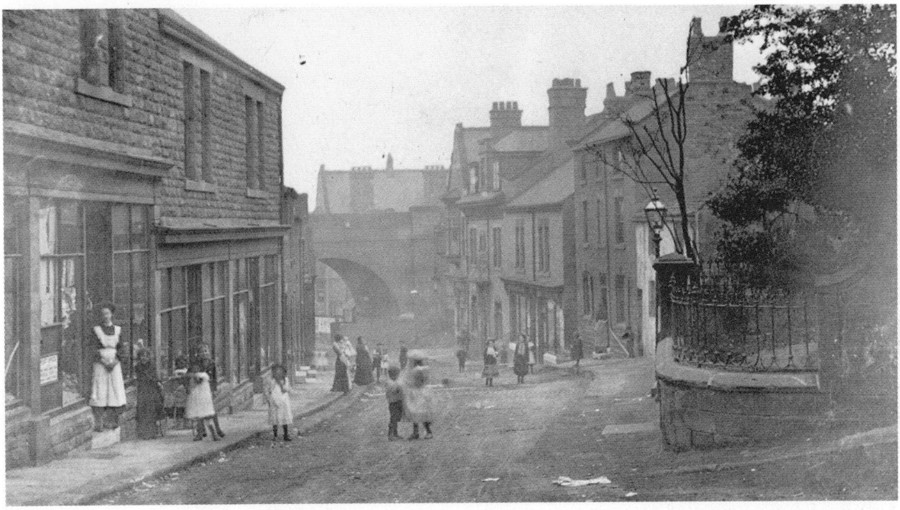

Catcliffe, like so many settlements in the Rotherham area, was a small hamlet until coal mines were developed in the area in the 19th century. The children standing around in the street suggest that, in the early years of the 20th century, traffic was light. [10861]

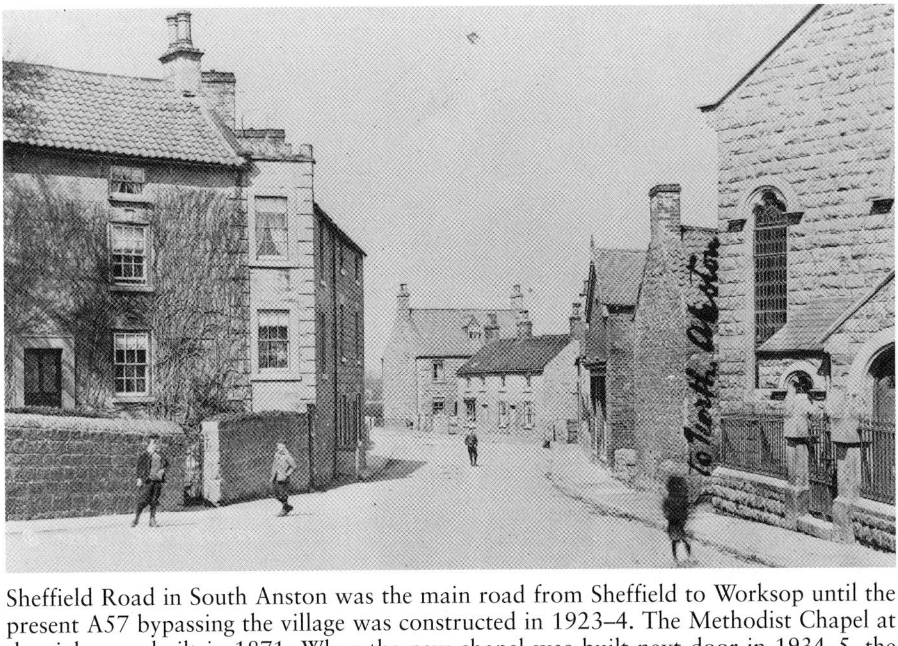

Sheffield Road in South Anston was the main road from Sheffield to Worksop until the present A57 bypassing the village was constructed in 1923–4. The Methodist Chapel at the right was built in 1871. When the new chapel was built next door in 1934–5, the old chapel continued in use as a hall. [581]

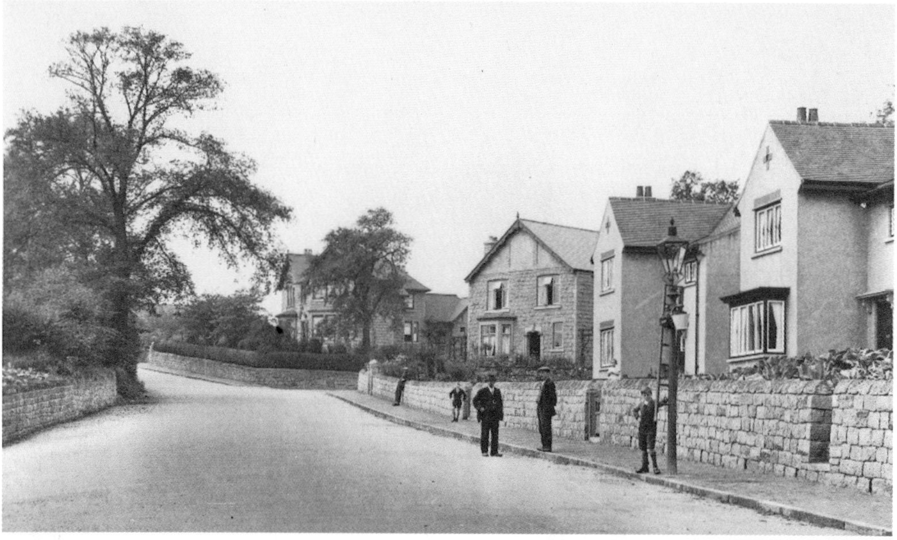

Judging by the ladder and bucket, the boy leaning against the gas lamp in Crowgate, South Anston, during the 1920s, had been engaged in cleaning the lamp before the photographer appeared. Axle Lane leads off to the right in the distance. The two houses either side of Axle Lane were reputedly the last two in the village to be built from local stone. The houses at the right were built in the mid-1920s. [576]

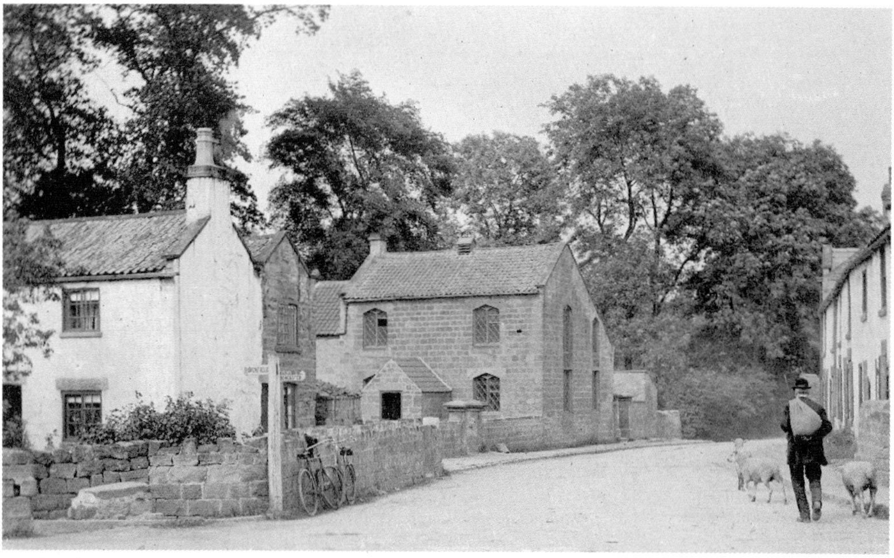

In the first decade of the century there was little chance of any passing motor traffic disturbing these sheep being driven through Bramley. The shepherd is driving his small flock along Lidgett Lane in the direction of Bramley Grange. Moor Lane leads off to the left towards Ravenfield. The building in the centre of the picture served as the village school until 1909. [1035]

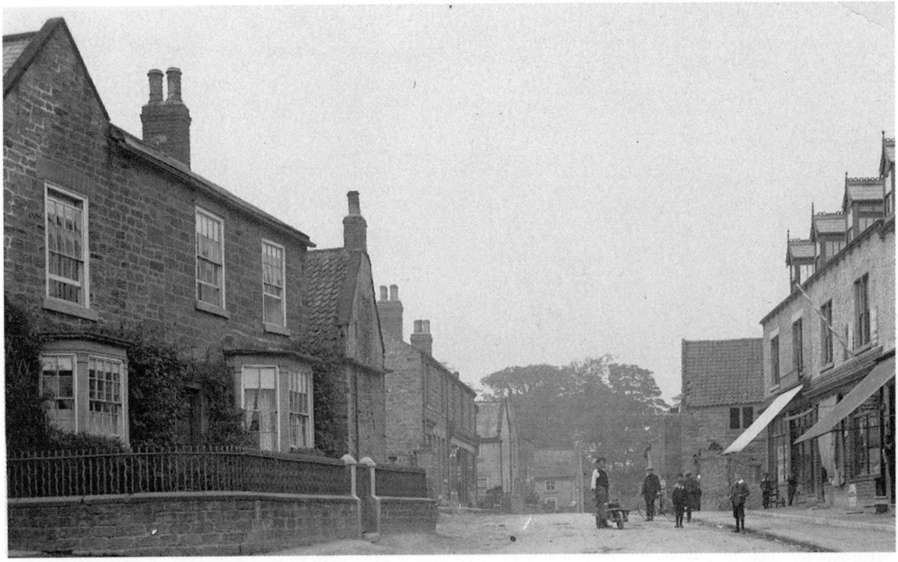

Even in Main Street, Bramley, it was quiet enough to trundle a wheelbarrow down the middle of the road, *c.* 1910. Note the prominent barber's pole at the right. [1025]

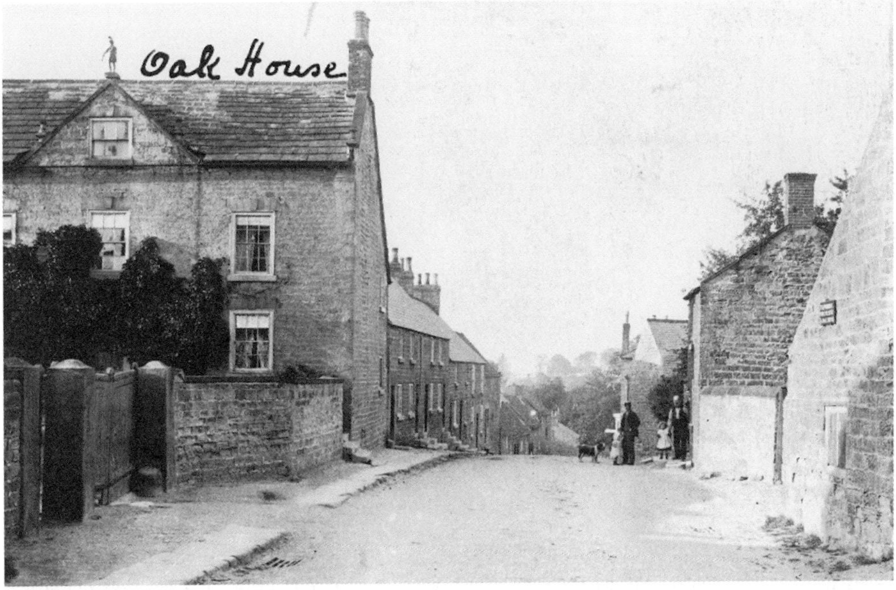

A view down the main street at Ravenfield in the early years of the century. Oak House (left) was one of several farmsteads in the village. The lead figure on the gable, said to be a Roman soldier, disappeared after the farm was sold by the Bosvile estate. [5857]

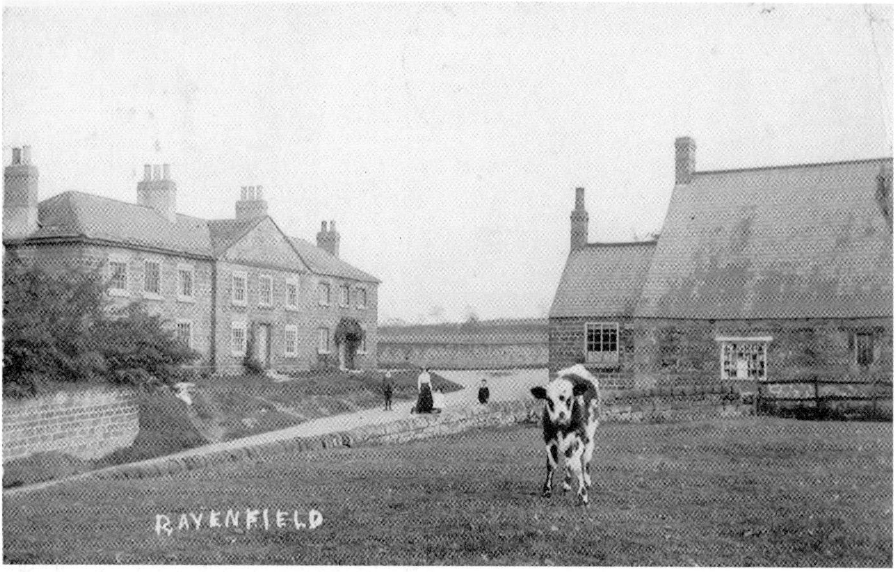

The row of three cottages at the left of this view of Ravenfield, *c.* 1903, was erected in about 1824 on the site of a small farmstead. Behind the middle cottage was a workshop used as a boot and shoemakers by William Wilson until his death in 1883. The inquisitive cow is standing in front of the village shop, off-licence and post office on the corner of Pingle Lane. [6381]

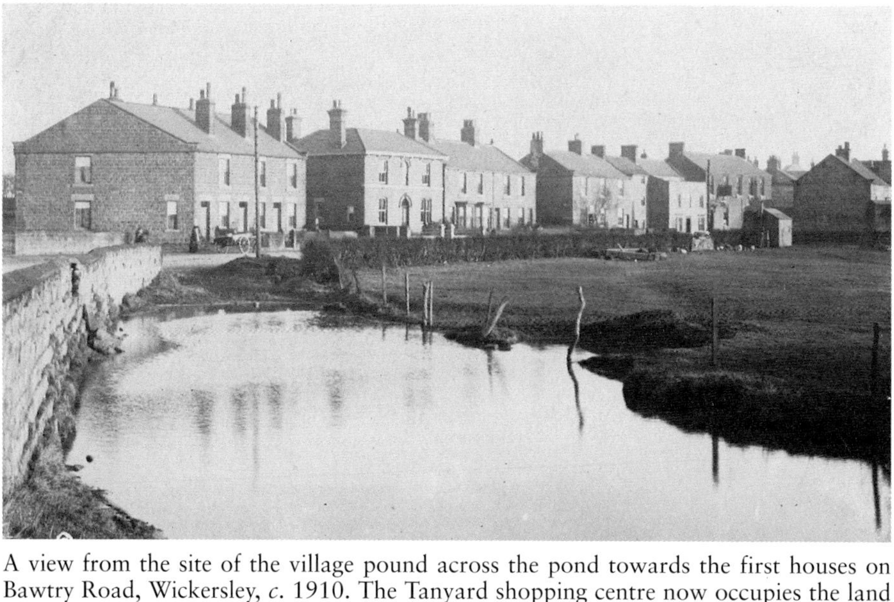

A view from the site of the village pound across the pond towards the first houses on Bawtry Road, Wickersley, *c.* 1910. The Tanyard shopping centre now occupies the land on the right-hand side of Bawtry Road. [84]

Although telegraph poles have been erected along Doncaster Road, Thrybergh, by about 1905, the road has still to be properly surfaced. A pony and trap makes its way towards Dalton. Houses have now replaced the trees at the left, while the barns in the background house Foster's garden centre. [4458]

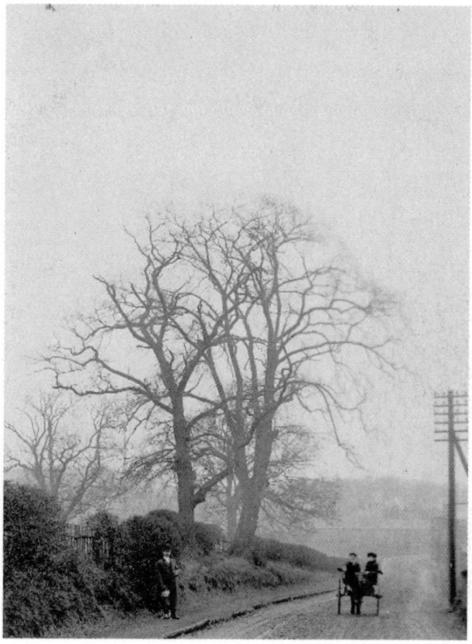

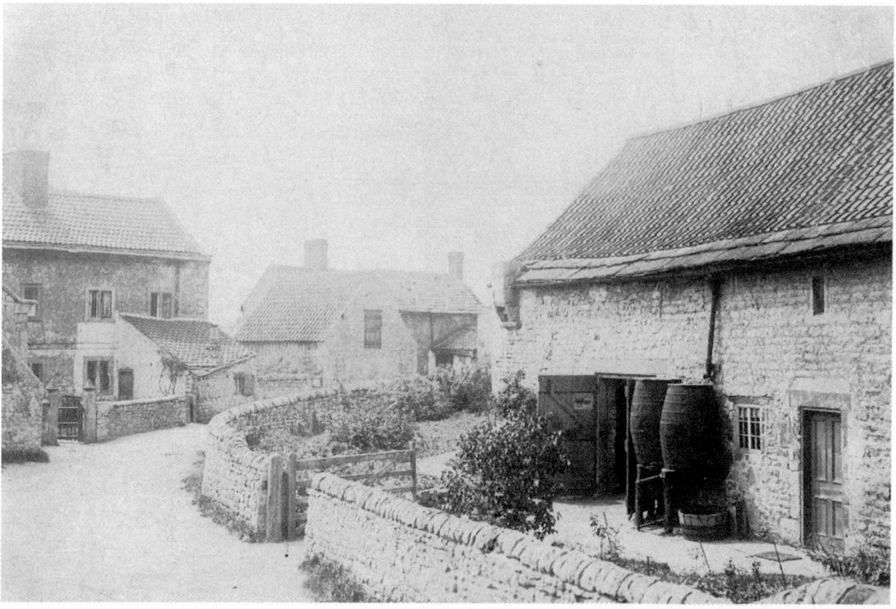

The cottages at Church Corner, Laughton-en-le-Morthen, seen here in about 1905, are built from local limestone with pantile roofs. The water in the area is naturally hard and the large water butts would have been used to maintain a supply of soft rainwater for laundry and washing. [13769]

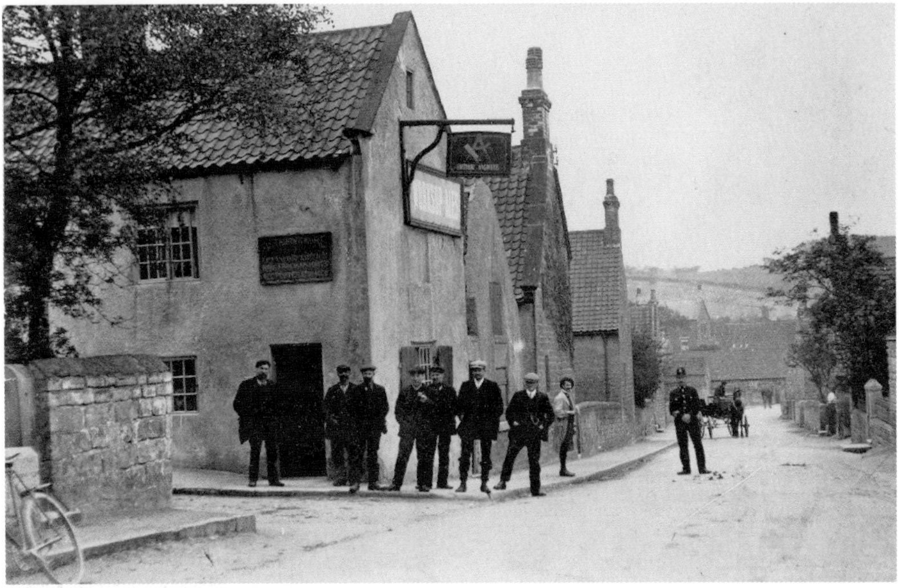

The village constable seems to be holding himself aloof from the group of villagers posing outside the Square and Compasses at Harthill, *c.* 1910. [2688]

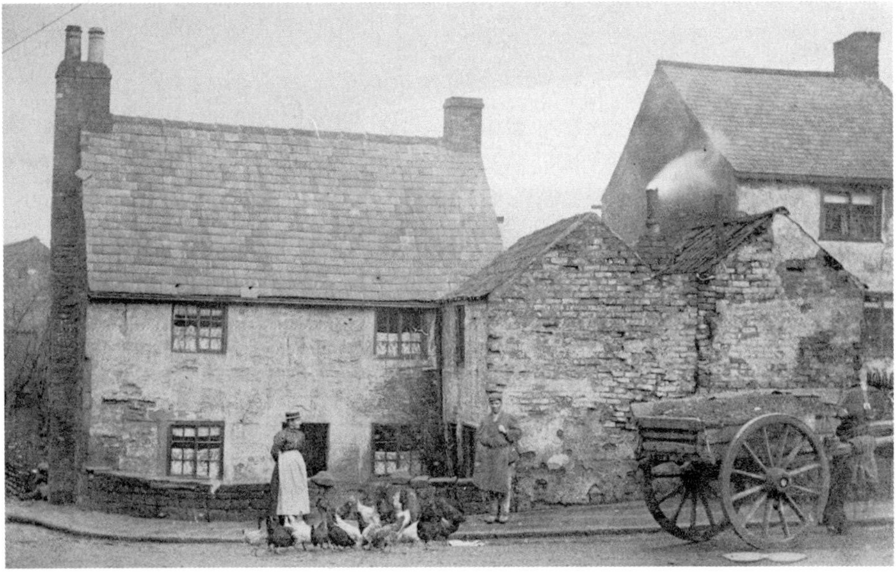

Front Street, Treeton, *c.* 1910, when it was still possible to feed the chickens in the road. [3105]

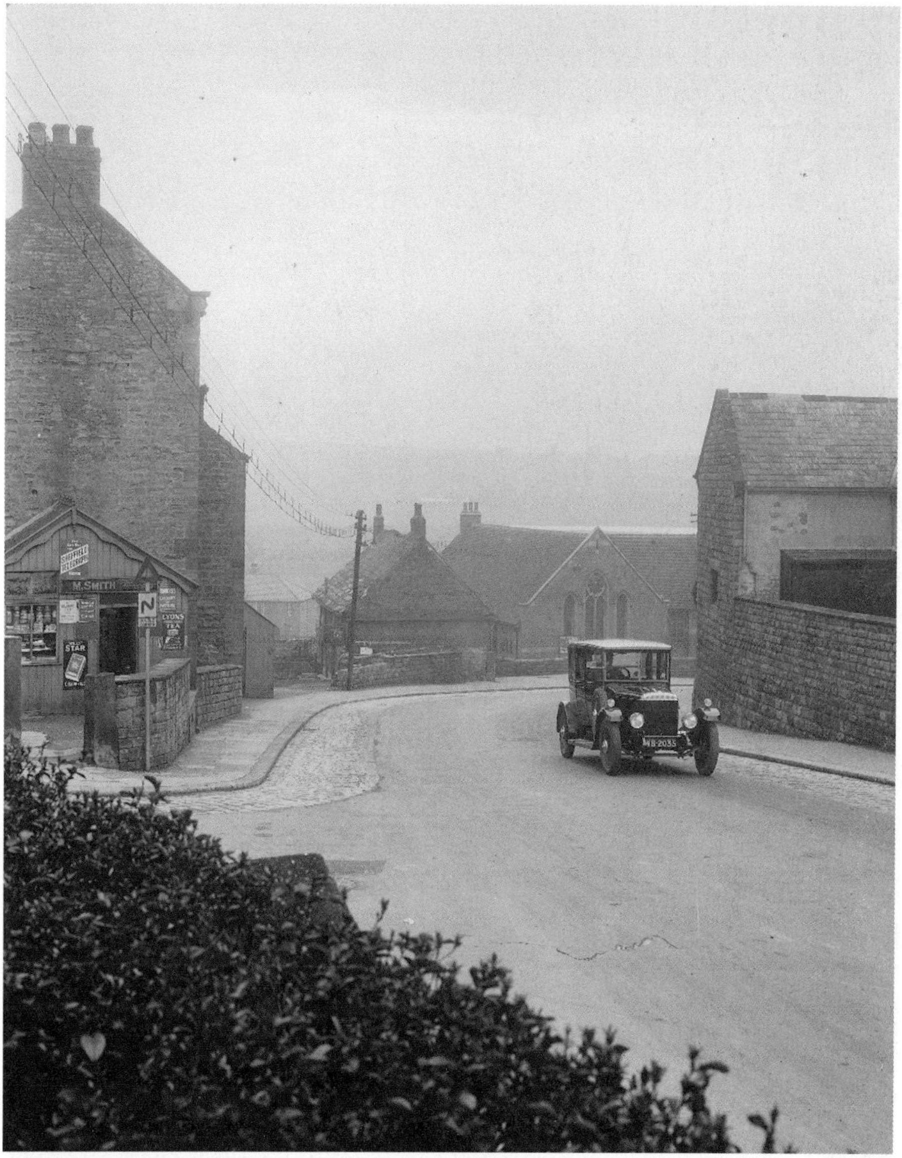

Station Road, Treeton, leads from the River Rother up to the village. Only the edges of the road were paved in 1930 and the photographer's Daimler would be asking for trouble if it was parked at that point today. Behind the car is the Baptist church, opened in 1924. At the left, M. Smith's general store occupies a small wooden building. [8759]

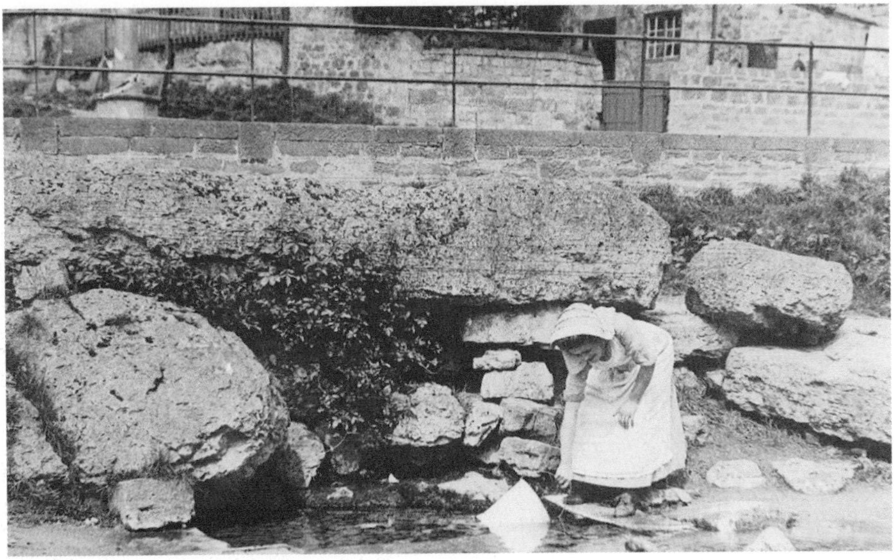

Fetching water was a continuous chore in the days before piped water supplies. This girl is filling her bucket at the Town Well in Blyth Road, Maltby, one of several public wells in the village, seen here in about 1905. [3527]

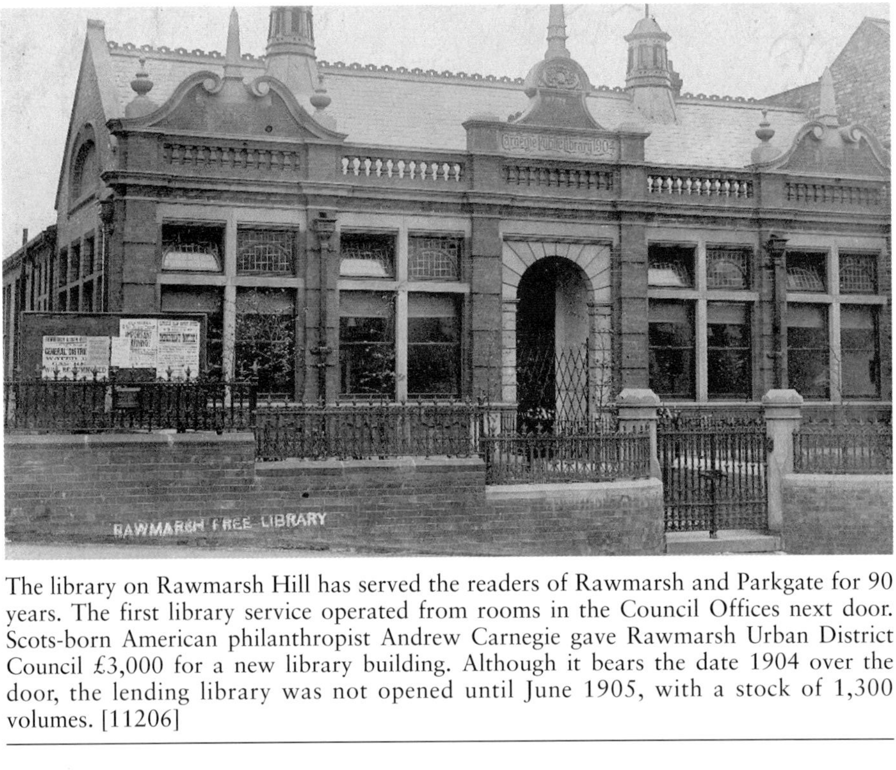

The library on Rawmarsh Hill has served the readers of Rawmarsh and Parkgate for 90 years. The first library service operated from rooms in the Council Offices next door. Scots-born American philanthropist Andrew Carnegie gave Rawmarsh Urban District Council £3,000 for a new library building. Although it bears the date 1904 over the door, the lending library was not opened until June 1905, with a stock of 1,300 volumes. [11206]

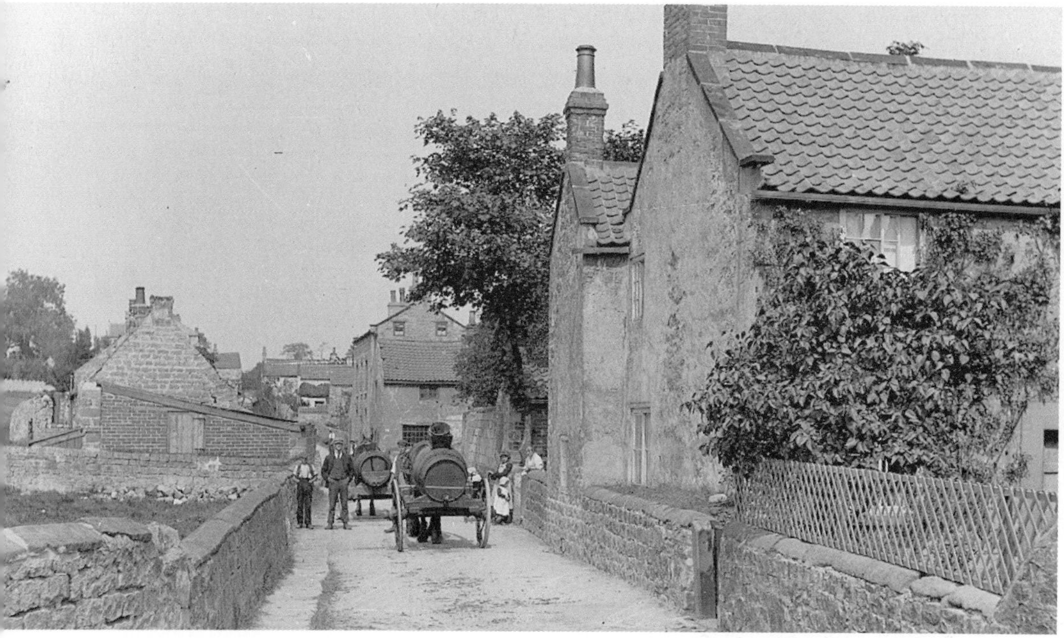

Millindale, Maltby, was much narrower in 1910 than it is today. The two water carts emphasise the problems in maintaining an adequate supply from wells and pumps in the days before piped water. [3574]

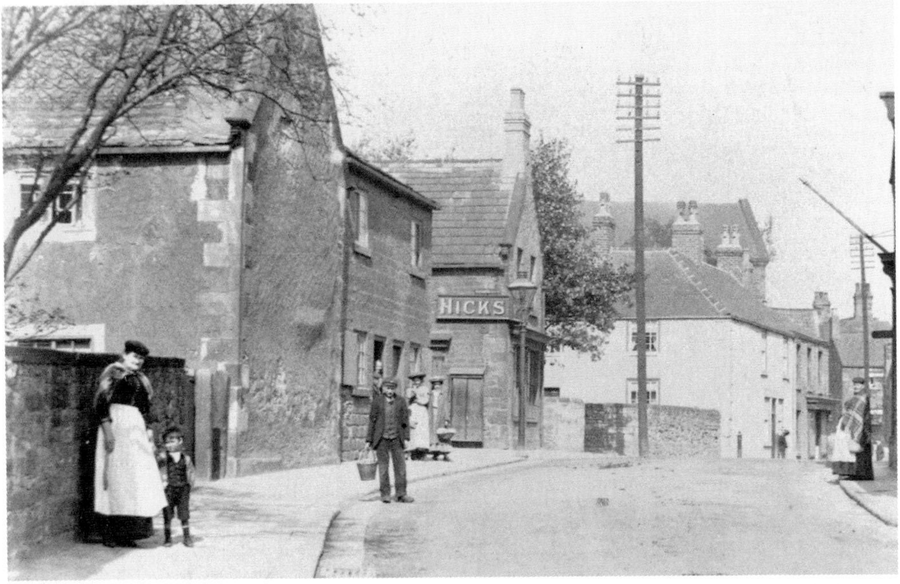

Henry Hicks's saddler's shop is prominent in the centre of this view of High Street, Rawmarsh, in the early years of the century. Immediately beyond the shop is Rawmarsh Manor House, above which can be seen the roof of the Wesleyan chapel. Hicks's shop and the Manor House were demolished for road widening in 1966. [11153]

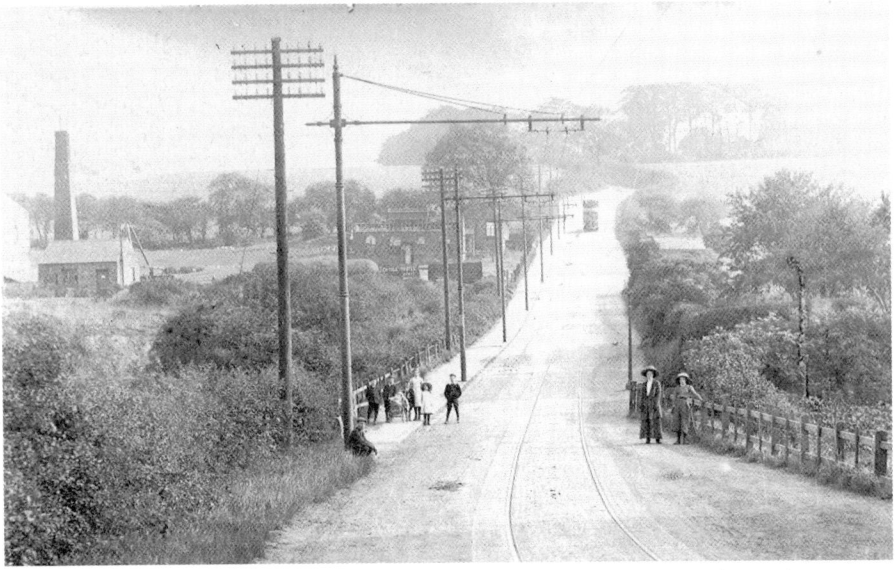

Warren Vale lies between Rawmarsh and Swinton. This view dating from about 1910 shows a Mexborough and Swinton Tramways car in the distance and the former Warren Vale Colliery on the left. The present road at Warren Vale was constructed in 1928–31 to bypass the old, winding road. [11150]

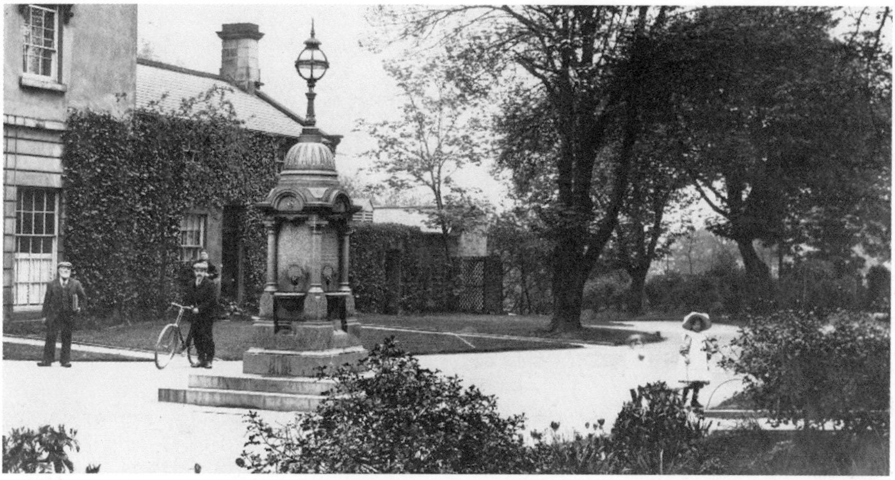

The Town Hall at Wath was originally a private house, erected in 1770, and was purchased by the Wath Local Board for £2,500 in 1891. The elaborate drinking fountain was erected by the townspeople in 1901 as a memorial to Wath brewer Spedding Whitworth, 'as a token of their appreciation of his generosity and the many services rendered by him; also as a personal tribute to his character and personal worth'. The fountain is now to be found in the Market Place on the High Street. [3310]

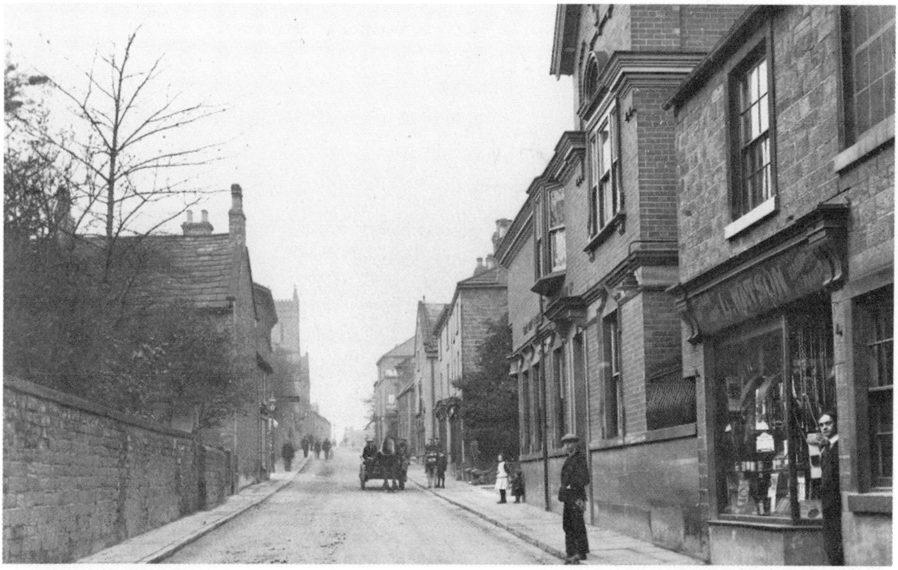

Wath-upon-Dearne was once known as the 'Queen of Villages', but with the sinking of collieries in the Dearne Valley it was transformed into a bustling town. This view up the High Street in about 1910 shows L. Watson's harness-making shop on the right. Tanning was an important industry in Wath so he could well have been using locally produced leather. The tower of Wath Wesleyan church can just be seen at the top of the hill. [3317]

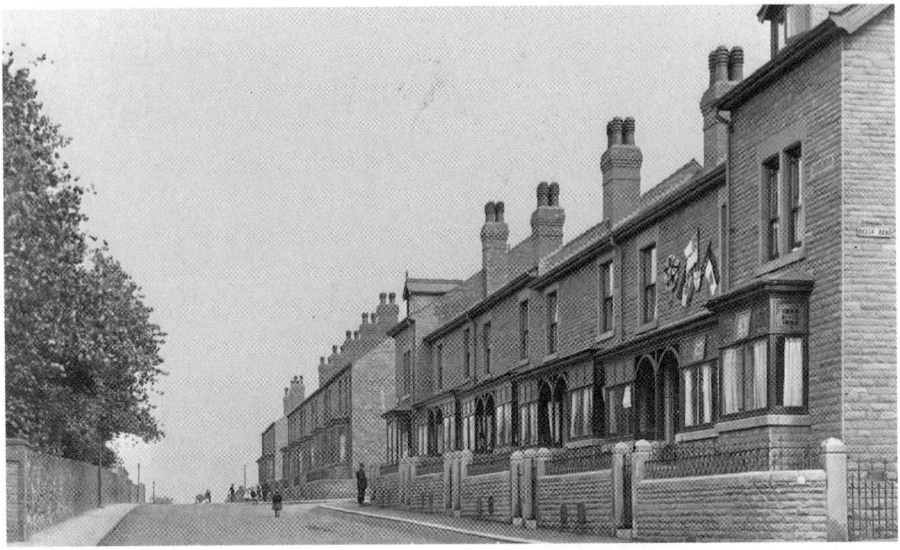

Judging by the clean nature of the stone, this terrace of houses on Doncaster Road, Wath, cannot have been up for long when this photograph was taken, *c.* 1910. A postman is standing at the corner of Avenue Road (centre). The reason for the flags on the house at the right is unclear. [3309]

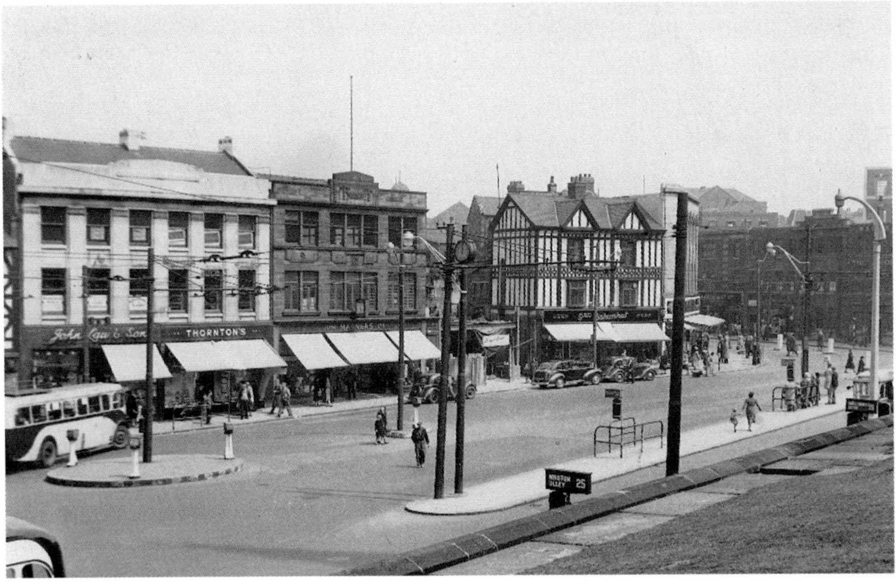

All Saints Square in the centre of Rotherham was formed in the early 1930s by the demolition of the property between College Street and the churchyard. Until 1972 it was the main bus and trolleybus interchange, but it is now pedestrianised. Thornton's sweetshop is still there but the other shops have changed ownership since this view was taken in about 1955. [13141]

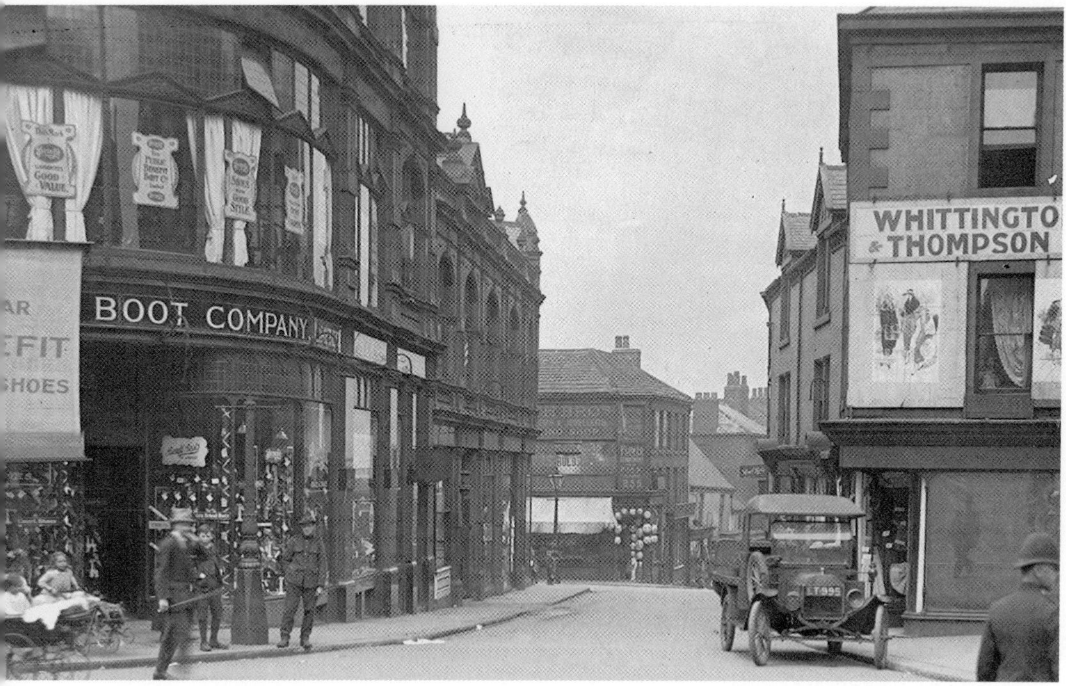

A Model T delivery van stands outside Whittington and Thompson's outfitters shop in Church Street, Rotherham, in the early 1920s. At the left is Imperial Buildings, erected in 1907 on the site of the medieval Shambles. The Public Benefit Boot Company occupies the corner shop. In the centre of the picture is the shop of Albert F. Upstone, seedsman, with displays of dried flowers around the door. [1348]

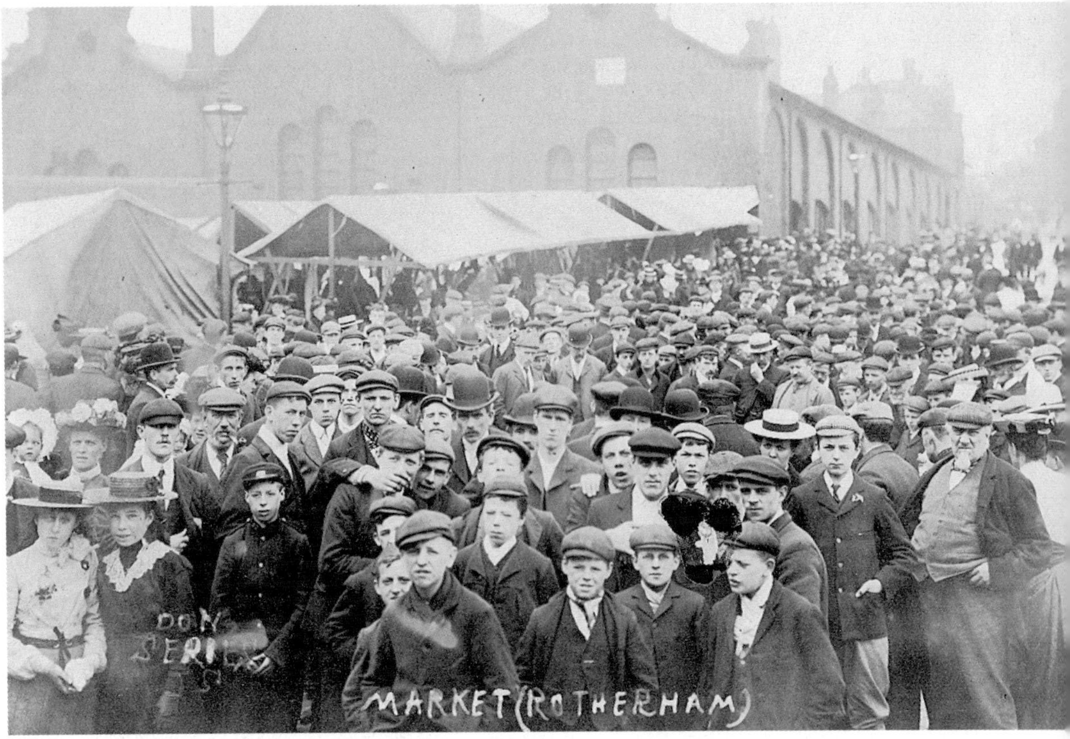

The odd straw boater can be seen among the sea of flat caps thronging Rotherham Market Place, *c.* 1905, suggesting that this photograph was taken in early summer. At the rear is the Market Hall, which was opened in 1889 and closed in 1971. The rear gables survived from its predecessor which burned down in 1888. [4472]

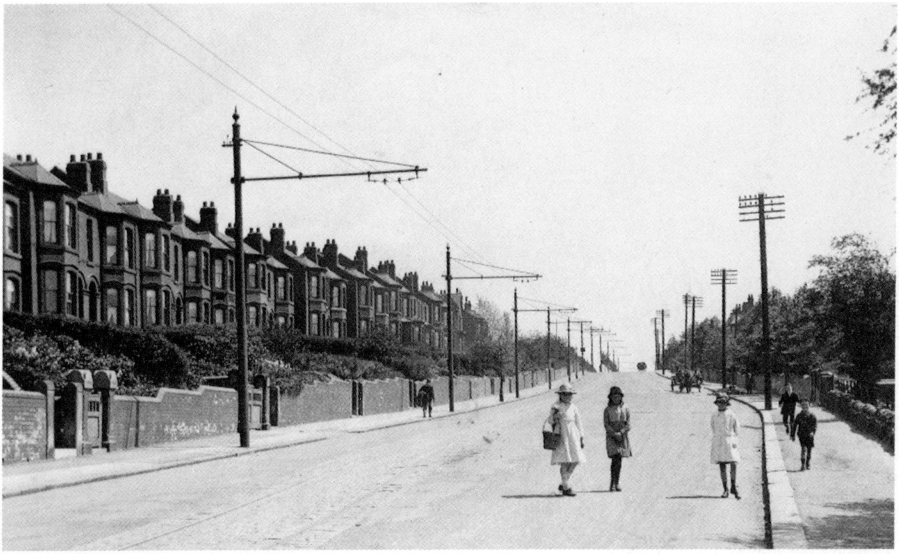

Broom Road, Rotherham, in the mid-1920s, with tramlines running towards the terminus at the Stag. The trolley bus wiring was extended from the Stag into the town centre in 1924, but the trams continued to run until the trolley bus service was extended into the town centre in 1929. The houses on the left-hand side of the road, erected in 1904–7, were designed by local architects Edward Hutchinson and Son. [4492]

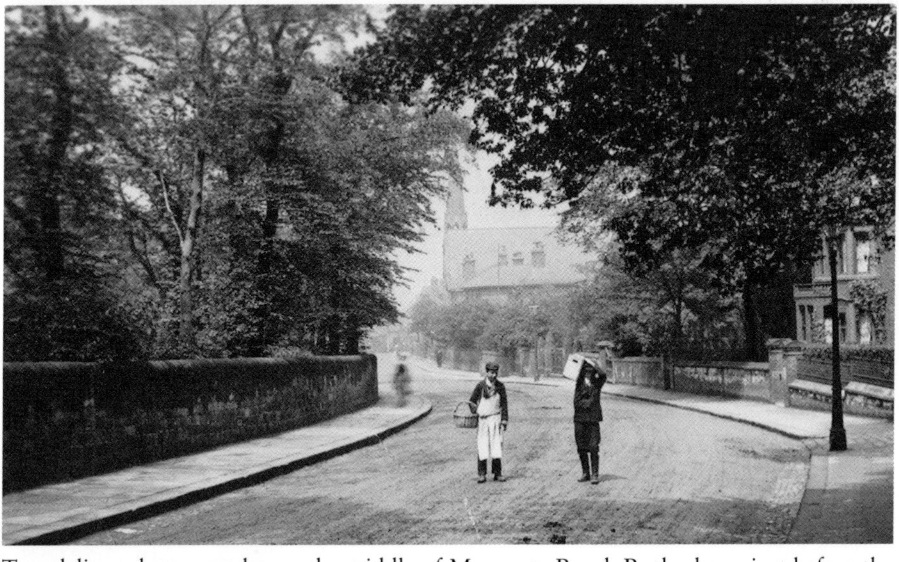

Two delivery boys wander up the middle of Moorgate Road, Rotherham, just before the First World War. South Grove School lies out of picture behind the wall to the left. The spire in the centre of the photograph belongs the Church of Our Father, a Unitarian chapel opened in 1880, and now used as a mosque. [4527]

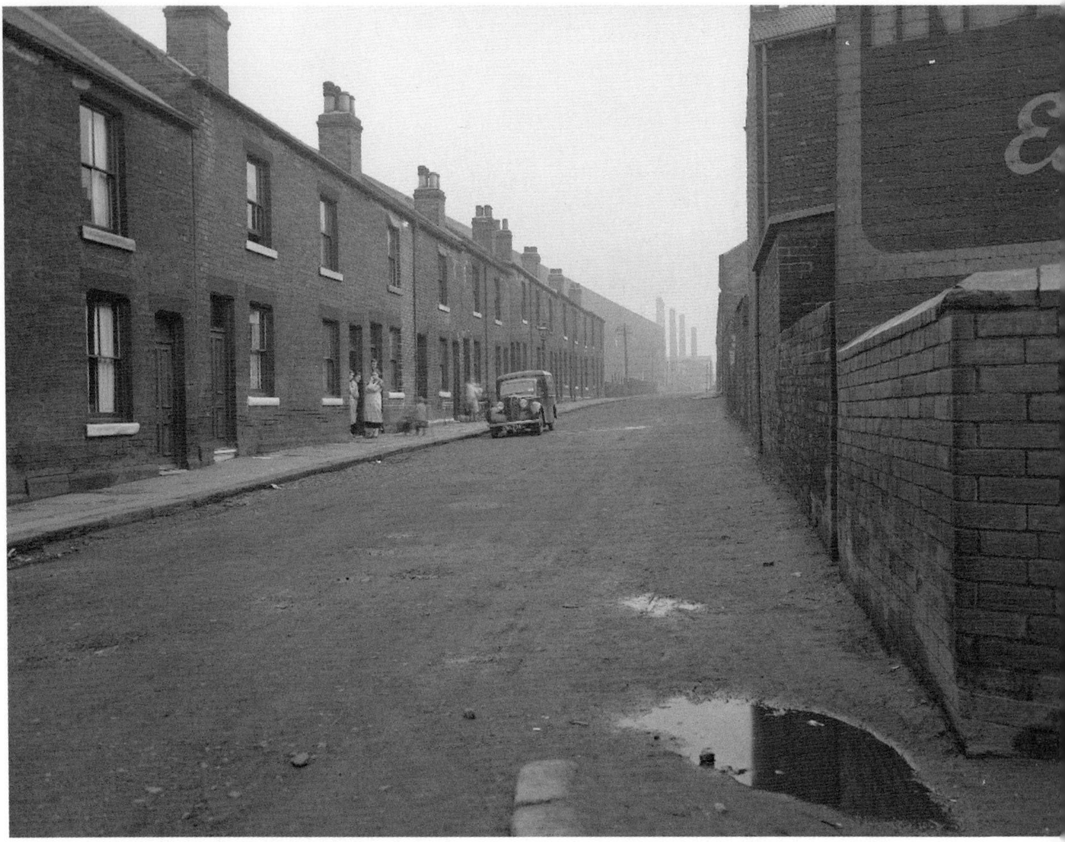

Most of the male inhabitants of Radcliffe Street at Templeborough would have worked at Steel, Peech and Tozer's steelworks, which overshadowed their houses. The houses were built in 1906–8 and are seen here in 1937. [8670]

Section Two

HOUSES, GREAT AND SMALL

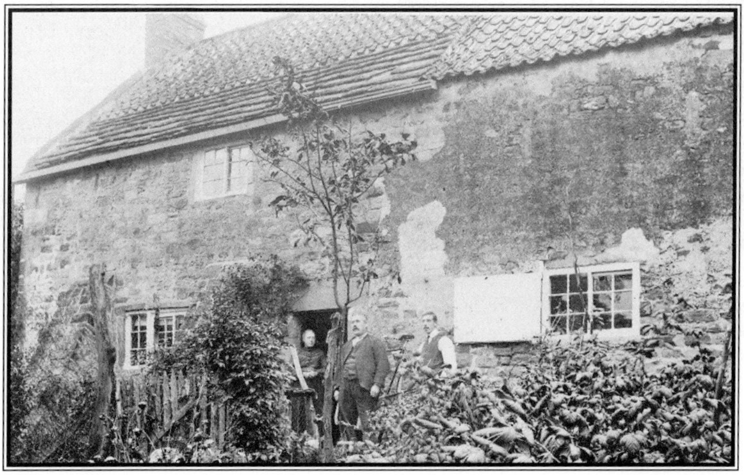

Spring Cottage, Ravenfield, disappeared in 1907 when it was demolished to allow the new railway line from Silverwood to Dinnington to be squeezed between Ravenfield Hall and the village. The cottage took its name from the nearby spring that was one of the main water supplies in the village. [5864]

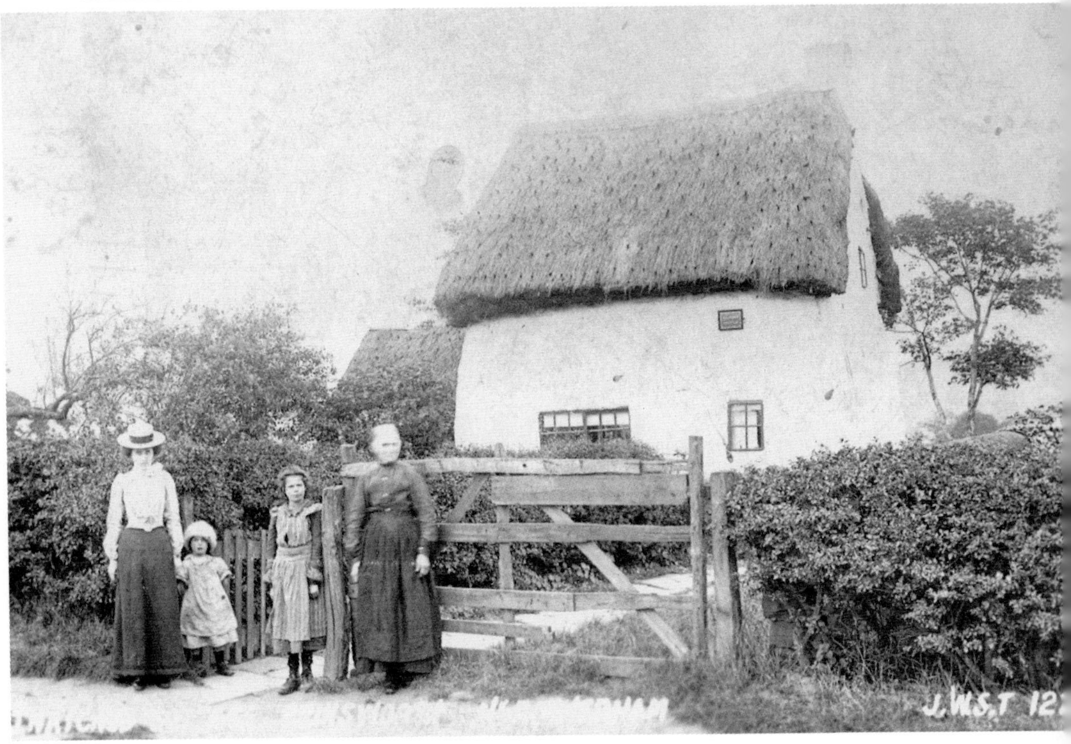

This thatched cottage in Bonet Lane, Brinsworth, was occupied by the Badger family. Pictured outside are Helen Badger, the two Sturman children and Mrs Ann Badger, who unfortunately moved as the photographer released the shutter. The postcard is dated 1904 and was sent to Mrs Badger by the photographer, J.W. Stobbs. [4359]

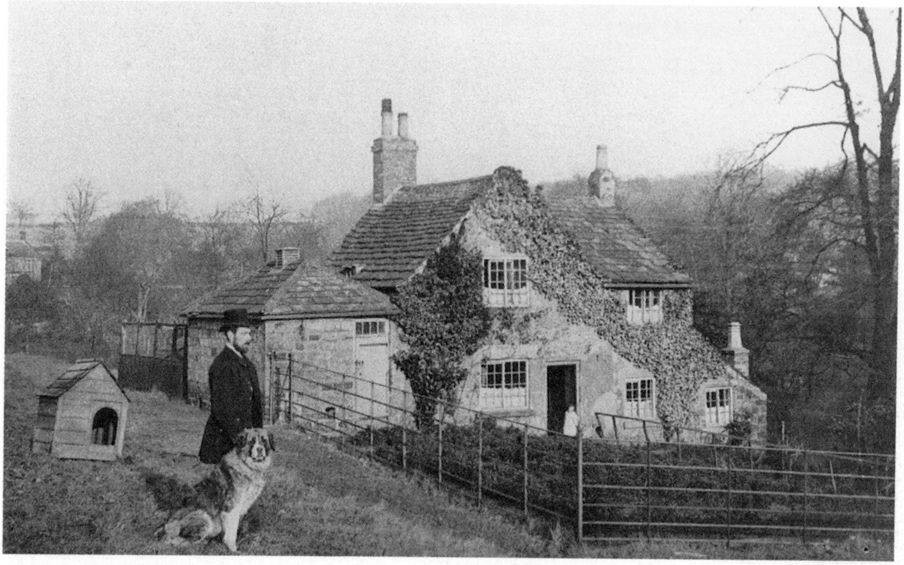

The Park Keeper's Cottage at Wentworth, from a postcard postmarked 1904. The keeper's dog looks more than capable of seeing off any trespassers in the park. [251]

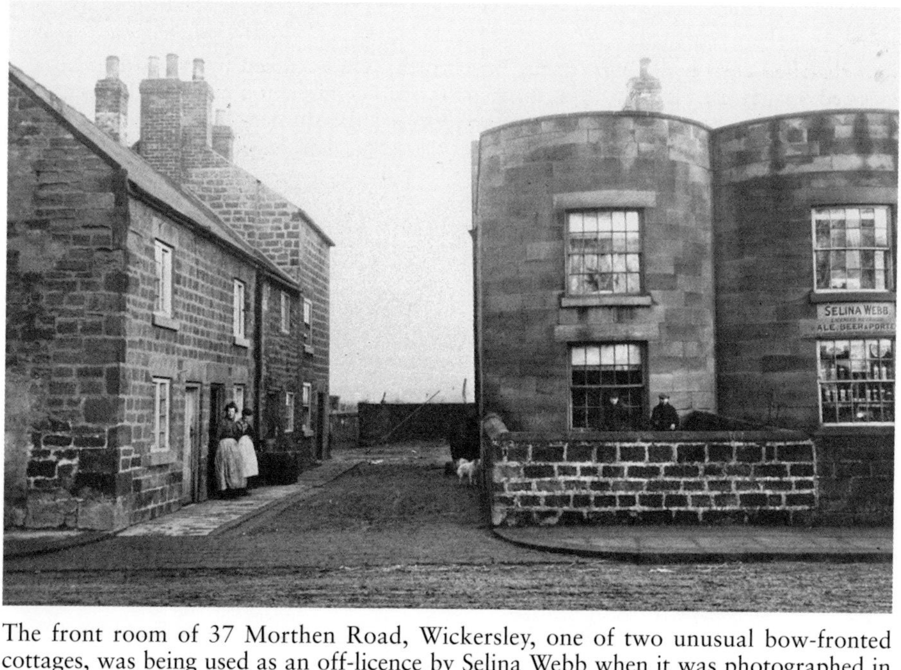

The front room of 37 Morthen Road, Wickersley, one of two unusual bow-fronted cottages, was being used as an off-licence by Selina Webb when it was photographed in about 1905. [91]

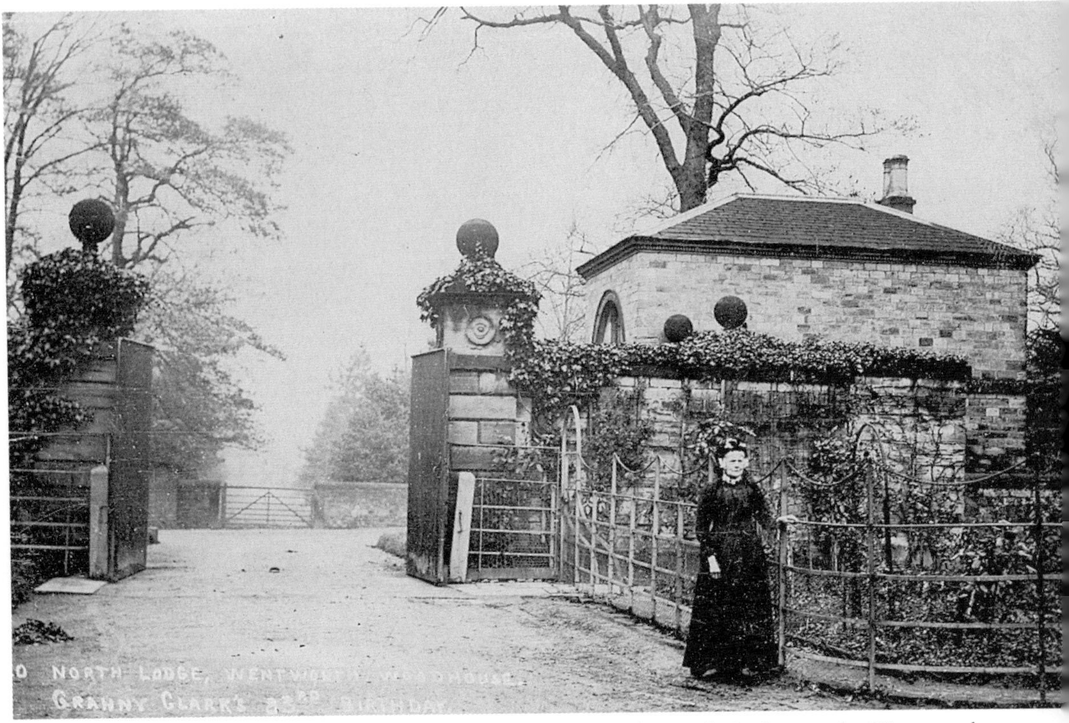

Granny Clark was lodge keeper at the North or Rainborough Lodge on the Wentworth Woodhouse estate, and had her picture taken on her 83rd birthday in 1905. She and her husband Charley, a carter, were then the oldest servants on the estate. The road through the gates led across Rainborough Park, via Needle's Eye, to Wentworth Woodhouse 2 miles away. [236]

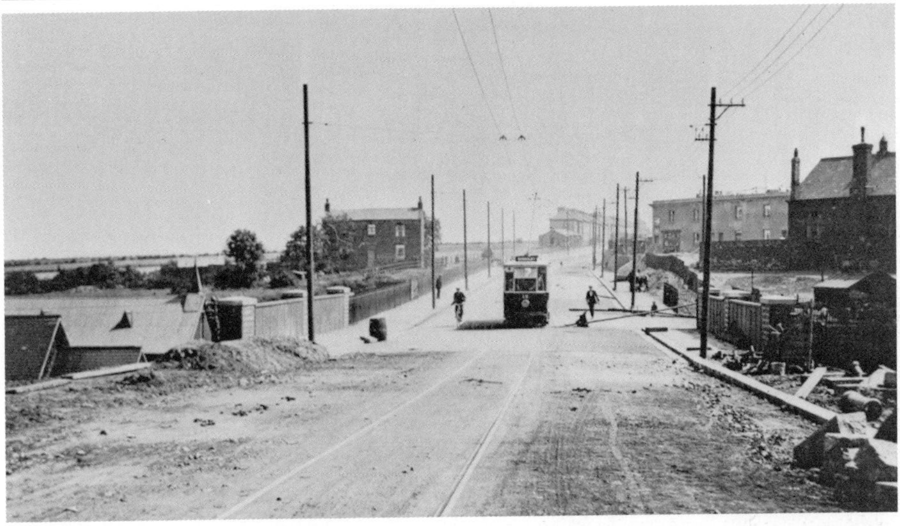

A Dearne District Light Railways tramcar, photographed at the boundary between Brampton Bierlow and Wombwell in the 1920s. The flat-topped houses, right of centre, can be seen in more detail below in a photograph of 1953. This development was known as Concrete Cottages and was built in 1873 to house miners at Cortonwood Colliery. There were 106 three-bedroom cottages in eight rows. The colliery also provided a school for the children. Alternatively known as 'Little Palestine', the cottages were an early example of the use of concrete in house building and survived until 1958. [1075,1079]

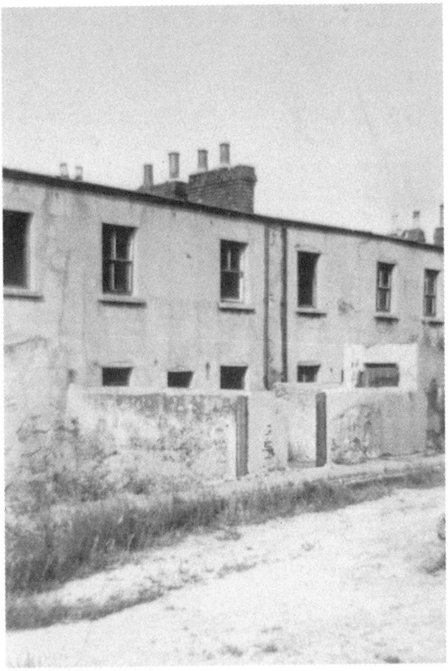

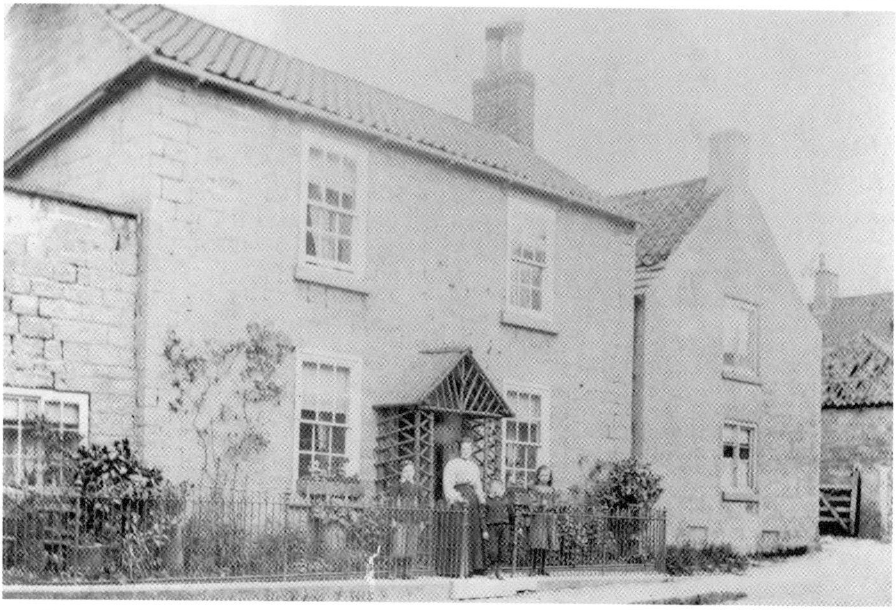

Mr Brewer's house in Laughton Road, Dinnington, *c.* 1910. It lay opposite the church. The frontage was later demolished to allow the road to be widened. [4663]

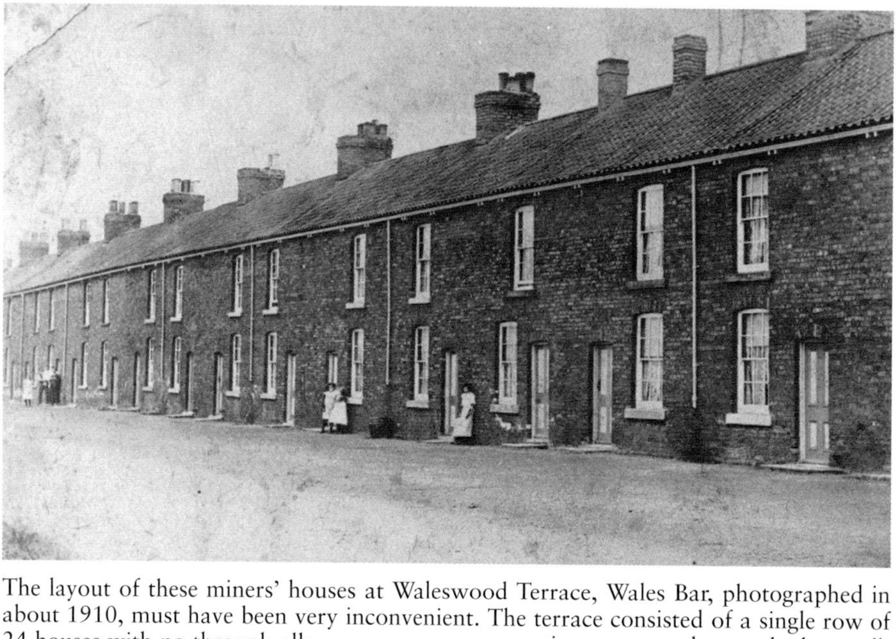

The layout of these miners' houses at Waleswood Terrace, Wales Bar, photographed in about 1910, must have been very inconvenient. The terrace consisted of a single row of 24 houses with no through alleyways, so anyone wanting to get to the rear had to walk right round the end or pass through one of the houses. [3936]

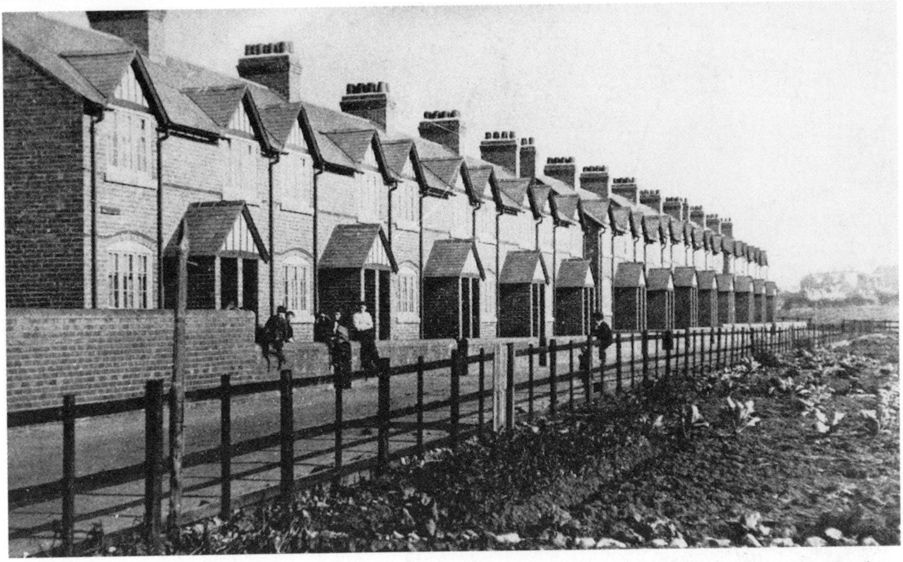

Hundreds of terraced houses were erected in the villages around Rotherham in the late 19th and early 20th centuries to house the workers needed by the new coal mines. These were among the first houses, known originally as 'the Barracks', added to the village of Dinnington after the pit was sunk in 1902–4. [4677]

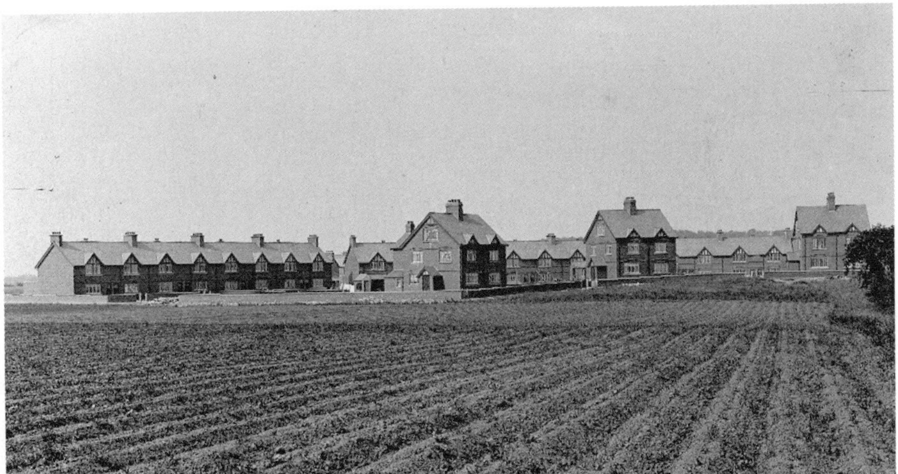

The sinking of Maltby Colliery between 1907 and 1910 more than doubled the population of the small village. To house the new workforce, the colliery company employed Herbert Mollekin to build the Model Village, consisting of two concentric circles of roads. The first quarter of the Model Village, shown here, was completed in 1910, with the miners' houses on Scarbrough Crescent at the rear and the larger deputies' and overmen's houses on Deacon Crescent in front. The potato field in the foreground was soon to disappear under the rest of the village. [3564]

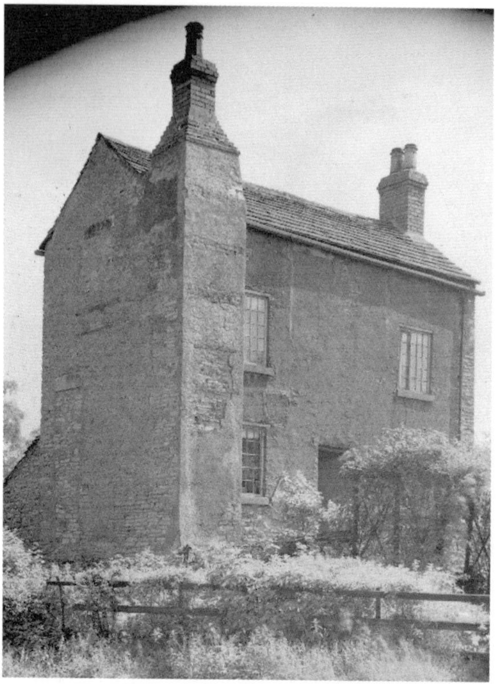

Both these unusual houses began life as colliery engine houses and were situated off Town Lane, Rockingham, near Greasbrough. The two-storey house was known as White Gates. The bricked-up hole through which the engine beam projected can be seen in the gable end. The three-storey house was known as Squirrel Castle. Both were photographed by H.G. Baker (of John Baker and Bessemer Ltd) in 1938, and were subsequently demolished. [4763, 4674]

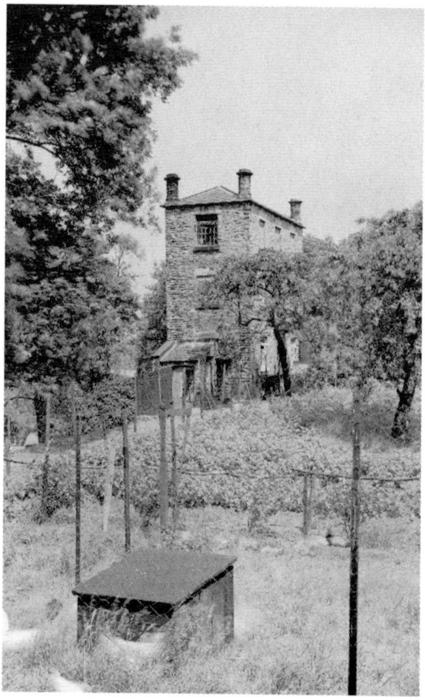

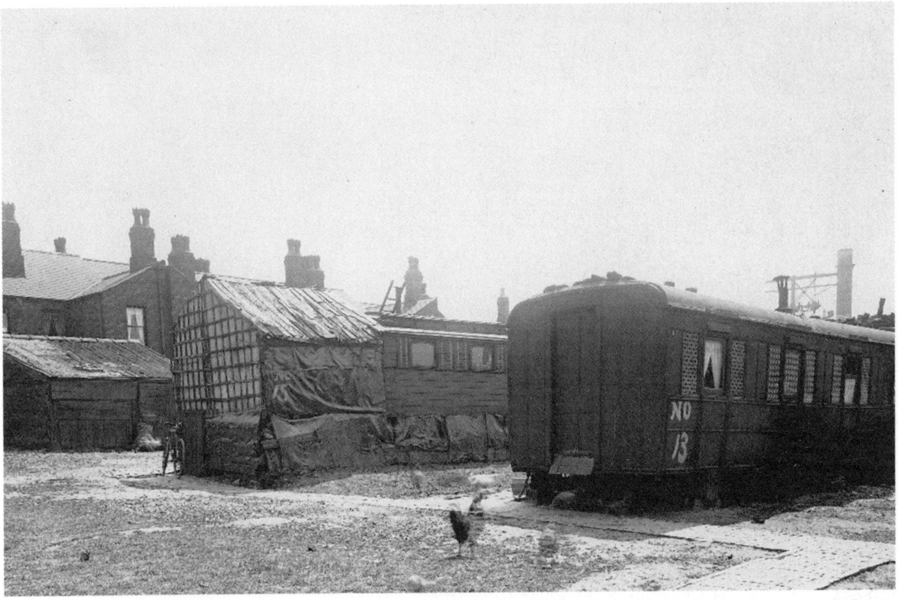

These 'houses', consisting of an old railway carriage and an extended gypsy caravan, were erected on land behind Naylor Street, Parkgate, during a housing shortage after the First World War. The photograph was taken in 1920 by Rawmarsh UDC's Medical Officer of Health, who was no doubt hoping to get them condemned. [8693]

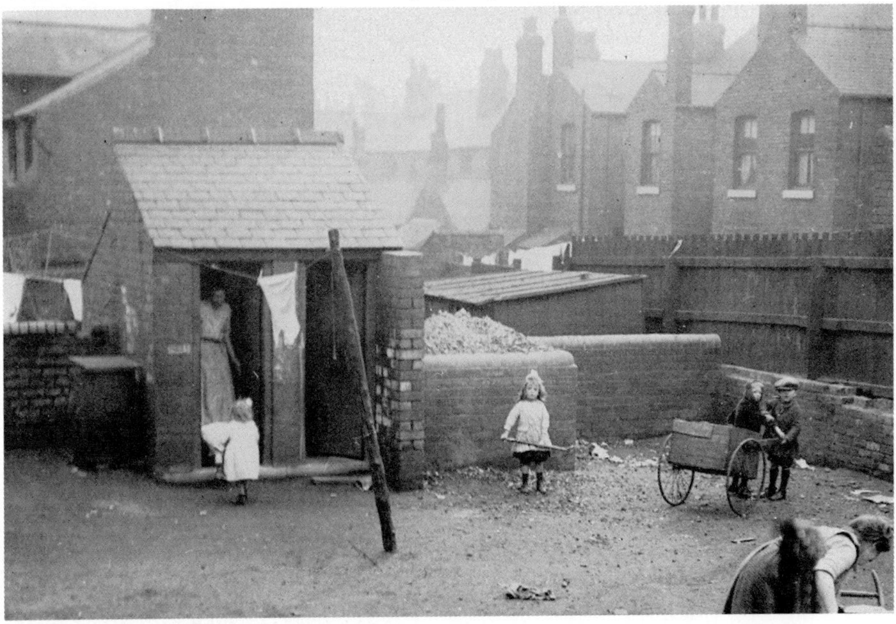

Children play among the ashes in the back yard of 28 Beartree Road, Parkgate, in February 1921. This is another Rawmarsh UDC photograph. [8697]

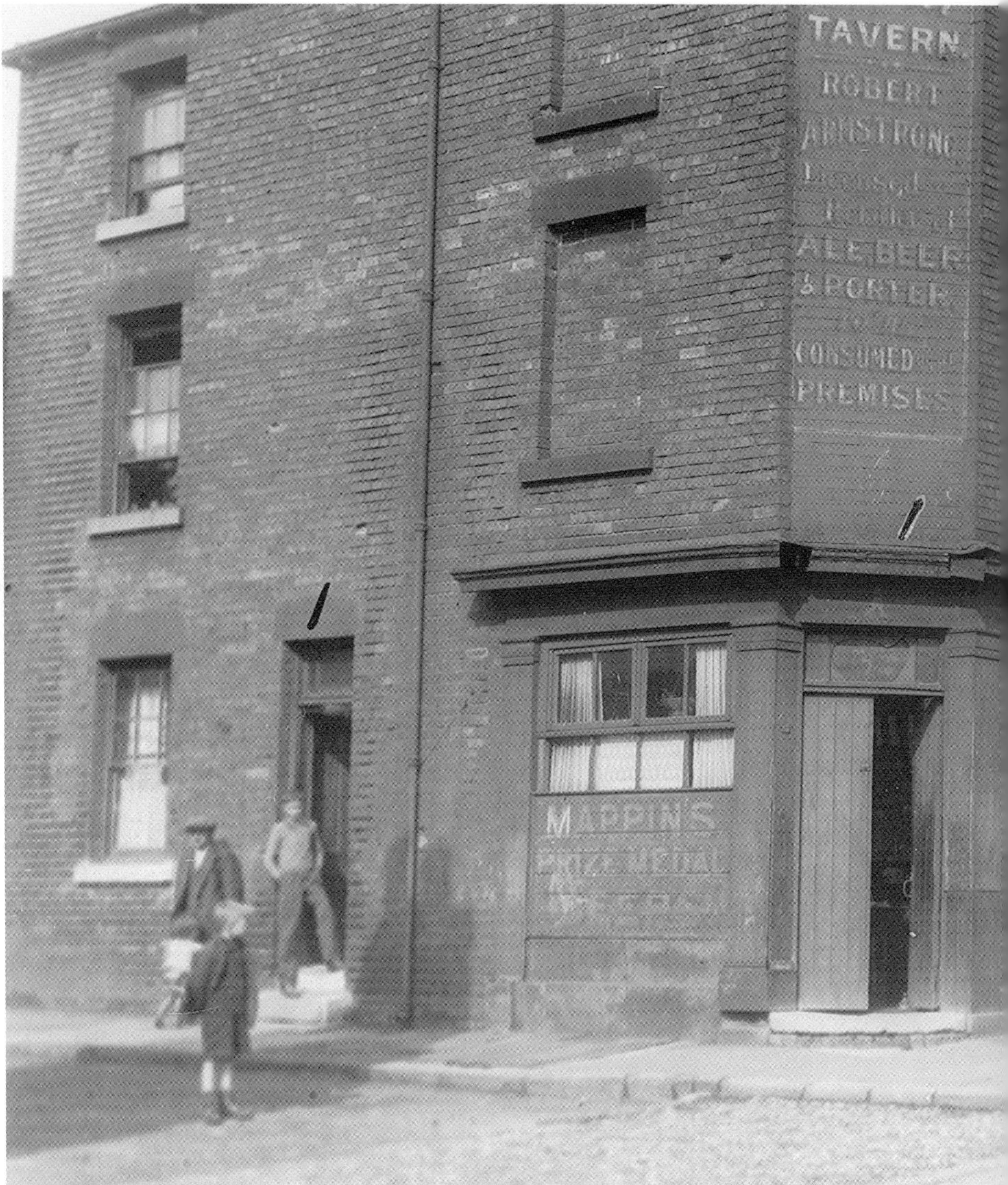

This is one of a series of photographs taken by Rotherham Borough Council as part of their slum clearance campaign in the mid-1930s. The inhabitants of these three-storey back-to-back houses in Albert Street, Masbrough, were no doubt looking forward to

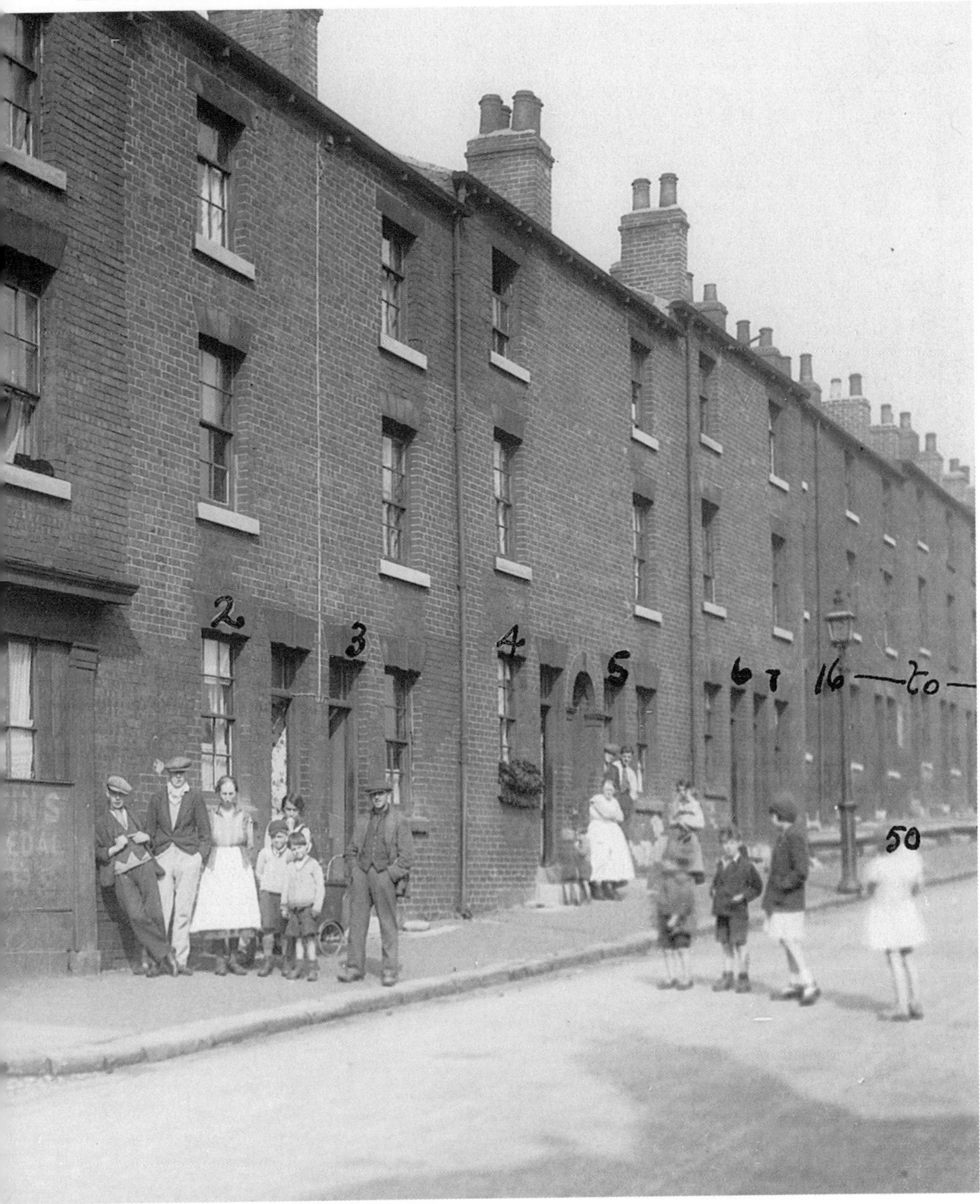

being rehoused in the new Council houses at East Dene. Robert Armstrong had pulled his last pint in the Albert Tavern in 1914, but the building remained in use as a dwelling. [467]

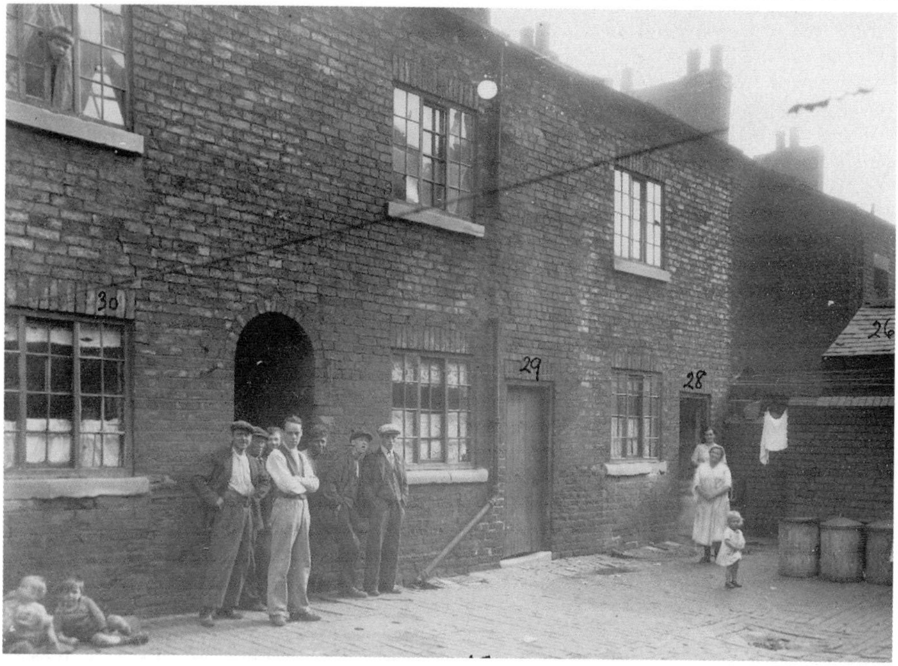

Mary Street at Masbrough was one of a large number of streets of sub-standard houses that were swept away by Rotherham Borough Council in their slum clearance campaign of the 1930s. Some of the occupants were captured by the Council's photographer in 1933. The young man at the left of the group standing in the archway was Staffy Brittle, a well-known local billiards player. [4984]

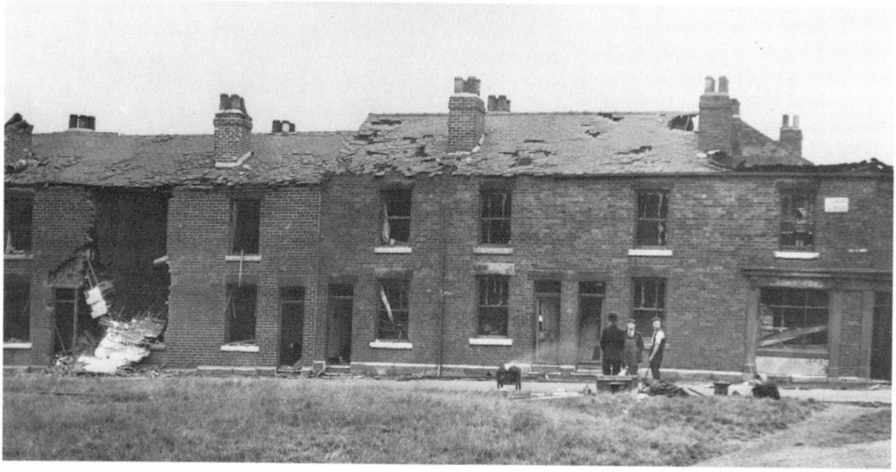

These houses in Harrison Street, Masbrough, were damaged in the air raid of 28–9 August 1940. A number of houses in the Holmes area were badly damaged but, luckily for Rotherham, the Luftwaffe made no further attempts to destroy the steel industry in the Don Valley, and the town was saved the ordeal suffered by Coventry and Sheffield. [3177]

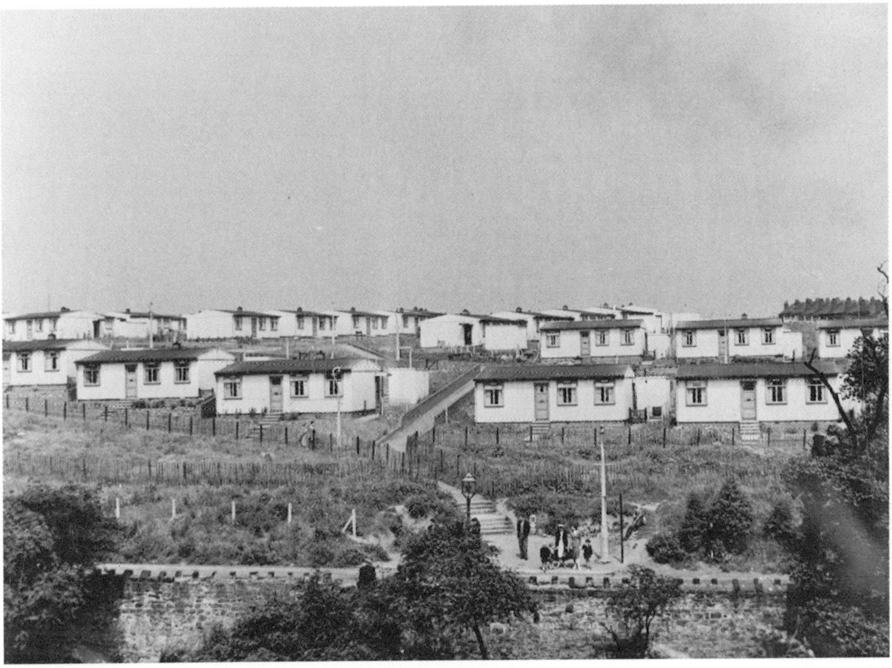

One answer to the postwar housing shortage was the erection of prefabricated houses. These prefabs at Brinsworth were still occupied in 1971. [8346]

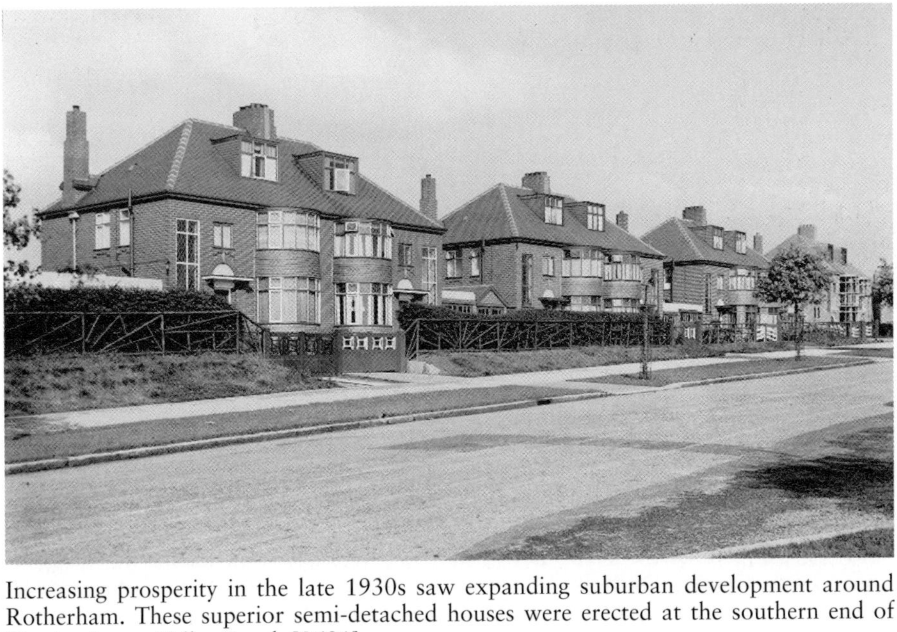

Increasing prosperity in the late 1930s saw expanding suburban development around Rotherham. These superior semi-detached houses were erected at the southern end of Herringthorpe Valley Road. [8681]

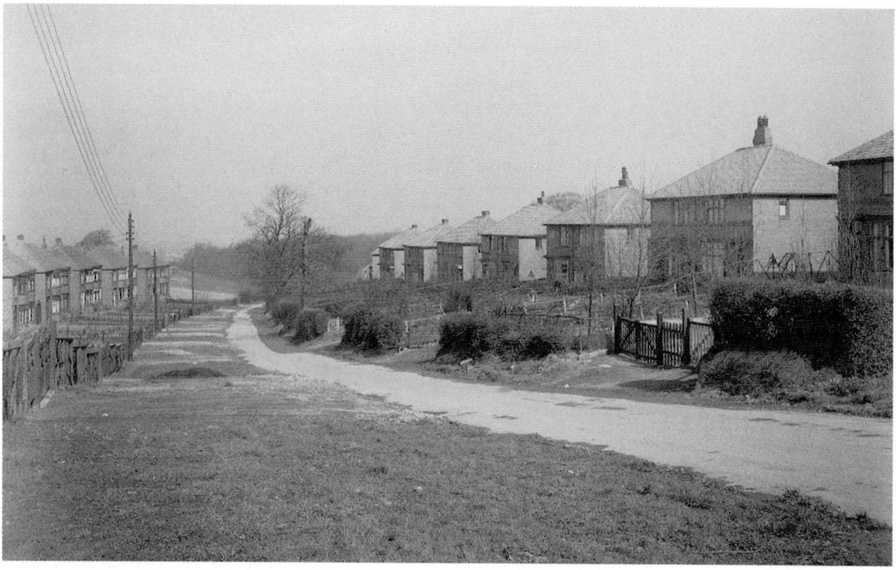

When these smaller semis were erected just outside the borough boundary in Brecks Lane, Dalton, in about 1938, the road was still the unimproved country lane it had always been. [1082]

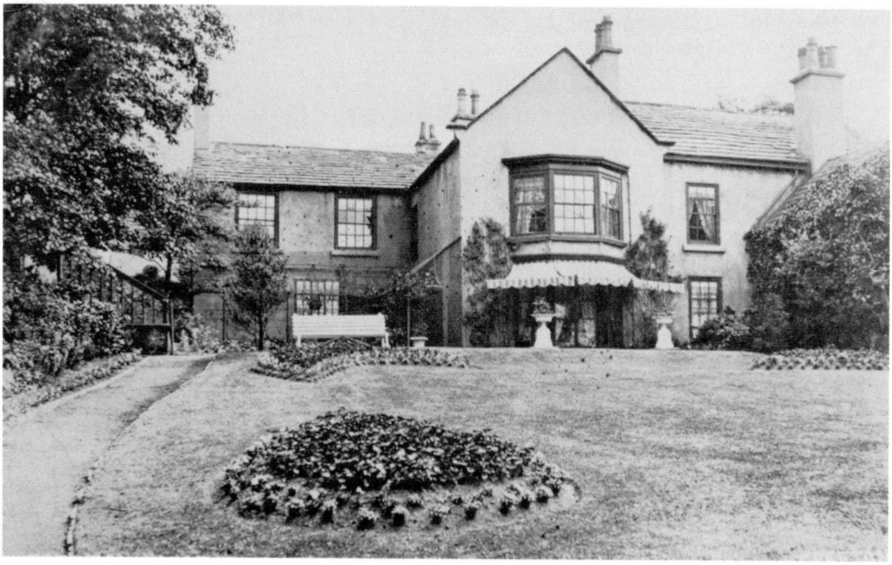

Treeton House at Treeton, *c.* 1910. Note the well-manicured lawns and regimented flower beds. In the late 19th century the house was the home of John Drought Kenny, the village's first resident doctor. It was the only freehold in the village that was not owned by the Duke of Norfolk. Dr Kenny moved to Wickersley in 1912 and Treeton House was then occupied by various officials of Rother Vale Collieries. It was demolished in the 1960s. [3095]

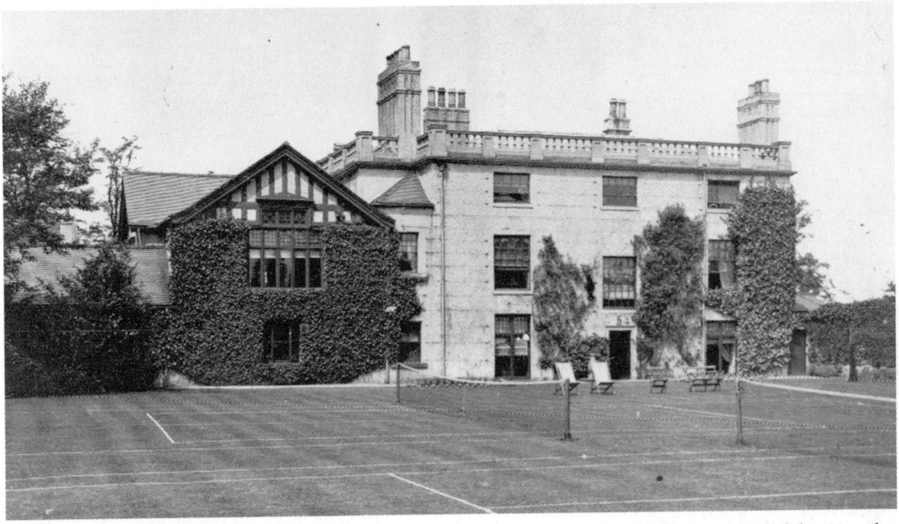

Tennis was obviously a popular pastime at Hooton Levitt Hall, near Maltby, in the early years of the 20th century. In the 19th century the estate was inherited by the lawyer William Fretwell Hoyle (1801–86). He was steward of the manors of Rotherham and Kimberworth and local solicitor to the Earl of Effingham. Although he lost much money investing in tin mines, he persisted in driving to his office in Rotherham in a carriage and pair with a footman in uniform with green facings. The Hall was replaced with modern housing in 1964. [4470]

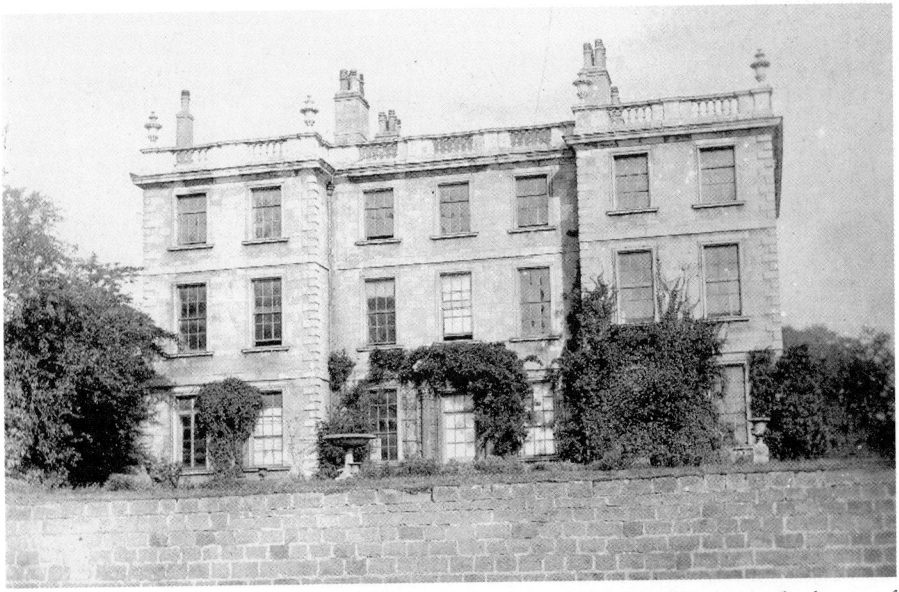

Aldwarke Hall lay between Parkgate and Dalton and for many years was the home of the Foljambe family. Photographed in the 1890s, the Hall was demolished in 1898, and a steelworks now covers the site. [3753]

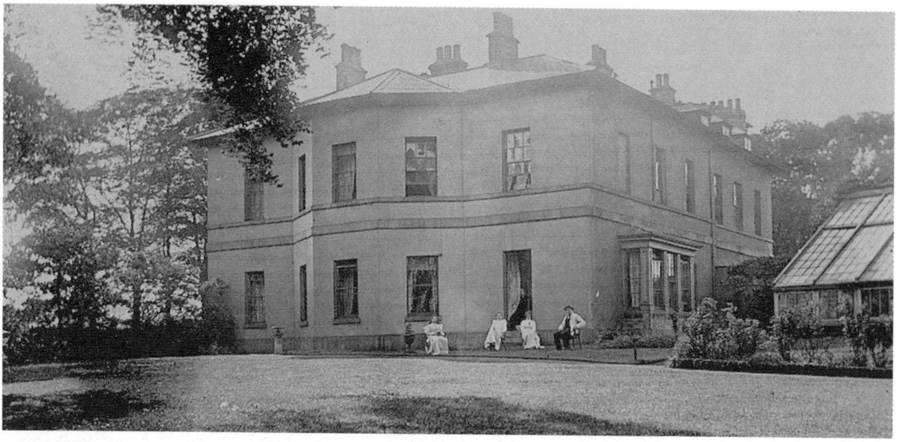

Barbot Hall between Rotherham and Greasbrough was built in about 1800 to replace the earlier Hall, which is now Barbot Hall Farm. The house was part of the Wentworth estate and was used at times as a dower house. At the time this photograph was taken the house was occupied by W.T. Freemantle (1849–1931), who can be seen sitting outside with his first wife and daughter in about 1910. A noted organist in earlier life, Freemantle later concentrated on collecting books and manuscripts, as the second photograph (of his library) shows. He met his second wife, who worked for Sheffield libraries, in 1926 when he was researching a book. He was then 77, his wife was 28. His best-known published work is *A Bibliography of Sheffield and Vicinity* (1911). [709, 714]

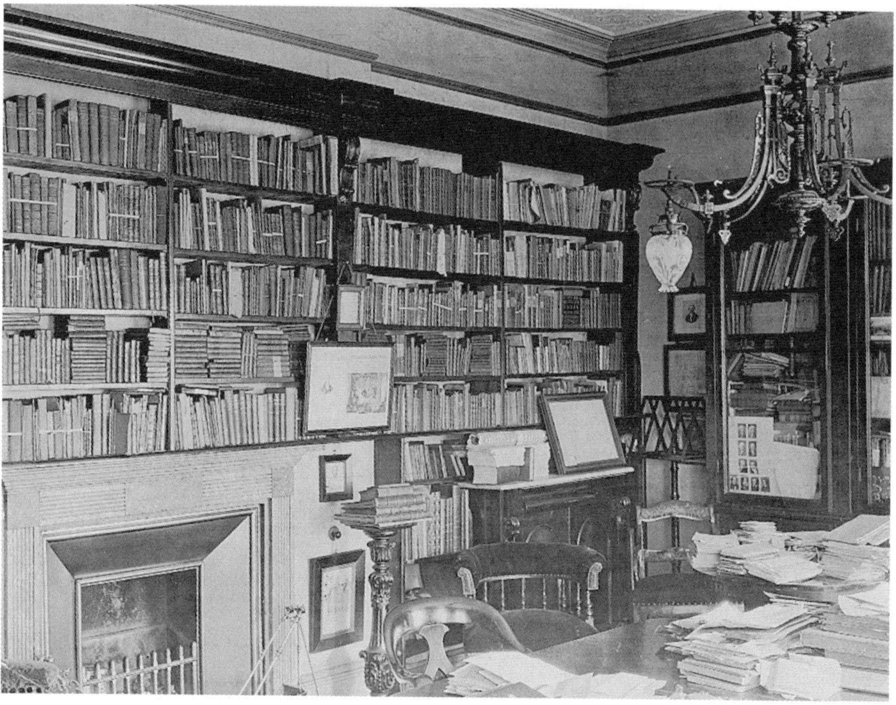

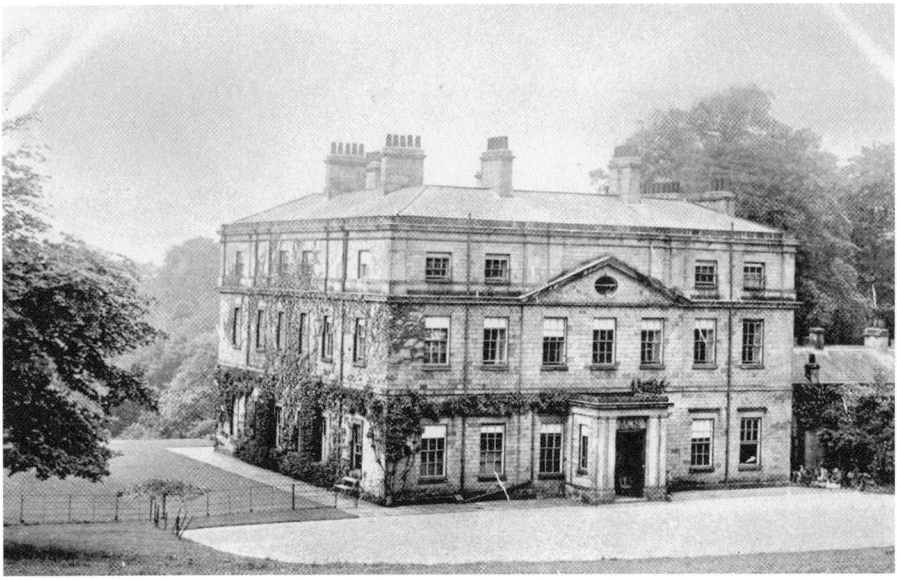

Thundercliffe Grange near Kimberworth was built by Rotherham architect John Platt for the Earl of Effingham in 1776–85 after his house at the Holmes became surrounded by industry. Originally two storeys, the attics were added later. When photographed, *c.* 1900, the house was a private mental home for ladies. It was later a home for mentally ill children and is now divided into apartments. [4948]

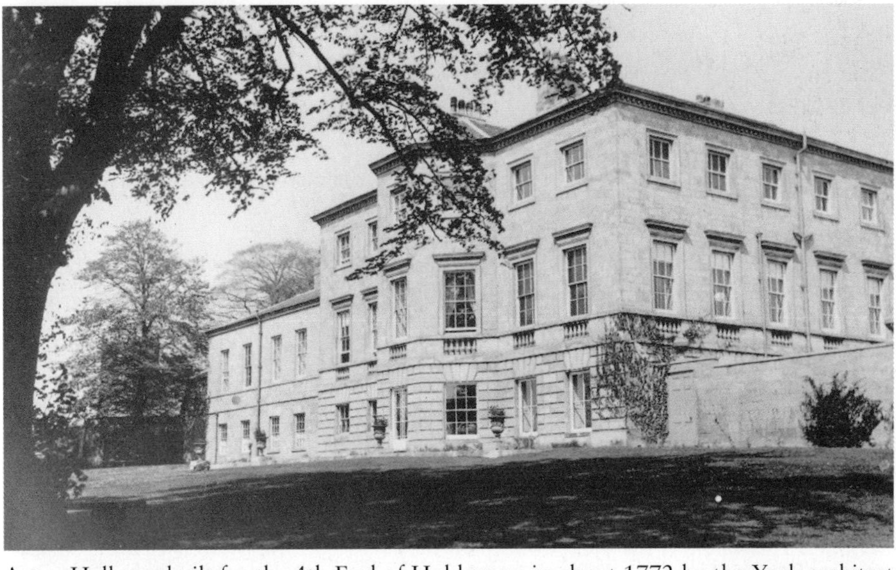

Aston Hall was built for the 4th Earl of Holderness in about 1772 by the York architect John Carr. Almost immediately the Earl sold the house and estate to Harry Verelst, a former Governor of Bengal. After many years as a hospital, under the name Aughton Court, it is now a luxury hotel. [3756]

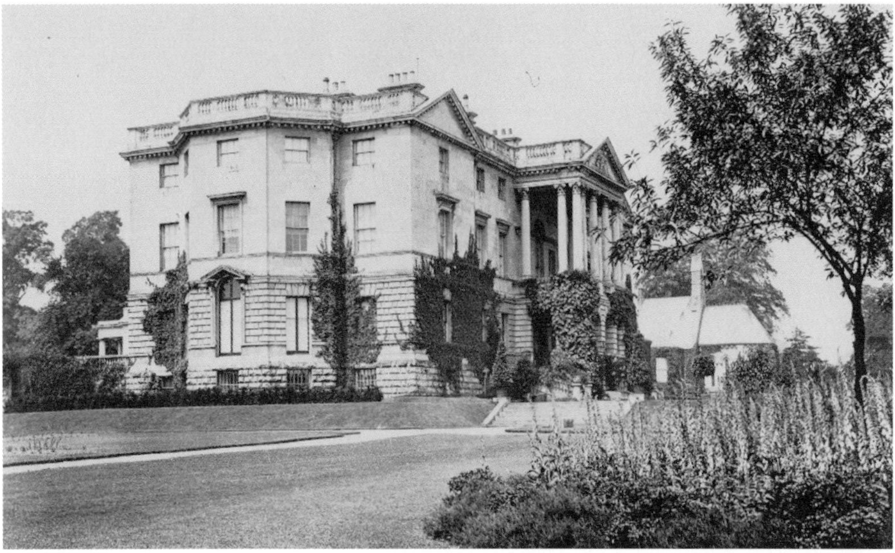

Sandbeck Park, near Maltby, seen here in about 1915, is still the home of the Earl of Scarbrough whose ancestors have lived on the estate since the 16th century. The present house dates from 1760 and was designed by James Paine. Beyond the house can be seen the private chapel of 1869. [4286]

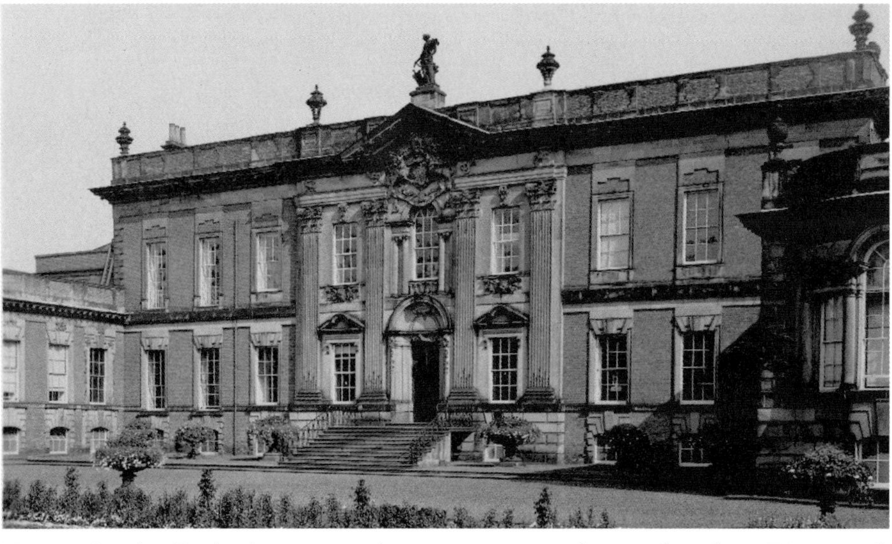

Houses in the Rotherham area do not come much grander than Wentworth Woodhouse, which has the longest façade of any house in England. This is the smaller West or Garden Front, built in 1725–35 for the first Marquis of Rockingham; it is seldom seen by the public. The great East Front was begun in 1734 and not finished until the 1770s. When the East Front became a teacher training college after the Second World War, the West Front was retained for use by the Fitzwilliam family. [295]

Section Three

CHURCHES AND CHAPELS

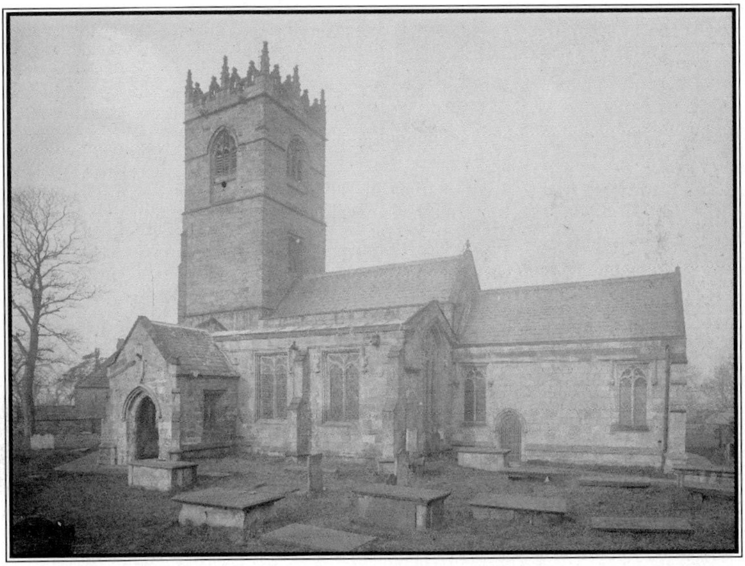

The earliest portions of the church of All Saints, Aston, date from the late 12th century. The tower and porch date from the Perpendicular period. In the chancel is an elaborate memorial to Sir John Darcy and his three wives. This photograph was taken in about 1905. [611]

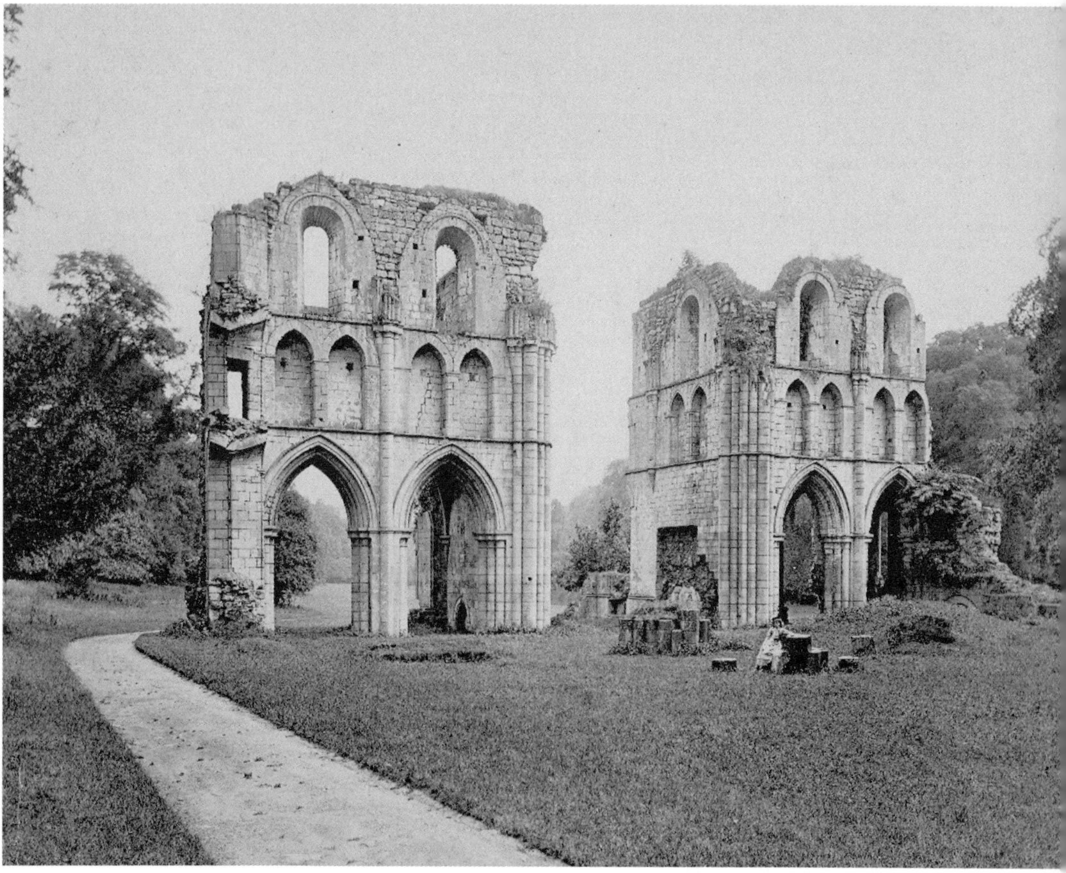

The Cistercian abbey at Roche was founded in 1147 and dissolved in 1538. It then became part of the Sandbeck estate and was landscaped by Capability Brown in the mid-18th century. It was a favourite site for romantic picnics in the 19th century but only one elegant young lady is posing for the photographer in this view from the 1880s. [7593]

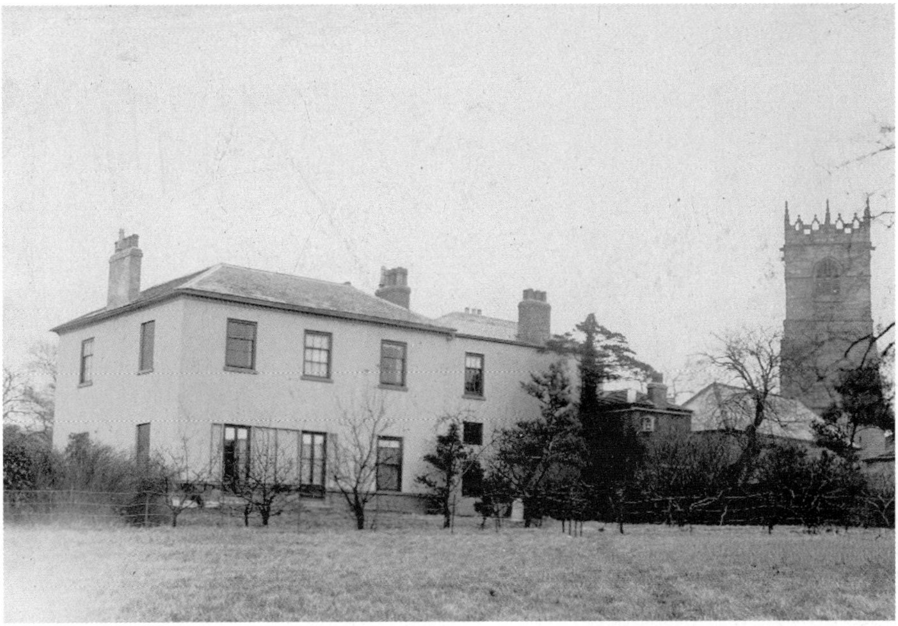

The most famous inmate of the Rectory at Aston was the Rev. William Mason (rector 1754–97), a well-known poet in his own right and a friend of Thomas Gray (of Gray's *Elegy* fame), who visited him at Aston. The Rectory was extensively rebuilt for Mason in about 1772 by John Carr, who was then building Aston Hall. [5961]

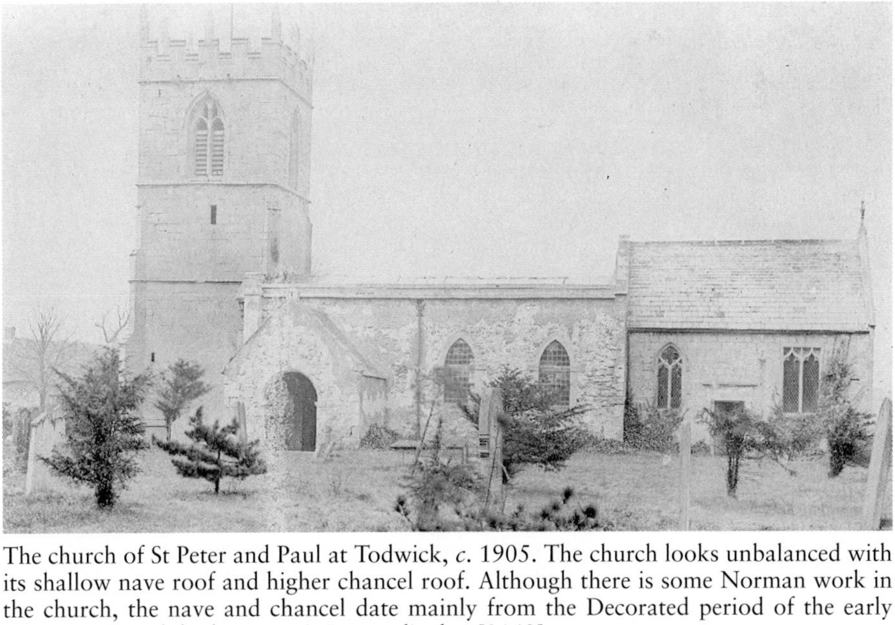

The church of St Peter and Paul at Todwick, *c.* 1905. The church looks unbalanced with its shallow nave roof and higher chancel roof. Although there is some Norman work in the church, the nave and chancel date mainly from the Decorated period of the early 14th century, while the tower is Perpendicular. [3142]

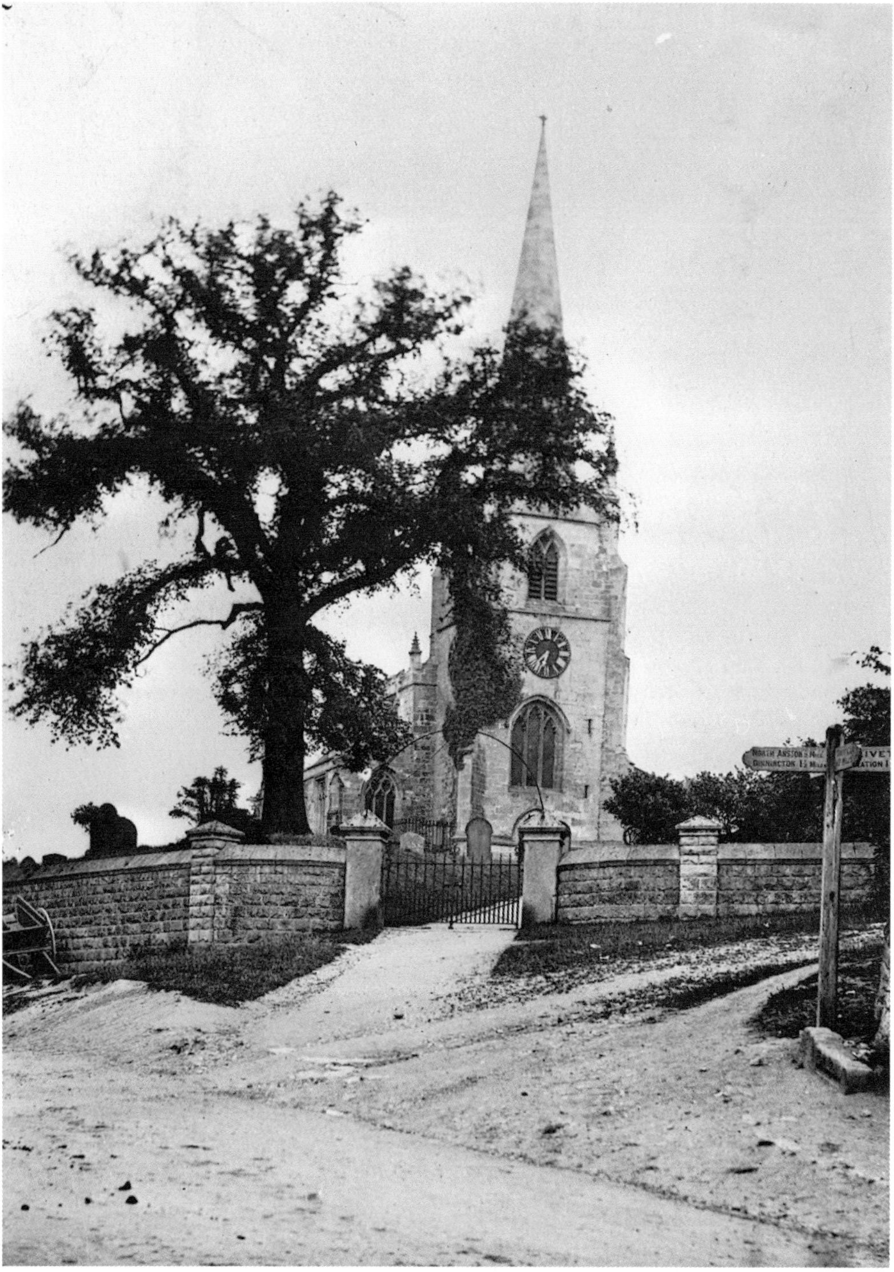

The church of St James at South Anston dates mostly from the mid-14th century. The tree disappeared in 1920 when the present lych-gate was erected as the parish war memorial. The original gate pillars were removed to the Welfare Ground. [588]

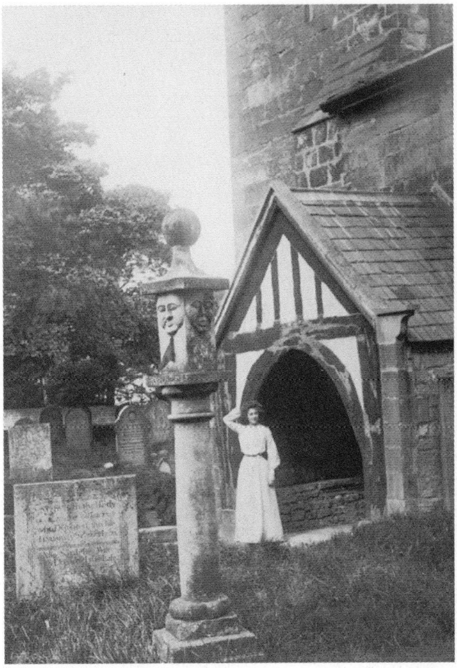

The Norman church at Thorpe Salvin, *c.* 1910. The church boasts a richly carved Norman font as well as this curious sundial in the churchyard. [10197]

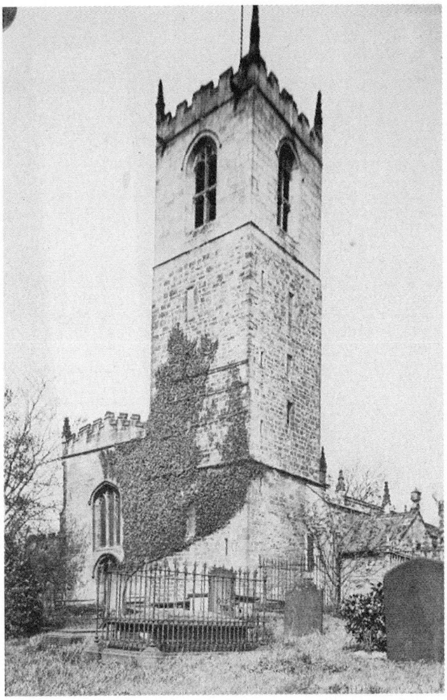

A view of St Helen's Church, Treeton, that was sent as a Christmas card by A.E. Butland, the village schoolmaster, in 1914. Pevsner describes the church as 'a confusing building'. The basic building dates from 1175–1200 with much later work, including an early 14th-century chancel. [3088]

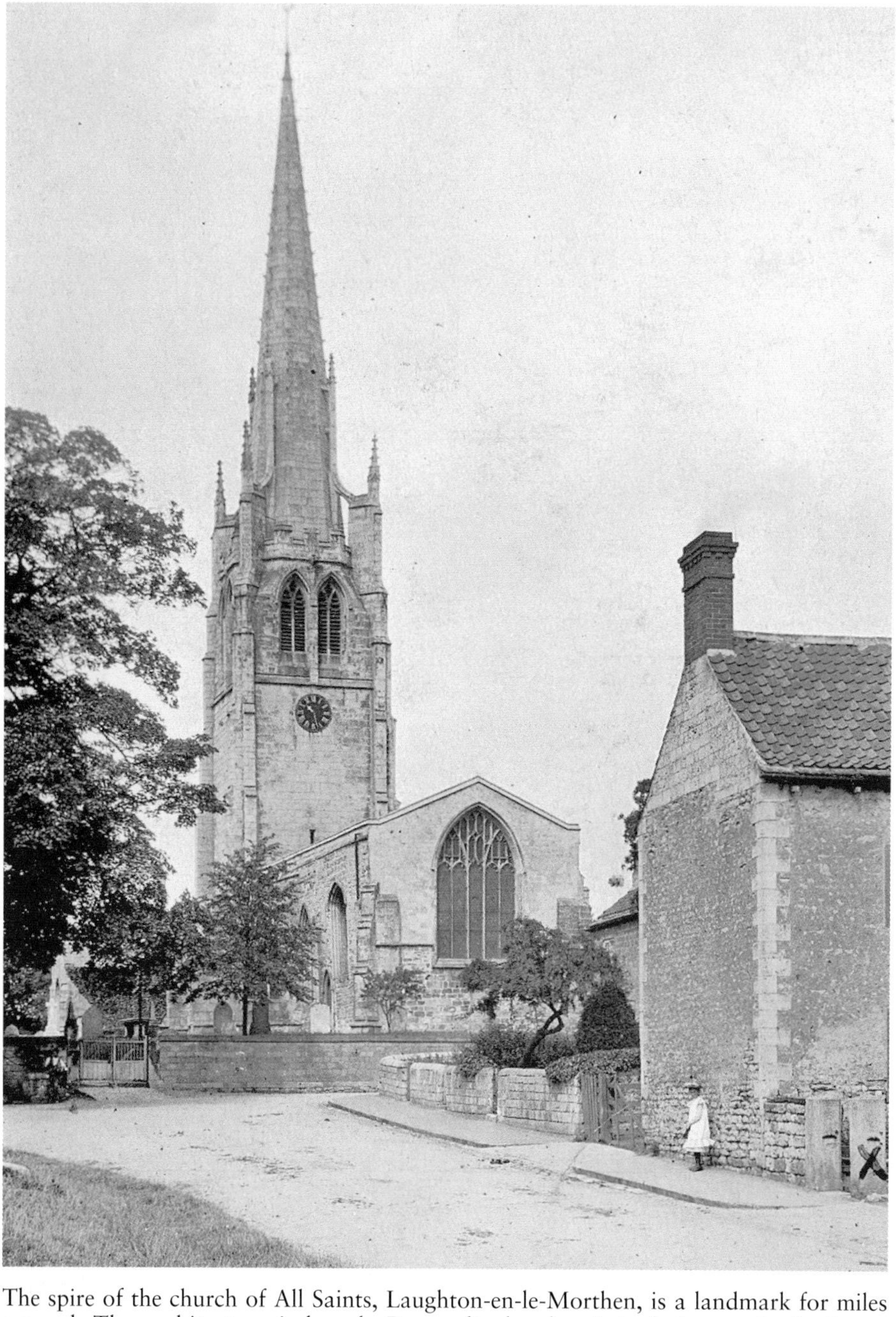

The spire of the church of All Saints, Laughton-en-le-Morthen, is a landmark for miles around. The architecture is largely Perpendicular, but it includes an Anglo-Saxon doorway and a late-Norman north arcade in the nave. This view dates from about 1910. [5565]

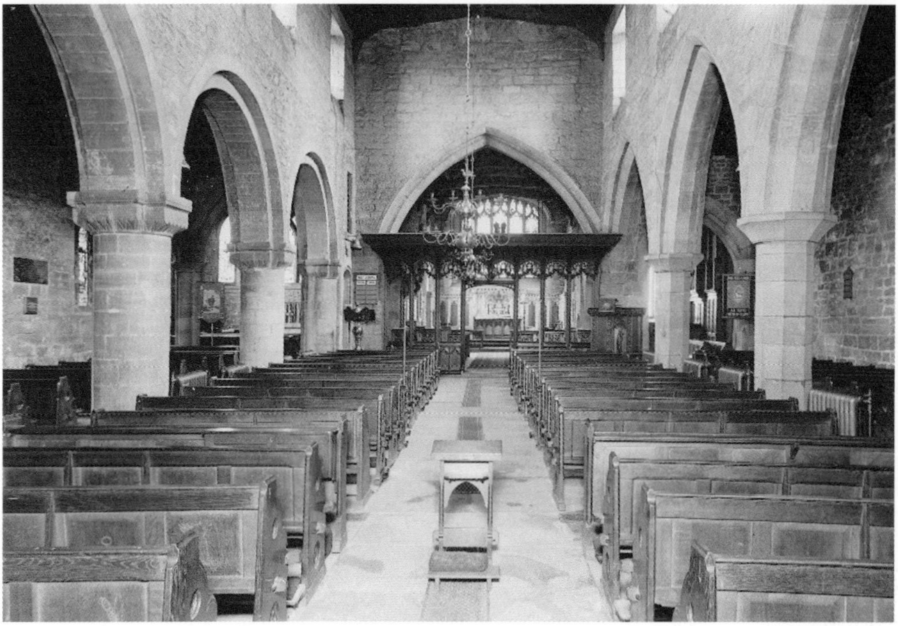

An interior view of All Saints' Church, Wath-upon-Dearne, in the 1950s. The nave arcade on the left is Norman while the chancel and north aisle are 13th century. The brass chandeliers in the nave date from 1823. [13007]

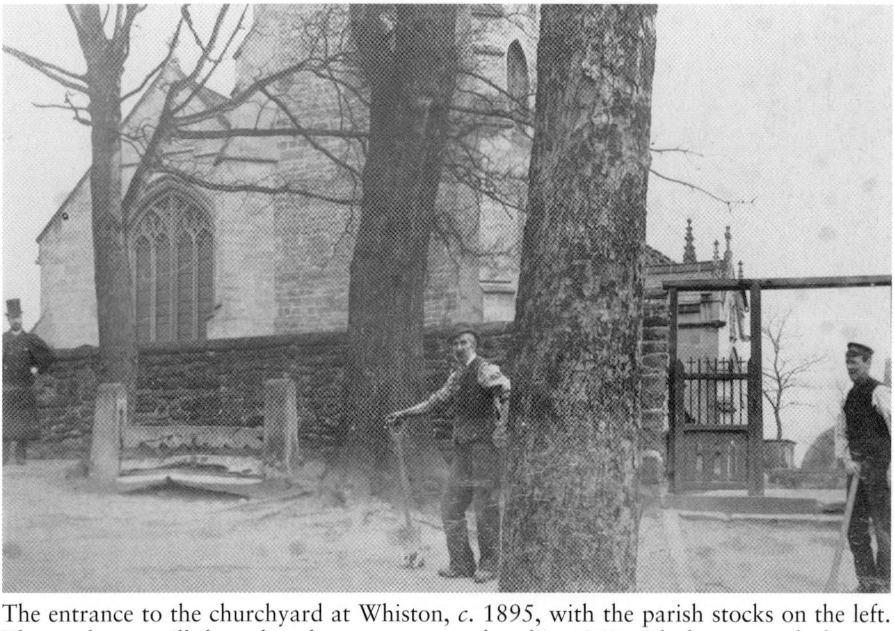

The entrance to the churchyard at Whiston, *c.* 1895, with the parish stocks on the left. The stocks are still there, but the gates were replaced in 1919 with the present lych-gate, which was erected as the parish war memorial. [5105]

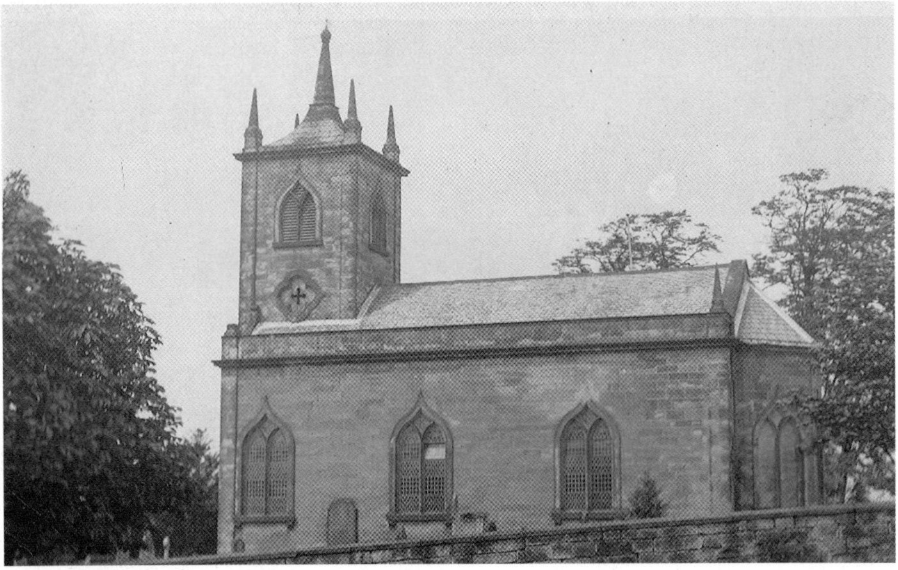

The small Gothic church of St James at Ravenfield was rebuilt in 1756 by John Carr for Miss Elizabeth Parkin, a successful businesswoman who had purchased the Ravenfield estate. There is a monument to Miss Parkin inside the church. [5876]

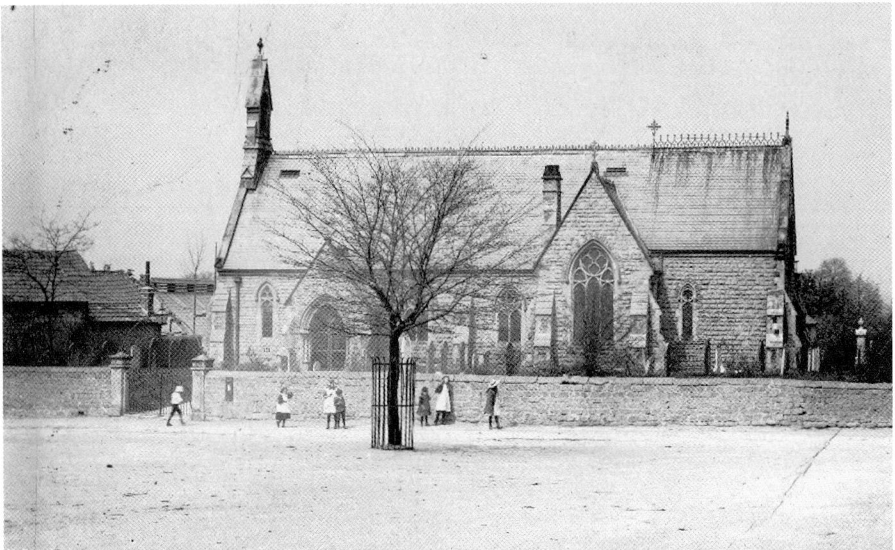

Dinnington is an ancient parish, but the present parish church of St Leonard dates only from 1886. The nave was extended westwards and a north aisle was added in 1906. The chancel was extended in 1911, dating this view to the period 1906–10. [8889]

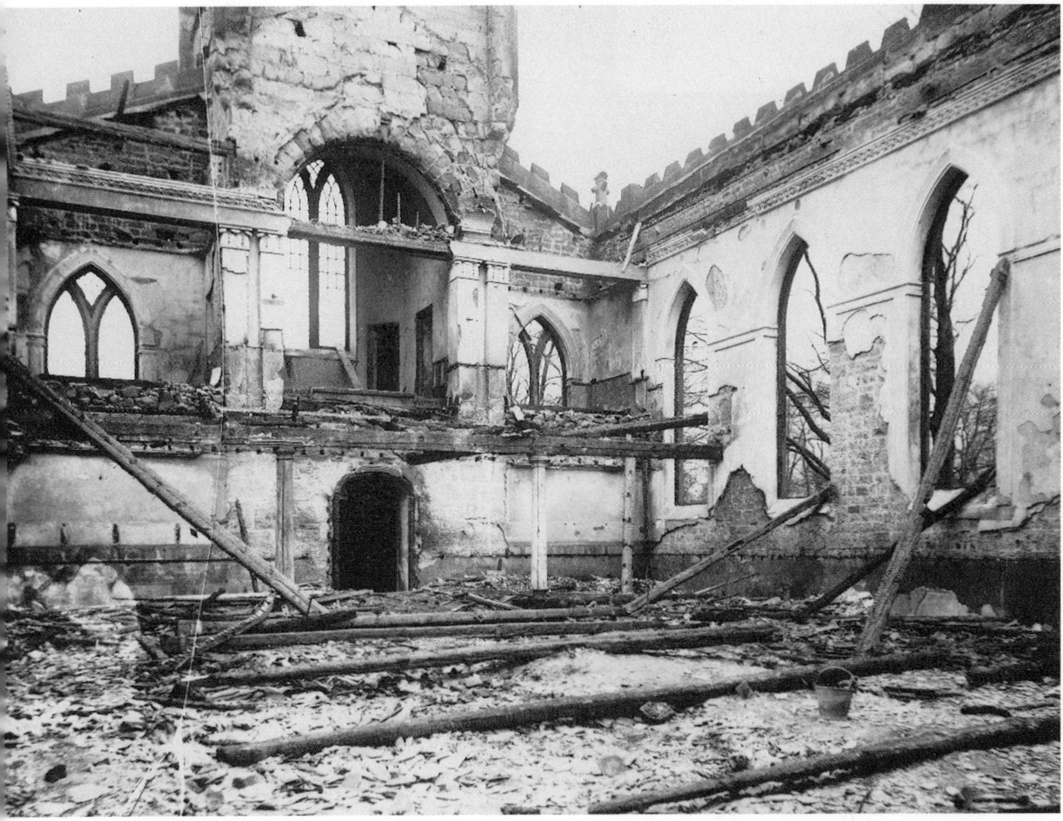

The original church at Swinton was a simple Norman structure. When it was rebuilt in 1816–17, much of the cost was subscribed by Earl Fitzwilliam. In 1896 tenders were invited to enlarge the church, but on 24 March 1897 fire broke out in the heating system. The combined efforts of the Swinton, Mexborough and Rotherham fire brigades were unable to prevent the building being gutted. The present church, consecrated in 1899, incorporates the surviving tower from its predecessor. [4162]

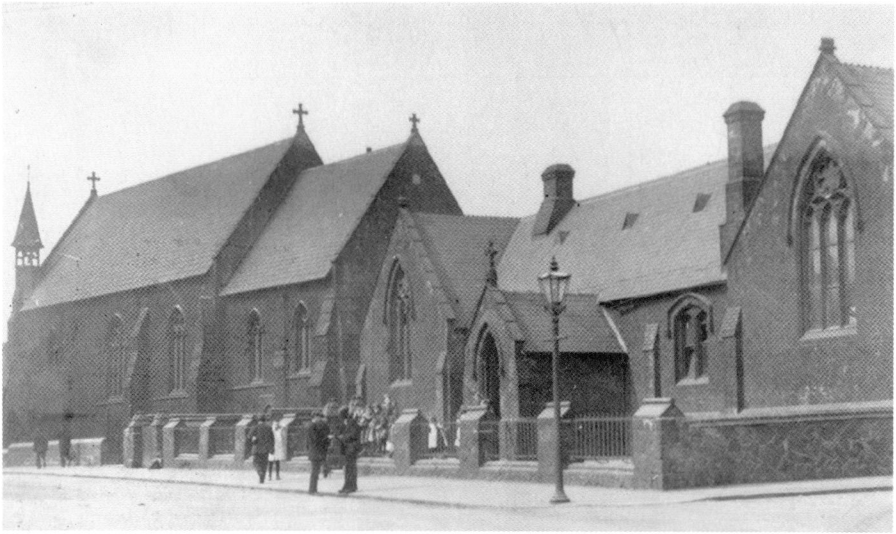

Christ Church in Aldwarke Road, Parkgate, was erected by subscription in 1867–8 to serve the growing settlement around the Parkgate steelworks. At the right is Christ Church School, later Parkgate Council School, which opened in 1901 and closed in 1938. The church was demolished in 1961. [3436]

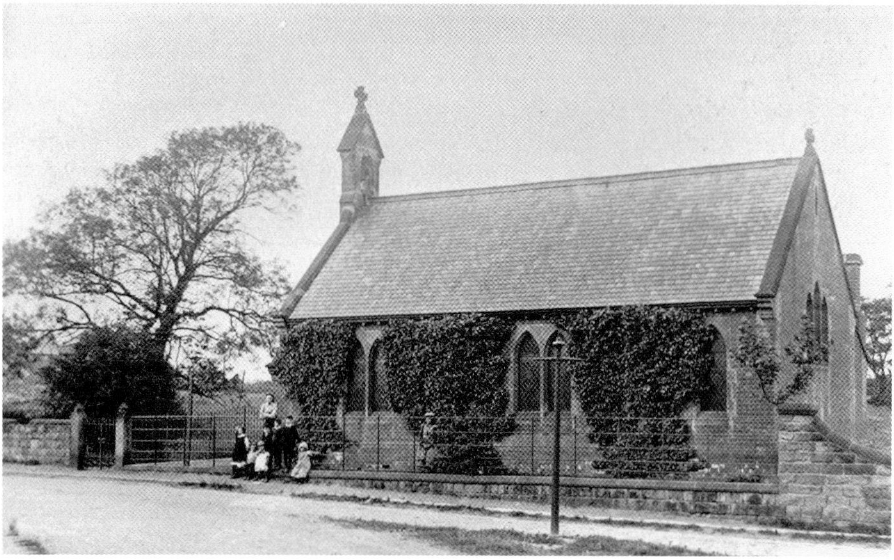

The small mission church of St Andrew, Brinsworth, was erected in 1886 to serve the growing village. When the larger St George's Church was built in 1898 St Andrew's became a chapel of ease, only to become the parish church when St George's was declared redundant in 1974. The bell cote disappeared when a small western extension was added in 1984. [6376]

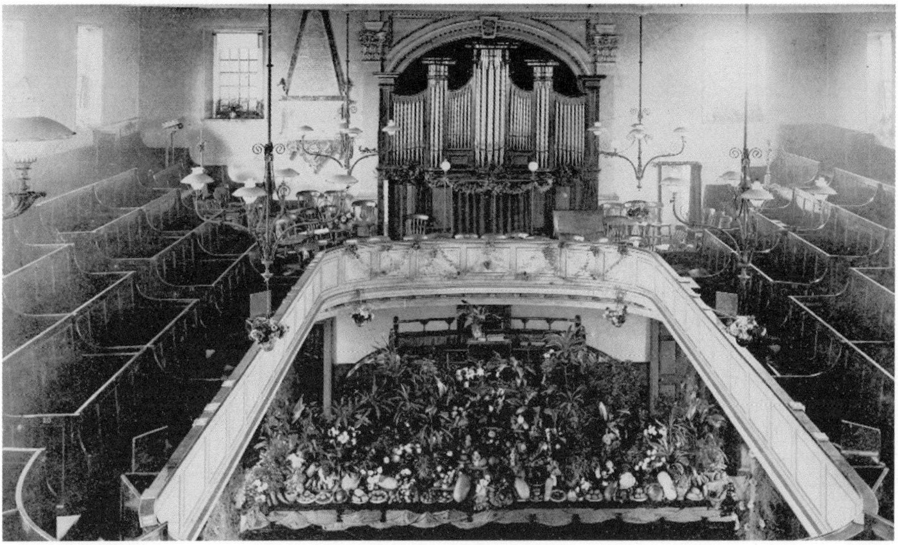

The Independent chapel at Masbrough, *c.* 1910. It was erected in 1764, and patronised by many of the leading industrial families in Rotherham. The monument to the left of the organ commemorates Samuel Walker (1716–82), one of the founders of the chapel. The building is now used as a carpet warehouse. [1163]

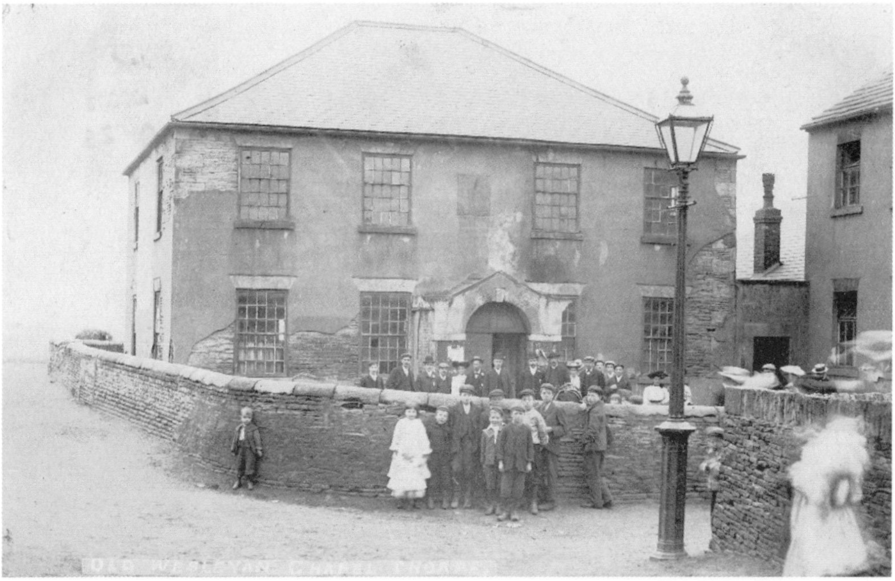

The Wesleyan chapel at Thorpe Street, Thorpe Hesley, looks rather down-at-heel on this 1906 postcard. Erected in 1795, the chapel was demolished soon after this picture was taken and replaced with a new chapel, designed by A.E. Lambert of Nottingham. The new chapel, together with the Sunday School and adjoining cottages, were put on the market in 1994. [4415]

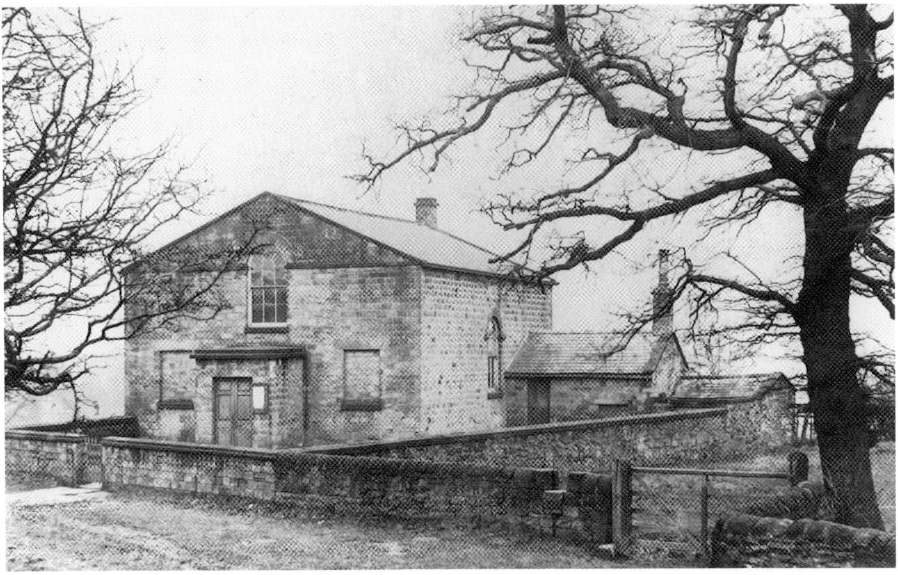

This small chapel was situated in Street Lane, Hoober. In 1833 Earl Fitzwilliam gave a plot of land for the erection of a building to be used as a day school and Sunday school for all denominations, which could be used as a Wesleyan place of worship when not needed for other purposes. In time it came to be used mainly as a Methodist chapel, but by 1937 the congregation had dwindled and the building was in poor condition. In later years the building was used as a village hall. [8339]

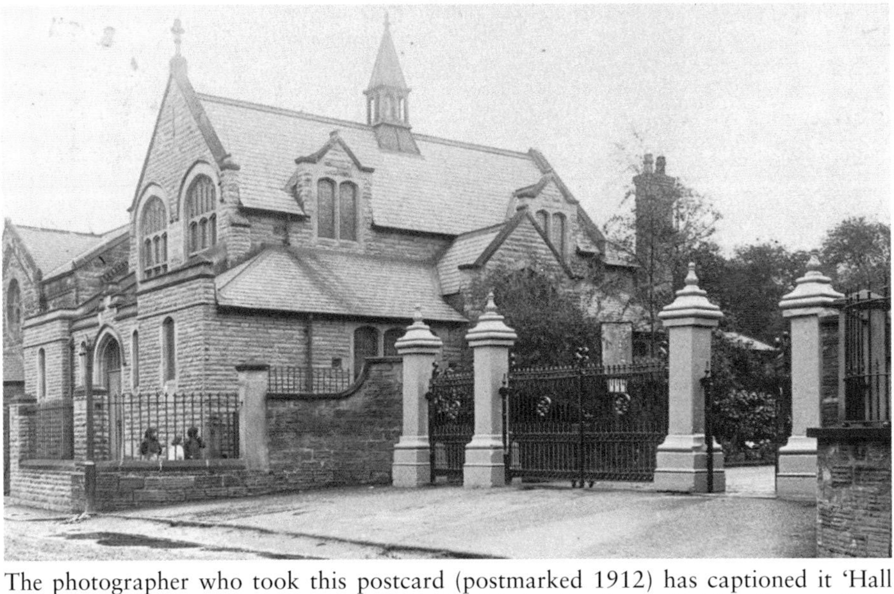

The photographer who took this postcard (postmarked 1912) has captioned it 'Hall Lodge'. The building is, in fact, the Primitive Methodist chapel in West Street, Wath-upon-Dearne. The gates at the right give access to the Town Hall Grounds. [3287]

Section Four

TRANSPORT

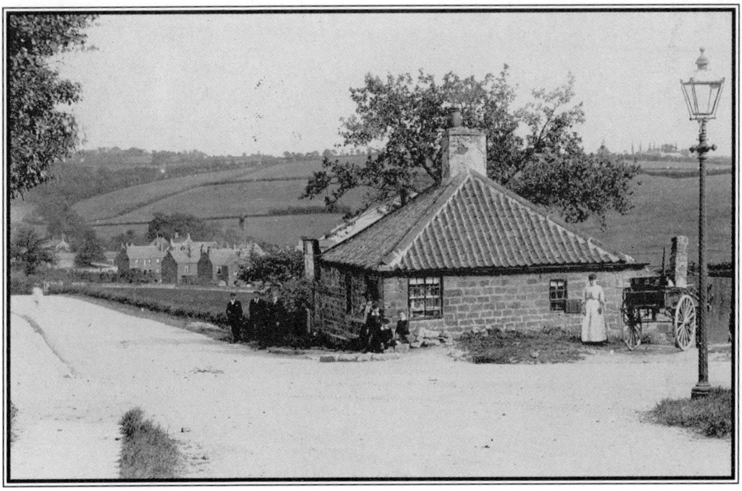

This former toll-house at Whiston crossroads controlled the Rotherham to Pleasley and Tinsley to Bawtry turnpikes. The roads were de-turnpiked in 1873 and 1878 respectively and by the turn of the century the building was inhabited by J. Evans, licensed tobacco dealer. Judging by the jars in the window, he also dealt in sweets. The houses in the distance are on the Pieces at Whiston. [56]

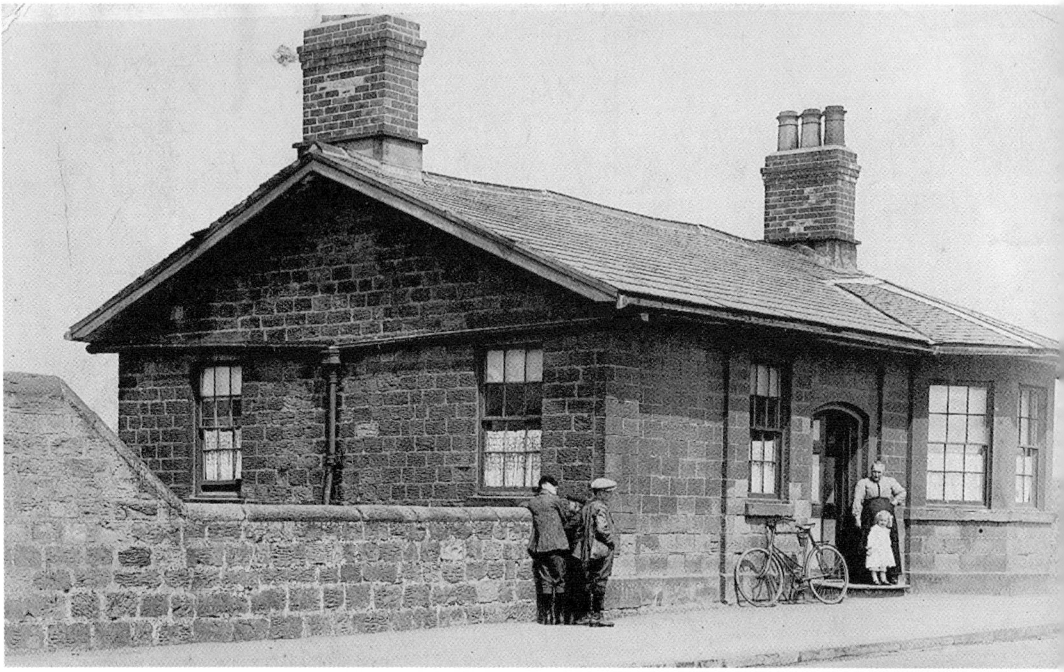

The toll-house on Doncaster Road, Rotherham, controlled the Sheffield and Doncaster Turnpike of 1764, and has the typical bow window allowing the toll keeper to keep an eye on the road in both directions while keeping warm and dry. Although the turnpike was abolished in 1873, the building, seen here in about 1913, remained in use as a dwelling until 1958. [3840]

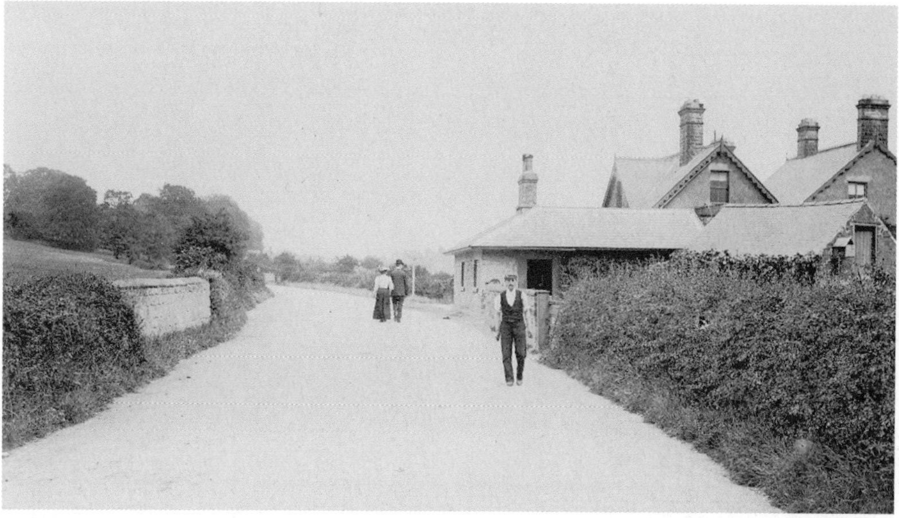

An elegantly dressed Edwardian couple stroll arm in arm along Rotherham Road, Maltby, past the old toll bar at the corner of Carr Lane. After it ceased to be used as a toll-house in 1878 it was renamed West Cottage. The roofs of Maltby Grange can be seen beyond the toll-house. [3610]

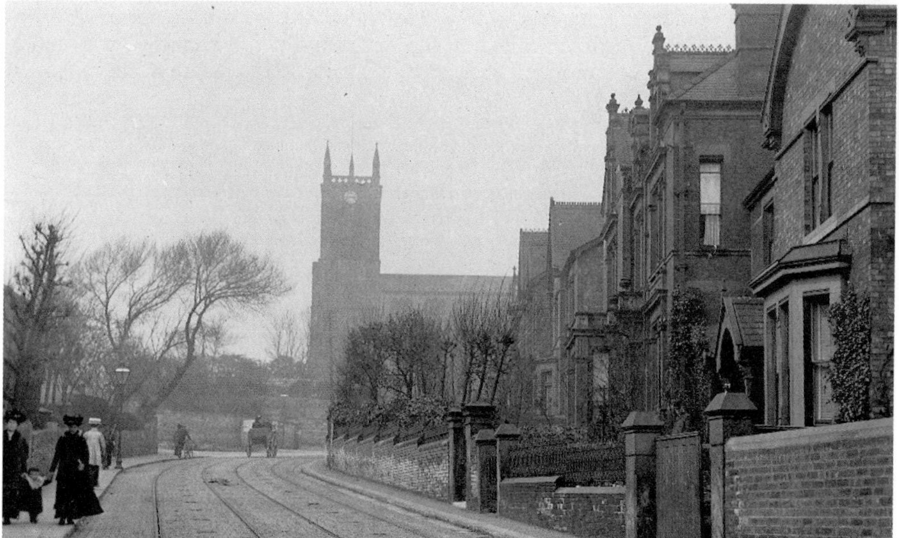

This view of Rawmarsh Hill, Parkgate, shows the lines of the Mexborough and Swinton Tramways, opened 1907, with the original Dolter stud pick-up system between the rails. In theory the studs rose up to energise the trams as they passed over, but the equipment frequently malfunctioned, resulting in electrocuted dogs and horses. Conventional overhead wires were installed in 1908. [3871]

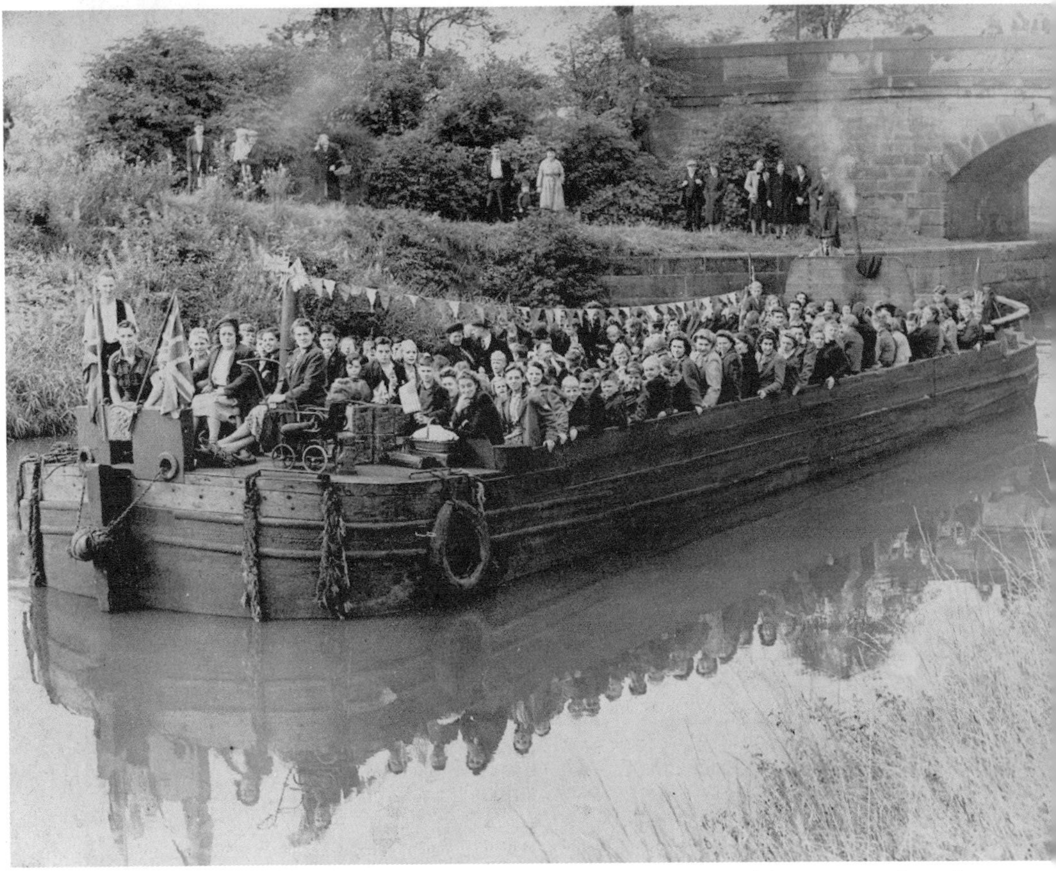

The Don Navigation reached Rotherham in 1740 and was one of the main catalysts for the industrial expansion of the area. The barges mostly carried bulk goods such as coal and grain, but were occasionally put to more social uses. The barge *Rowland* was built to carry coal to a glassworks at Mexborough. It was the first open barge on the navigation to be motorised and is seen here under the Aldwarke Canal Bridge on a canal excursion to celebrate VJ Day, 1945. [6077]

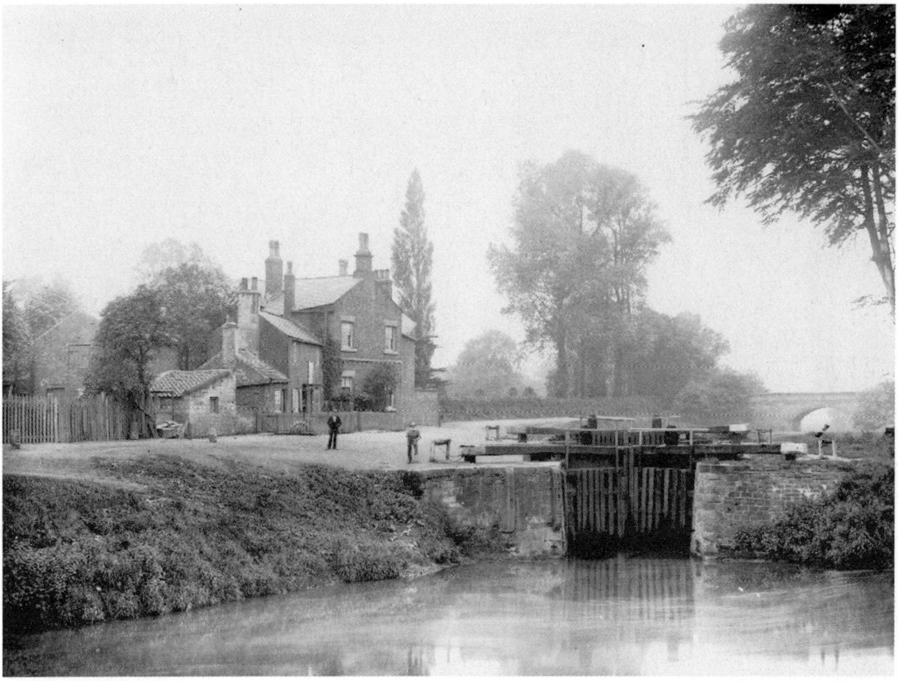

Two views of Aldwarke Lock on the Don Navigation, *c.* 1900. The lock lay on a short cut that bypassed a weir on the river and for a time, *c.* 1733, was the head of navigation. The upper view shows the downstream gates with Aldwarke House and the lock cottage at the left. In the lower photograph the crew of a typical Yorkshire keel work their craft out of the lock towards Rotherham. A close study of the two views shows that the same bearded gentleman is standing in the centre of the upper view and to the left of the lock in the lower. Could he have been the lock keeper? [14213, 14216]

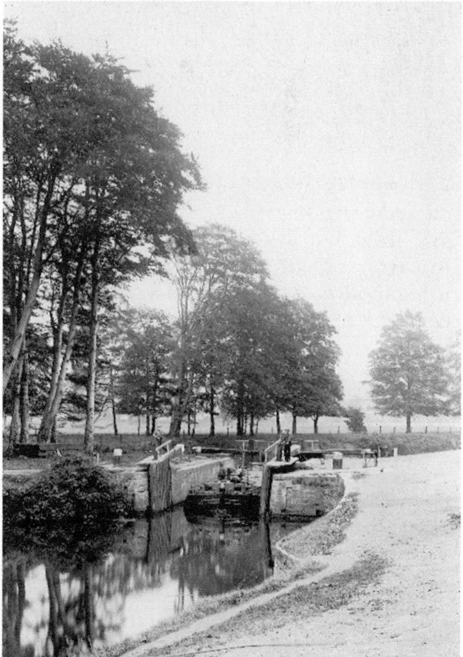

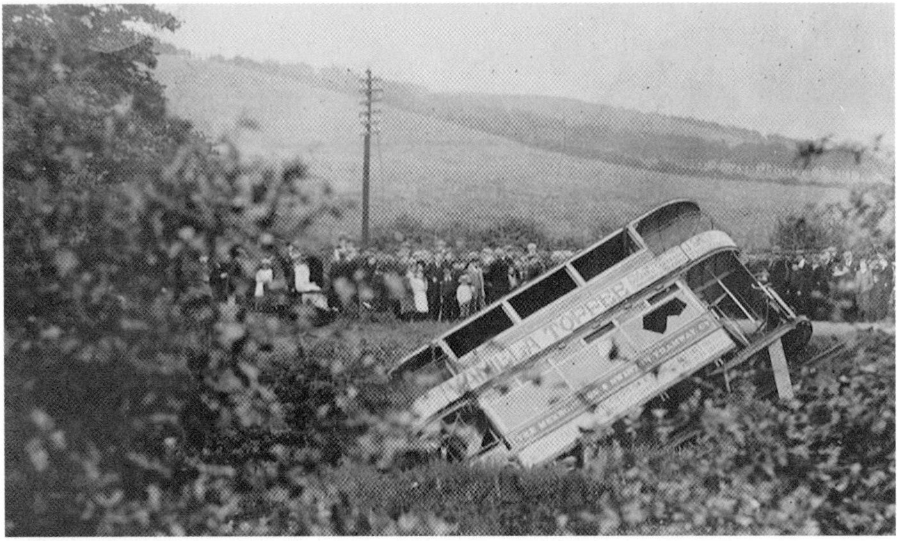

Mexborough and Swinton tram no. 14 came to grief when the brakes failed at Warren Vale in July 1908. The tram came off the tracks at the Swinton end of the passing loop and fell down the embankment. Of the 60 passengers, one suffered a broken collar bone, but the rest escaped with cuts and bruises. The trams on this route were replaced in 1928–9 by trolley buses, which survived until 1961. [11142]

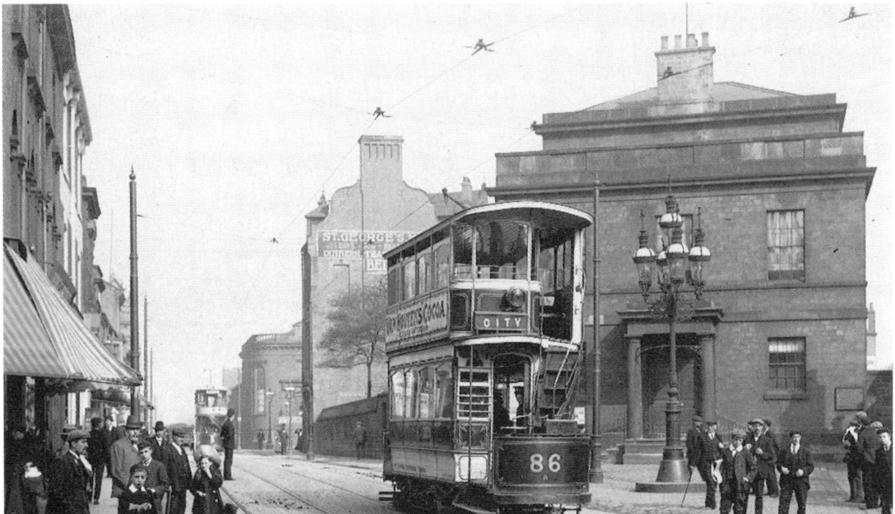

College Square and Effingham Street formed the main tram interchange in Rotherham; they are seen here in about 1910. The through service between Rotherham and Sheffield was operated jointly by the two tramways. Sheffield tram no. 86 waits to return to its native city. In the background is the Court House, erected in 1826 and demolished in 1929. Woolworths now stands on the site. [3872]

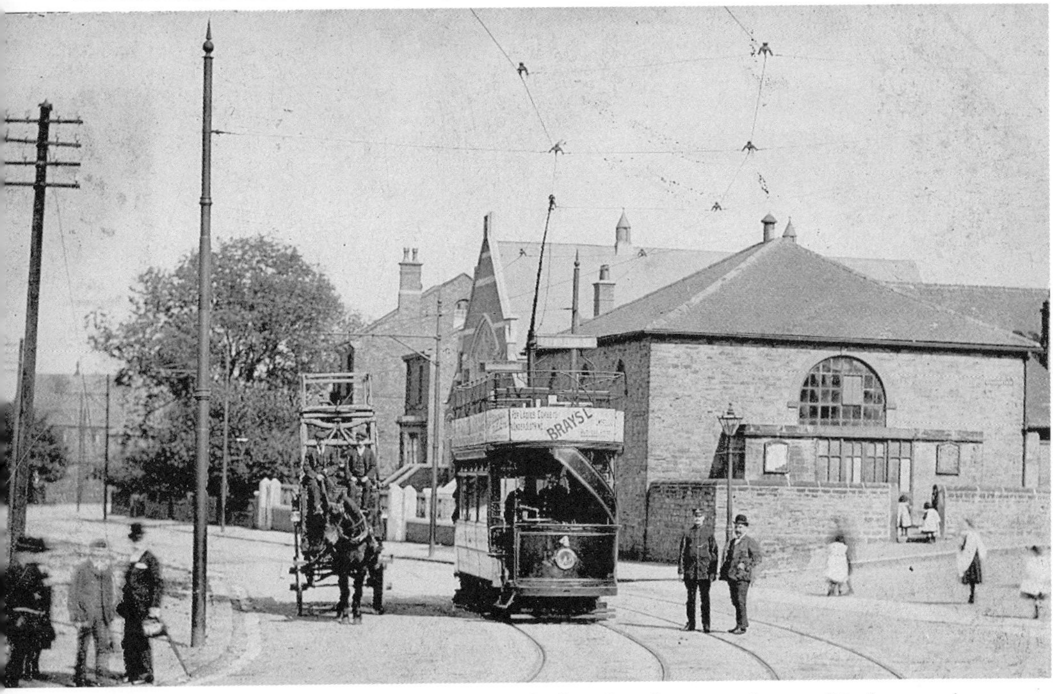

Rotherham Corporation tram no. 4 stands for the photographer at Kimberworth, *c.* 1905. Introduced in 1903, the trams were originally open topped, as here, but customer complaints soon forced the Corporation to fit top covers. Passing the tram is the Tramways Department's horse-drawn tower wagon, used for working on the overhead wires. Behind the tram is the original Kimberworth Wesleyan chapel of 1827, with the new chapel of 1903–4 behind. [5346]

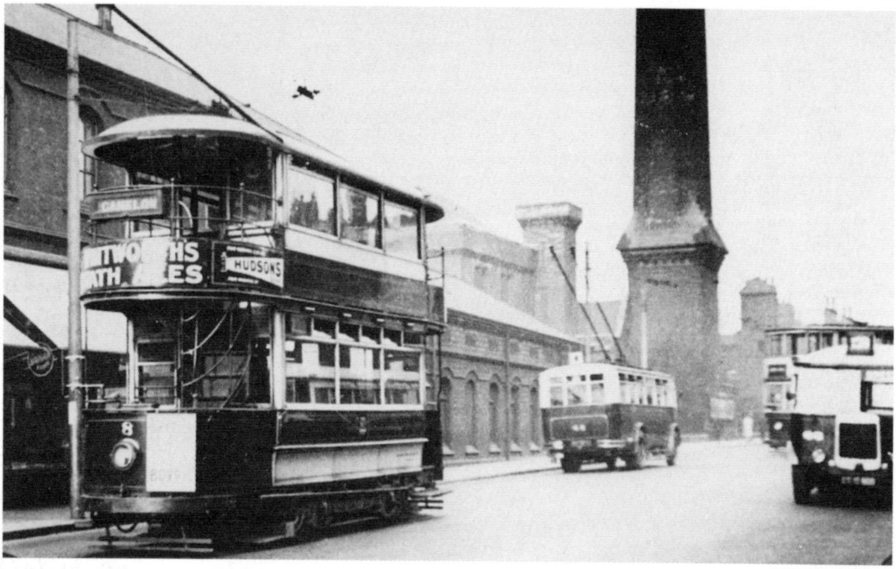

A busy day in Frederick Street, Rotherham, 1933, with two trams, a trolley bus and a motor bus in view. Tram no. 8 has just come into town from Canklow. The chimney belonged to the waterworks pumping station. The pumping station was demolished in 1964, but the chimney had gone some years before. [3960]

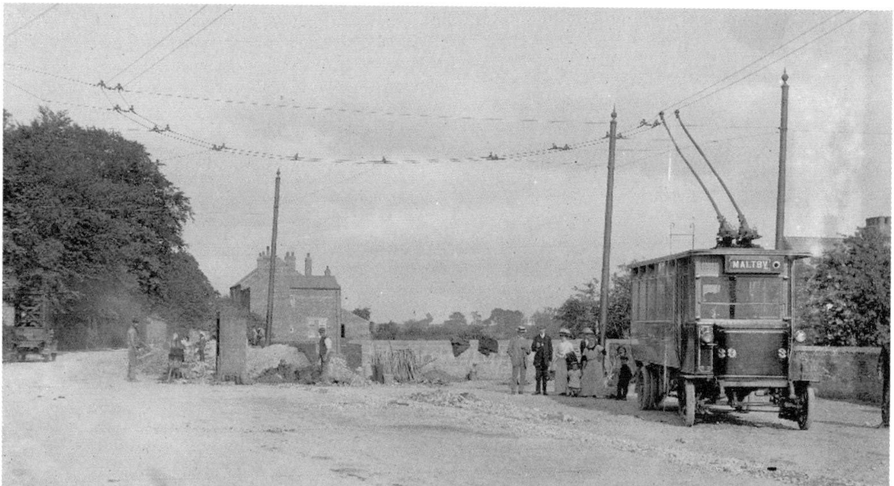

An early shot of the original trolley bus terminal on the outskirts of Maltby, soon after the service from Rotherham began in 1912, with no. 39, one of the initial fleet of 28-seater Roe vehicles. The service ran from the Herringthorpe tram terminus via Wickersley and Bramley to Maltby. In 1924, when the Maltby terminus was moved into the town centre, the 14 mile journey then cost 9d. and was claimed to be the 'cheapest ride in the United Kingdom'. The Borough Council's Halley tower wagon is parked in the background. [8712]

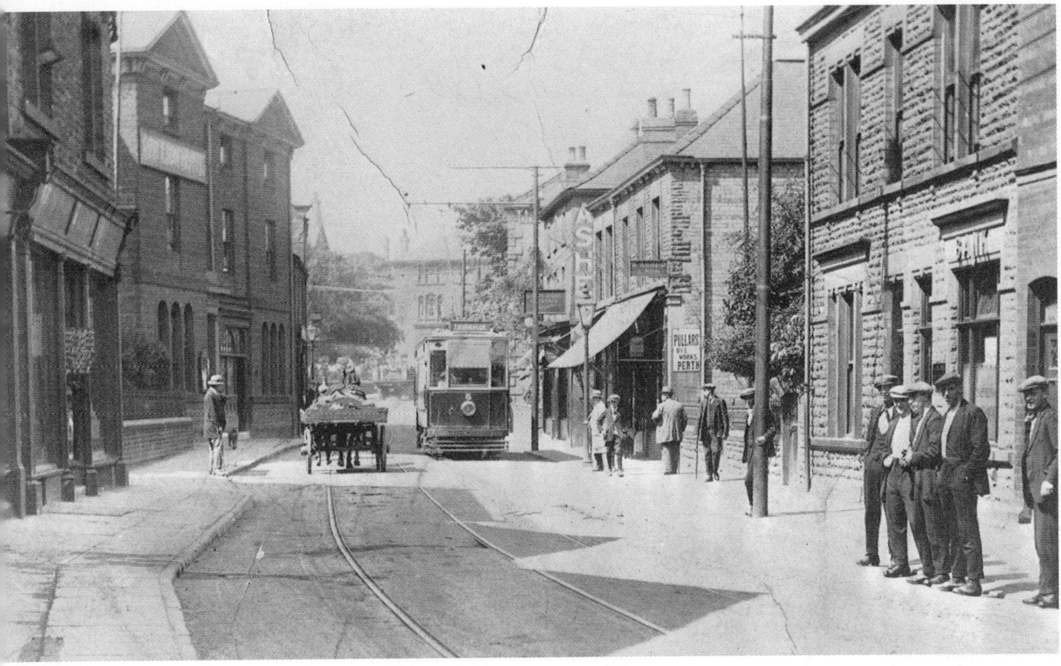

A single-deck tramcar of the Dearne District Light Railways makes its way along High Street, Wath, towards Thurnscoe in the late 1920s. The DDLR ran from Barnsley to Thurnscoe and the Woodman, Swinton. It had the dubious distinction of being the last urban tramway to open in England (1924) and the first to close (1933). [3532]

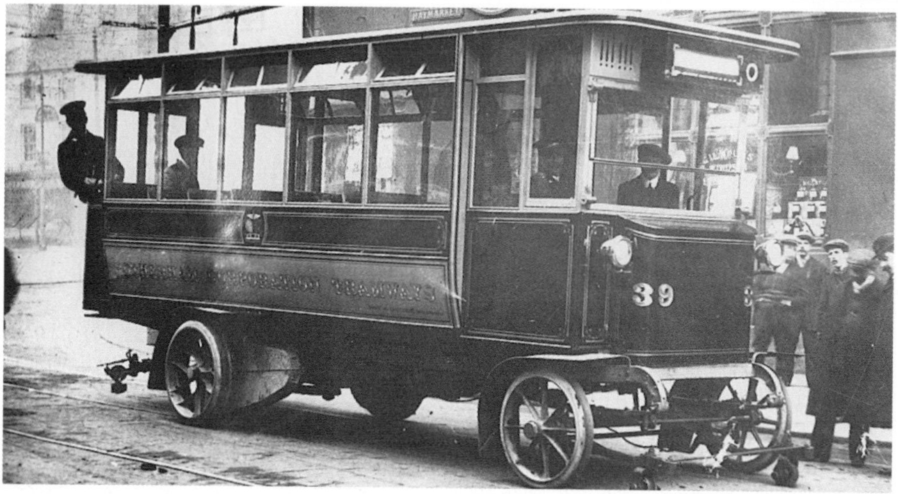

Rotherham trolley bus no. 39 again, this time in the centre of Sheffield in 1913. The vehicle is demonstrating the apparatus attached to the front wheels. Invented by Edward Cross, the General Manager of Rotherham's Transport Department, it enabled trolley buses to run on tram tracks. It does not seem to have impressed Sheffield Corporation, which never introduced trolley buses in the city. [3930]

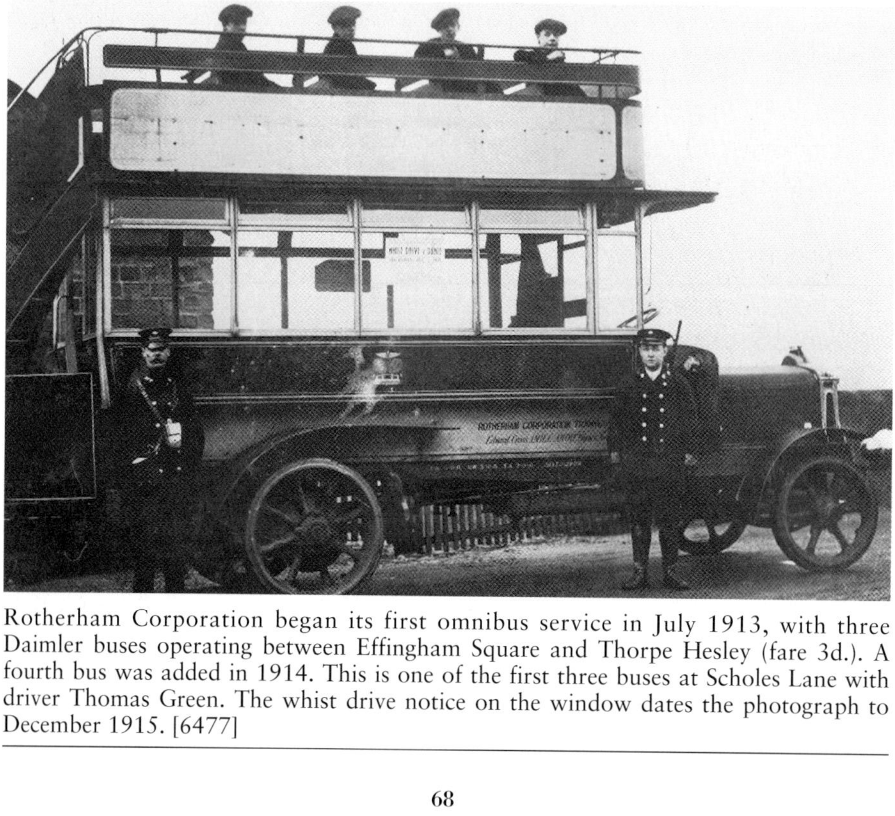

Rotherham Corporation began its first omnibus service in July 1913, with three Daimler buses operating between Effingham Square and Thorpe Hesley (fare 3d.). A fourth bus was added in 1914. This is one of the first three buses at Scholes Lane with driver Thomas Green. The whist drive notice on the window dates the photograph to December 1915. [6477]

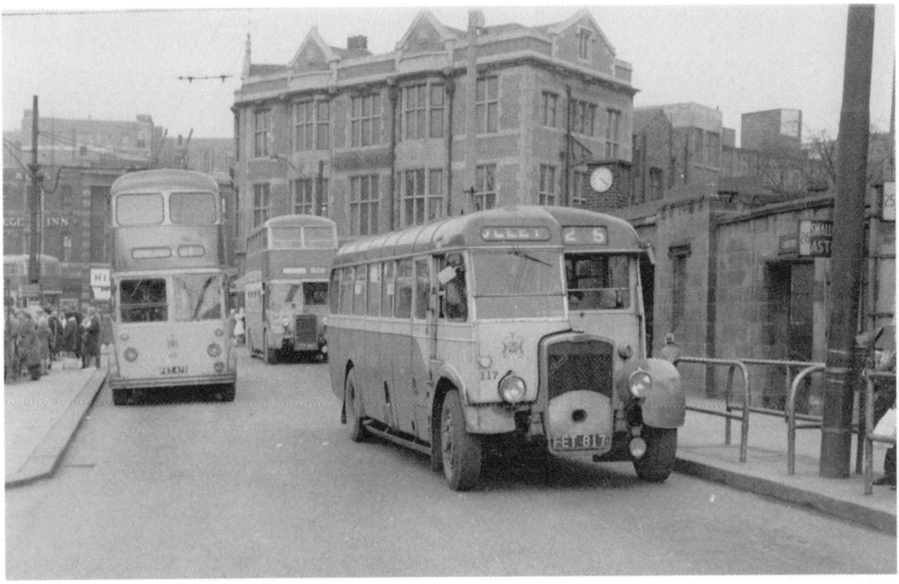

All Saints Square was Rotherham's main bus interchange from 1930 until the new bus station was opened in 1972. Single-decker FET 817, had an East Lancs. body on a Bristol chassis. New in October 1950, it was withdrawn in April 1967. A double-decker trolley bus stands at the left with a double-decker bus in front of Davy's café at the rear. [6454]

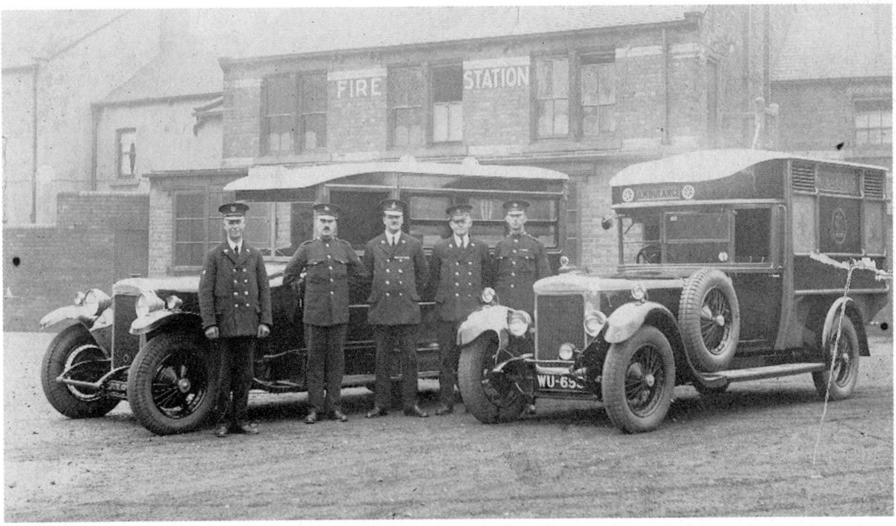

Ambulance patients travelled in some style in Rotherham in the 1920s. In 1924 the fire brigade could turn out three motor ambulances and a horse ambulance. These two Daimler ambulances were photographed in front of the original fire station in Rawmarsh Road. [4846]

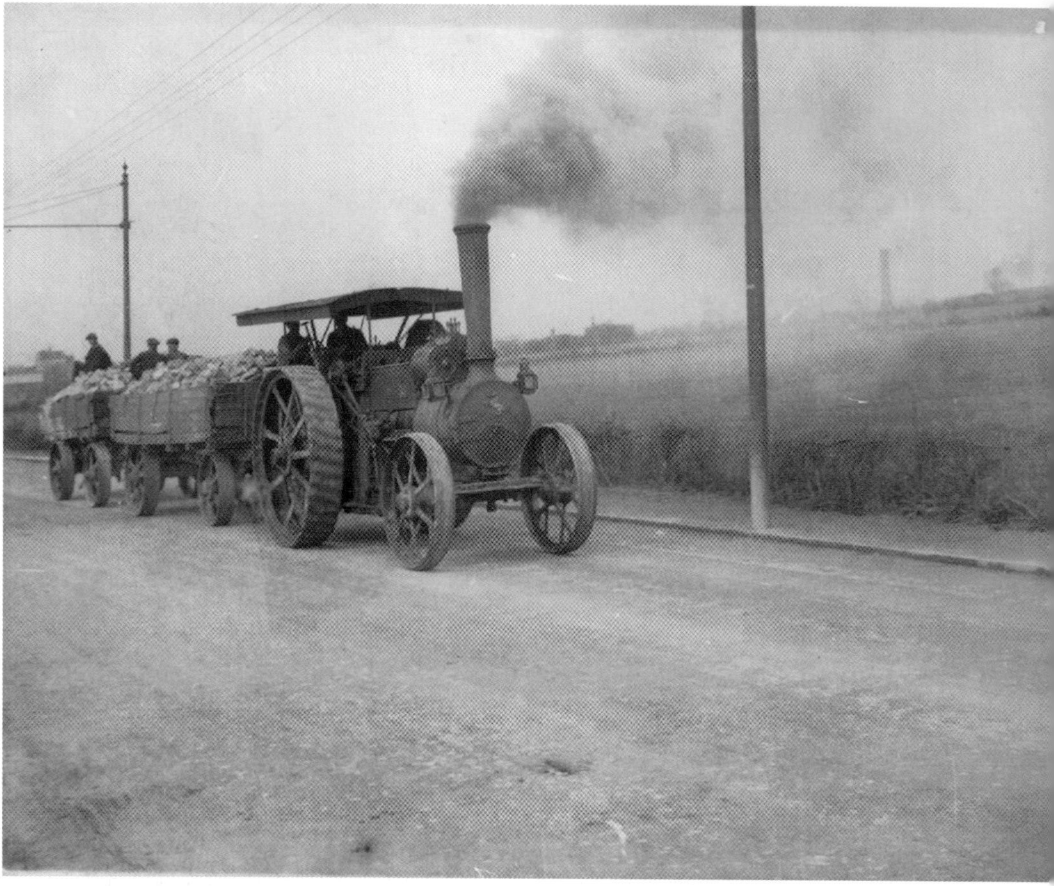

Steam road traction remained in wide use for moving heavy loads until well into the internal combustion era. This Invicta traction engine was photographed at Hellaby in 1913, hauling bricks from the Maltby Metallic Brick Co. The engine weighed 12 tons, the wagons 6 tons and the load 14 tons. The photograph was taken for Rotherham Borough Council. The Council was anxious to prove that it was the traction engines that were damaging the road and not the new trolley buses which had been introduced in 1912. [8715]

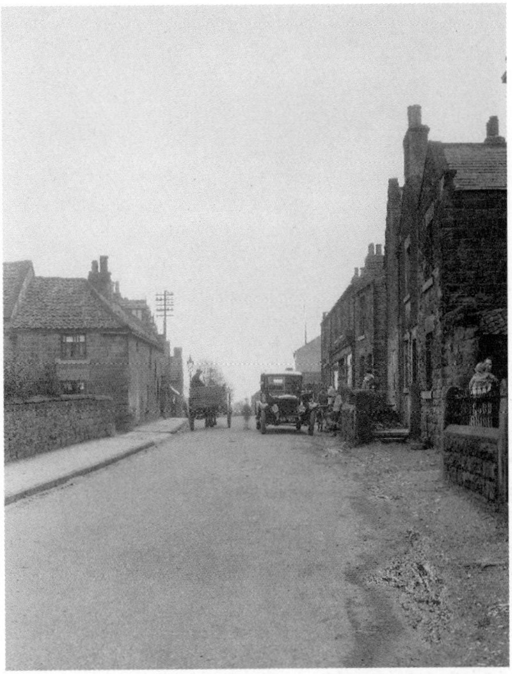

Two forms of private transport at Bramley, as the photographer's Daimler is slowly passed by a horse and cart. This was one of a series of photographs taken in 1930–1 to illustrate a proposed new Rotherham Corporation bus route. [8751]

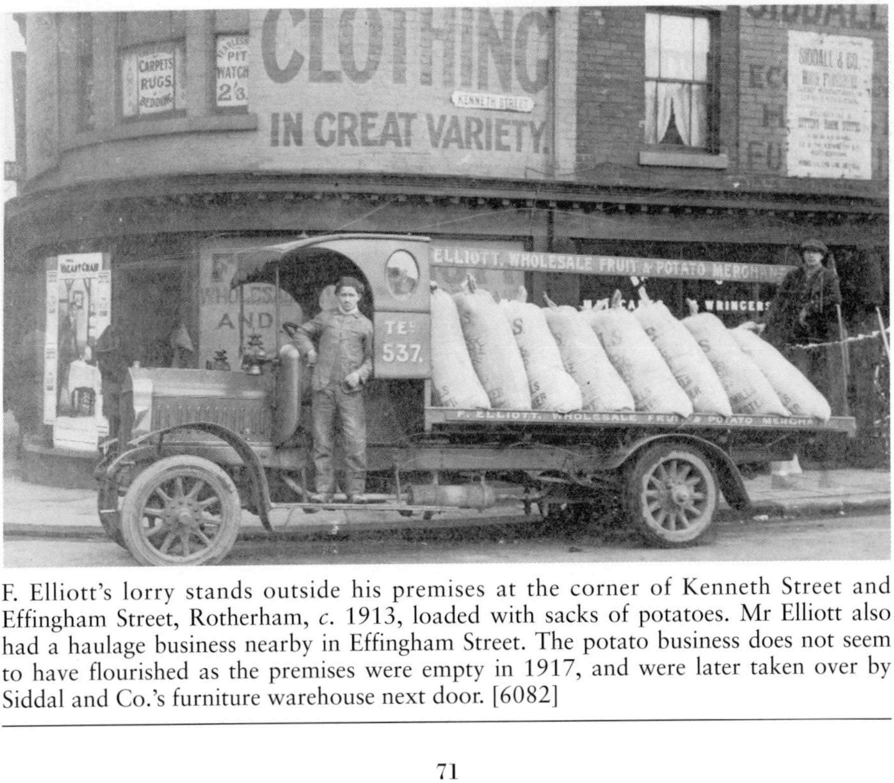

F. Elliott's lorry stands outside his premises at the corner of Kenneth Street and Effingham Street, Rotherham, *c.* 1913, loaded with sacks of potatoes. Mr Elliott also had a haulage business nearby in Effingham Street. The potato business does not seem to have flourished as the premises were empty in 1917, and were later taken over by Siddal and Co.'s furniture warehouse next door. [6082]

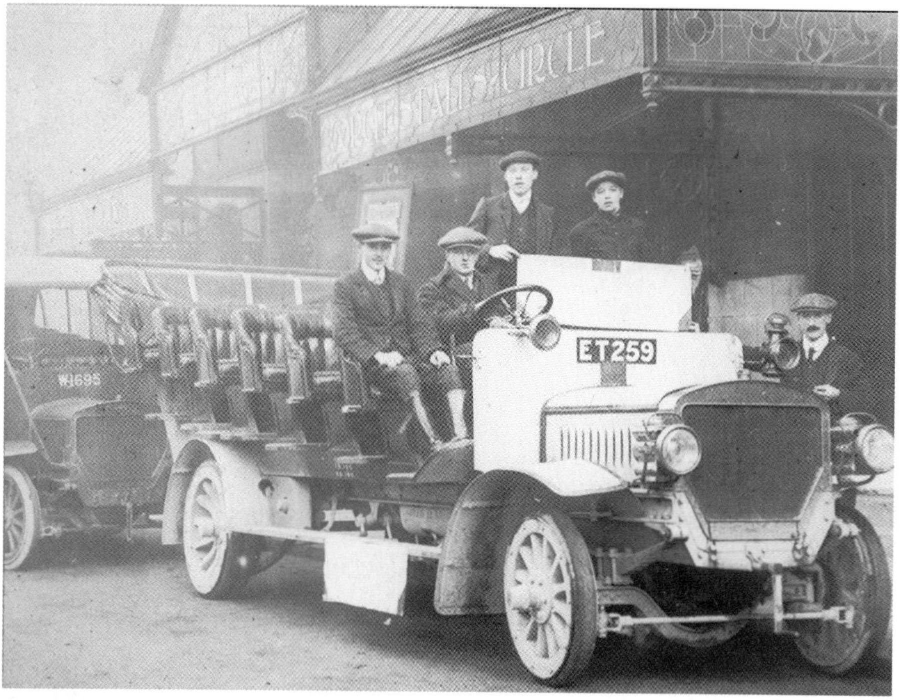

A Rotherham-registered, Sheffield-built Durham Churchill charabanc waits outside the Hippodrome on Henry Street, Rotherham, with a similar Sheffield-registered vehicle parked behind. ET 259 was registered to Rotherham cab and omnibus proprietor Moorhouse and Co. of Talbot Lane in 1910 and was painted red and black. Despite the folding hood, travel in these vehicles must have been uncomfortable in bad weather. [10310]

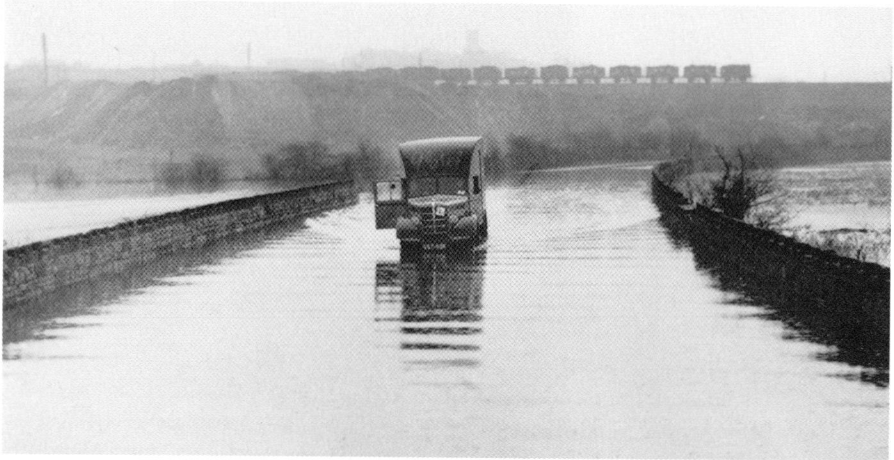

The Rother Valley has always been prone to flooding, as the driver of Vere's bakery delivery van discovered while making his way back to Rotherham in the early 1950s. The place is Treeton Lane, between Catcliffe and Treeton. [1868]

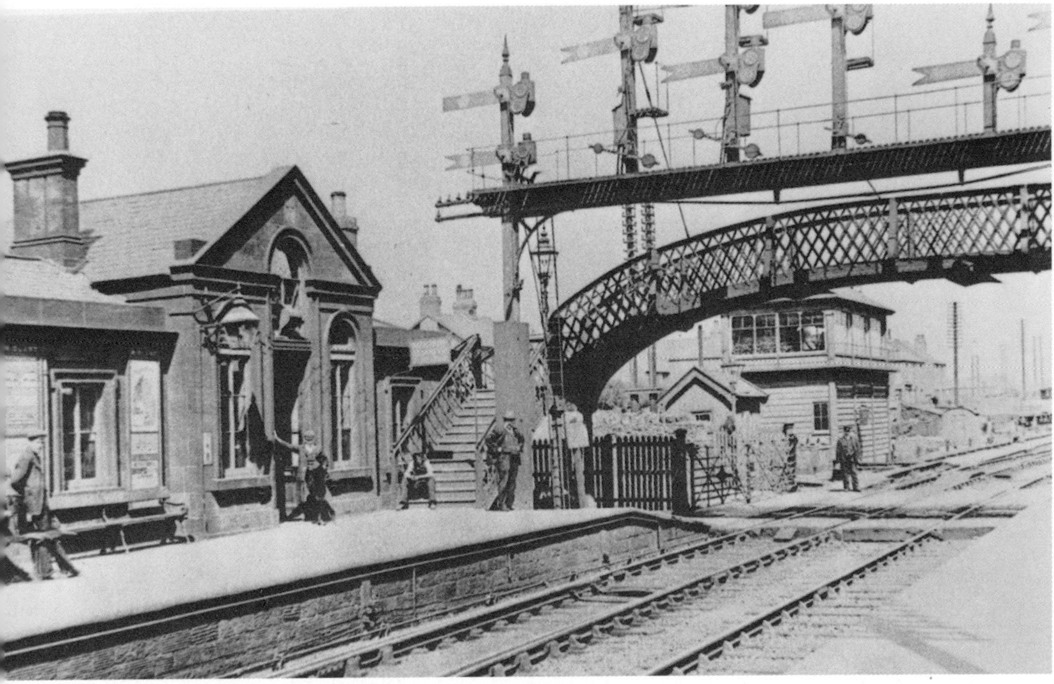

The station at the Holmes was the first stop out of Rotherham on the Sheffield & Rotherham Railway. The station buildings date from the opening of the railway in 1838. By the time this photograph was taken, in about 1910, the line had long been part of the Midland Railway. [6757]

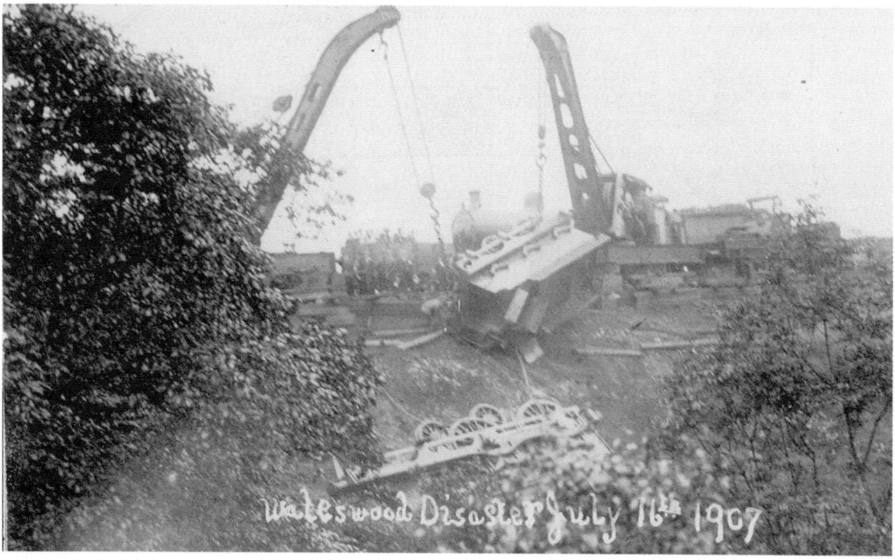

This railway accident at Waleswood looks spectacular but fortunately there were no fatalities. Late on 16 July 1907 a fast goods train became derailed on the Great Central line from Retford to Sheffield, and was struck by the 11 p.m. Sheffield–Retford passenger train. The train engine and first two coaches fell down the embankment. The driver and fireman had miraculous escapes and the sole passenger in the first carriage awoke with a sprained ankle to 'find the door to the carriage was the skylight'. [10027]

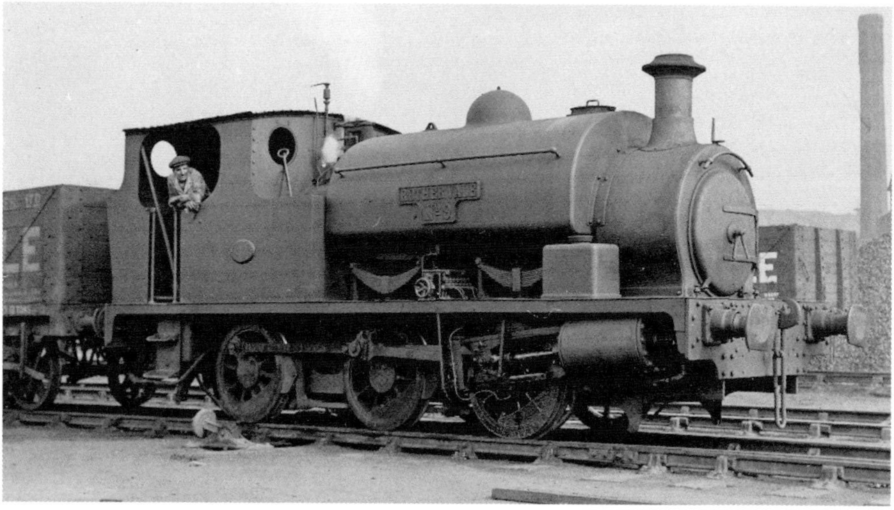

Most large local factories and collieries formerly had their own sidings and locomotives for shunting purposes. Aptly named *Rother Vale*, Rother Vale Collieries' no. 9, built by Hudswell Clark, takes a rest from its shunting duties. The company, which owned coal mines at Fence, Treeton and Thurcroft, became part of the United Steel Companies in 1918. [10064]

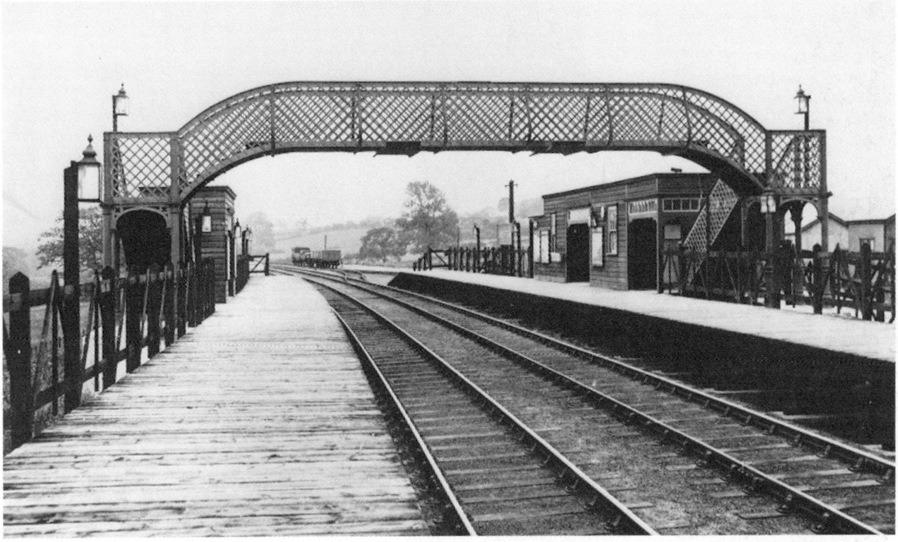

The deserted state of the station at Anston probably reflects the sparse nature of the passenger services on the line. On the jointly owned lines from Brancliff Junction to Dinnington Colliery, Silverwood and Doncaster, the passenger station at Anston opened in 1912 and provided a booking-office, waiting-room and ladies' room. The infrequent passenger service between Doncaster, Anston and Shireoaks lasted only until 1929. The unused station was removed during the Second World War to replace a blitzed station in Scotland. [6565]

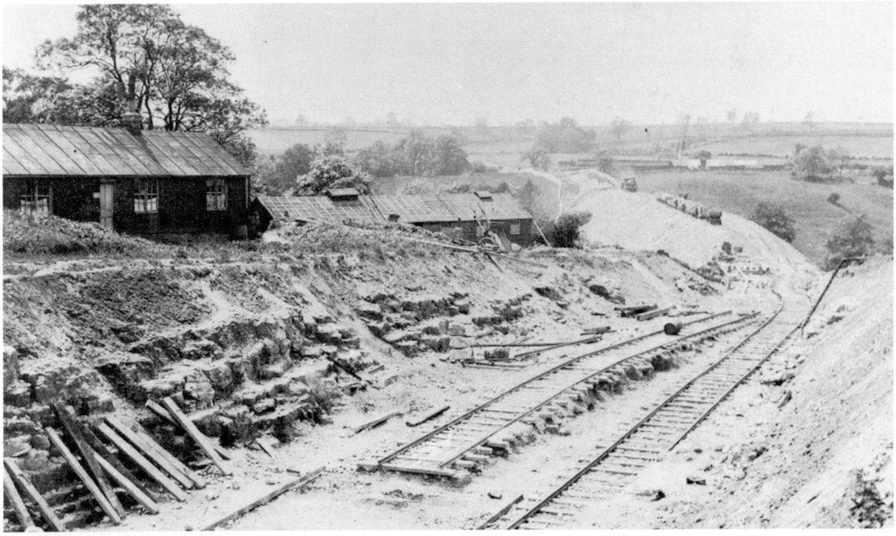

The South Yorkshire Joint Line under construction to the east of Maltby, *c.* 1908. A contractor's train is at work on the embankment near Mill Hill Holts in the middle distance. [6640]

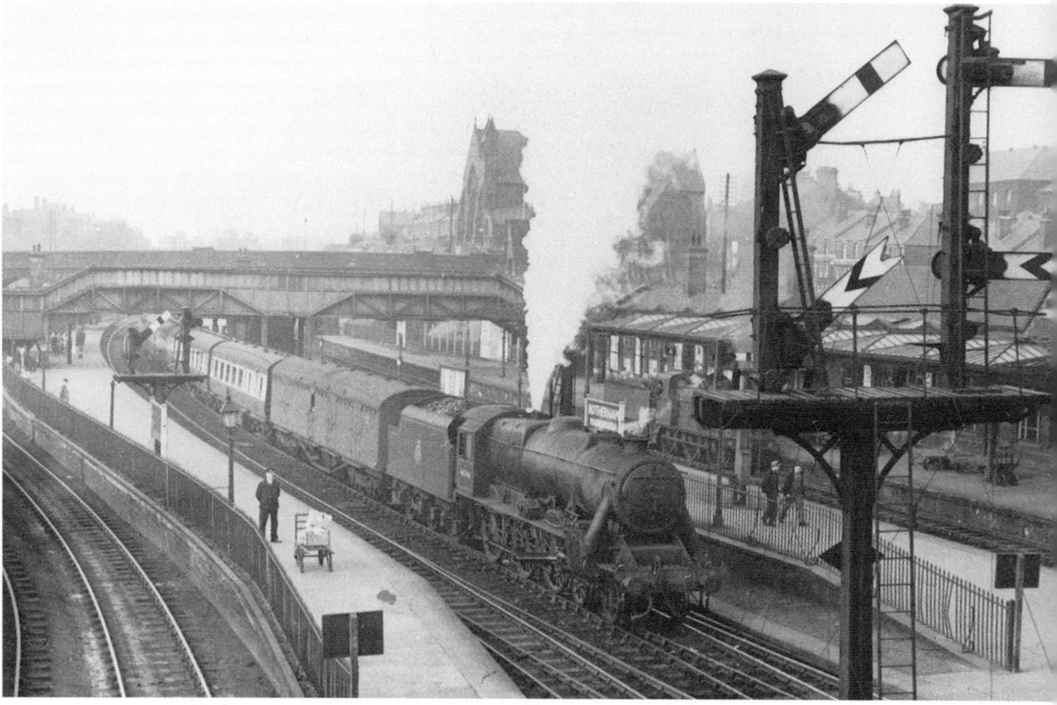

Ex-LMS 'Black 5', no. 44744, one of a batch fitted with Caprotti valve gear, waits to leave Masbrough station, Rotherham, in the 1950s. Stopping trains moved to the new Rotherham Central station in 1986, but the lines remain open for use by long-distance trains. The plume of steam obscures St John's Church, Masbrough, which opened in 1864 and was demolished in 1976. [6596].

Section Five

ENTERTAINMENTS

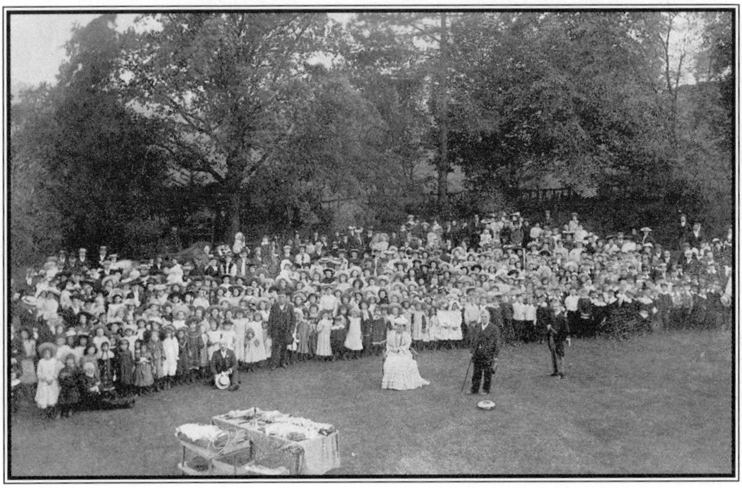

In 1901 the Sunday school at Masbrough Independent chapel held its annual picnic in the grounds of Howarth Hall between Brinsworth and Whiston. [4405]

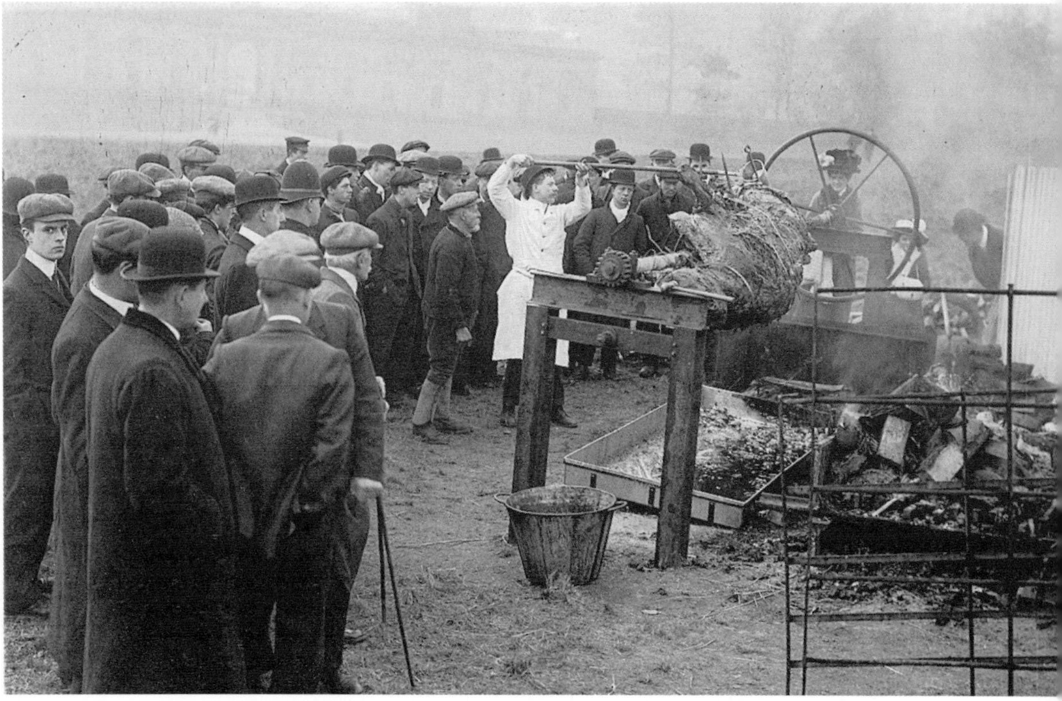

On 31 December 1910 Earl and Countess Fitzwilliam were finally blessed with a son, after four daughters. The christening of the young Viscount Milton, Peter Fitzwilliam, on 11 February 1911 was marked by great celebrations on the Wentworth Woodhouse estate, including an ox roast in front of the house and an evening firework display. The baby eventually became the eighth Earl, but was to die tragically in 1948 when the light aircraft in which he was travelling with his companion, Kathleen Kennedy (sister of John F. and Robert Kennedy), crashed in the south of France. [349]

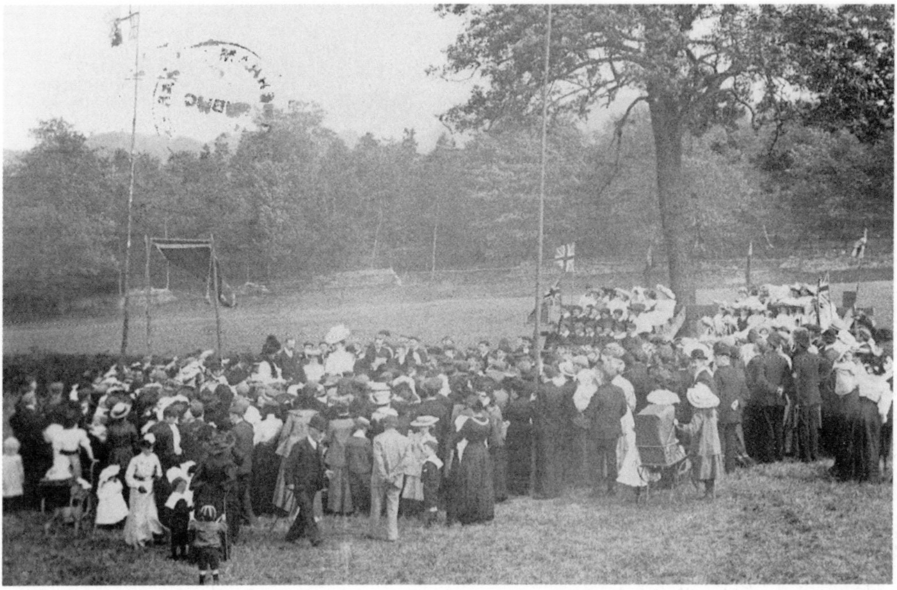

The hamlet of Scholes was owned lock, stock and barrel by Earl Fitzwilliam. It was therefore fitting that the opening ceremony for the new recreation ground was performed by Countess Fitzwilliam on 12 August 1905. She is left of centre in this postcard, wearing the large white hat. [4203]

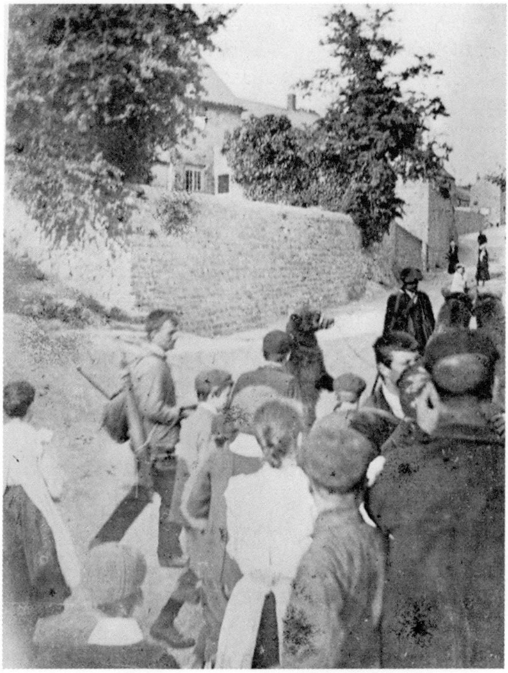

Travelling German musicians and entertainers were a common sight in Britain in the years before the First World War. This troupe visited North Anston with their performing bears in 1912. [558]

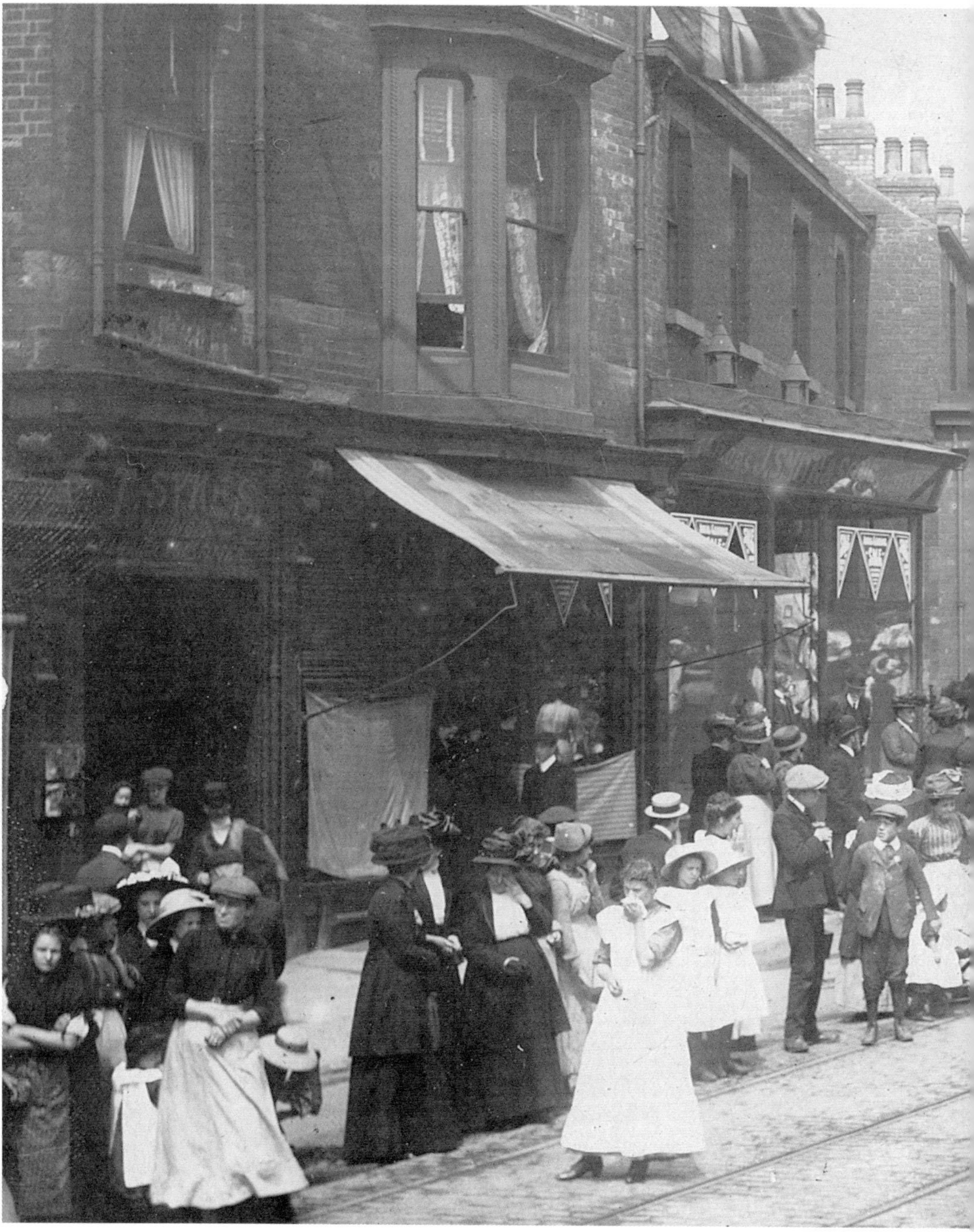

A royal visit can always be relied on to bring out the crowds. During July 1912 George V and Queen Mary stayed at Wentworth Woodhouse and made visits to a number of

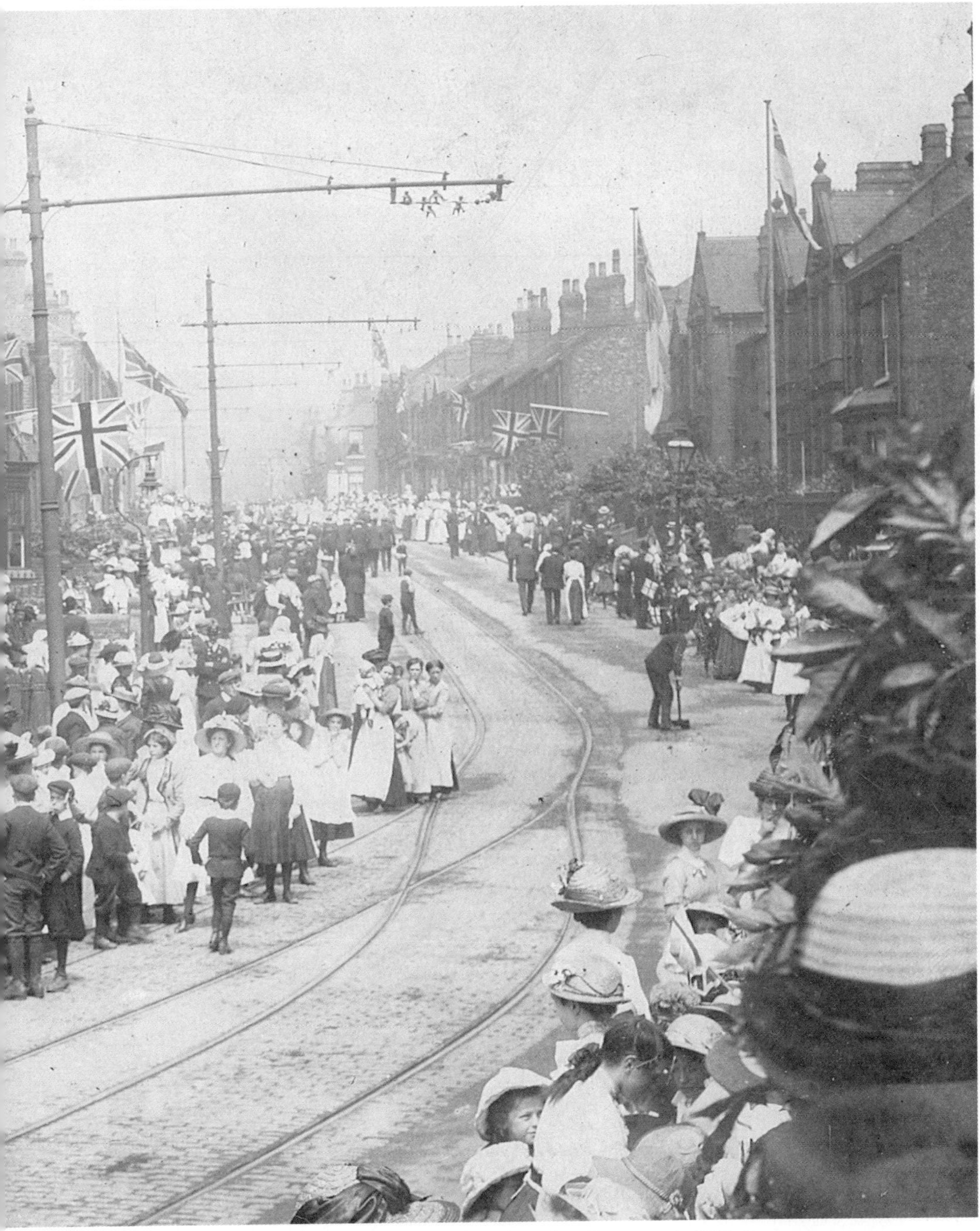

local collieries and factories. This crowd gathered in Rawmarsh Hill, Parkgate to await the passage of the royal party en route to Swinton. [3869]

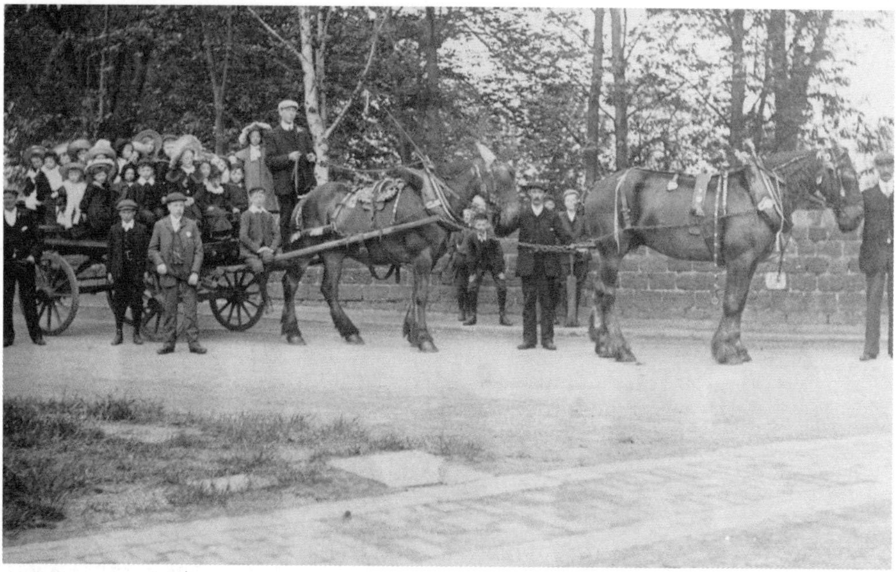

Whitsun was formerly a favourite period for church parades and outings. A wagon-load of Sunday school children from Brampton Bierlow pose for the photographer before setting out on their outing on Whit Monday, *c.* 1905. [1070]

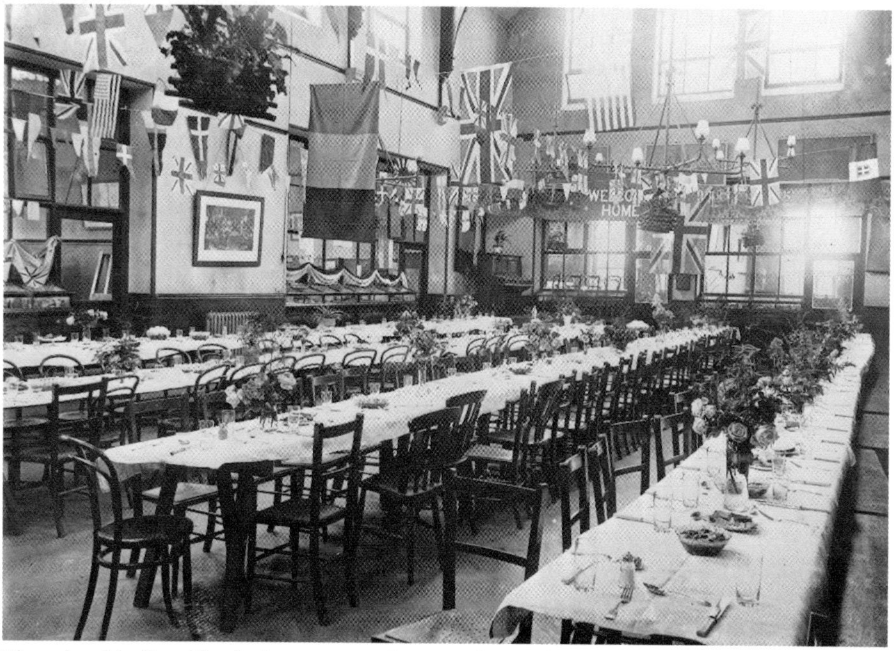

The school hall at North Anston was decorated to welcome back local soldiers in 1918 or 1919. Among the Union Jacks, Stars and Stripes and Tricolours is a solitary Japanese flag, Japan having been one of the Allies in the First World War. [511]

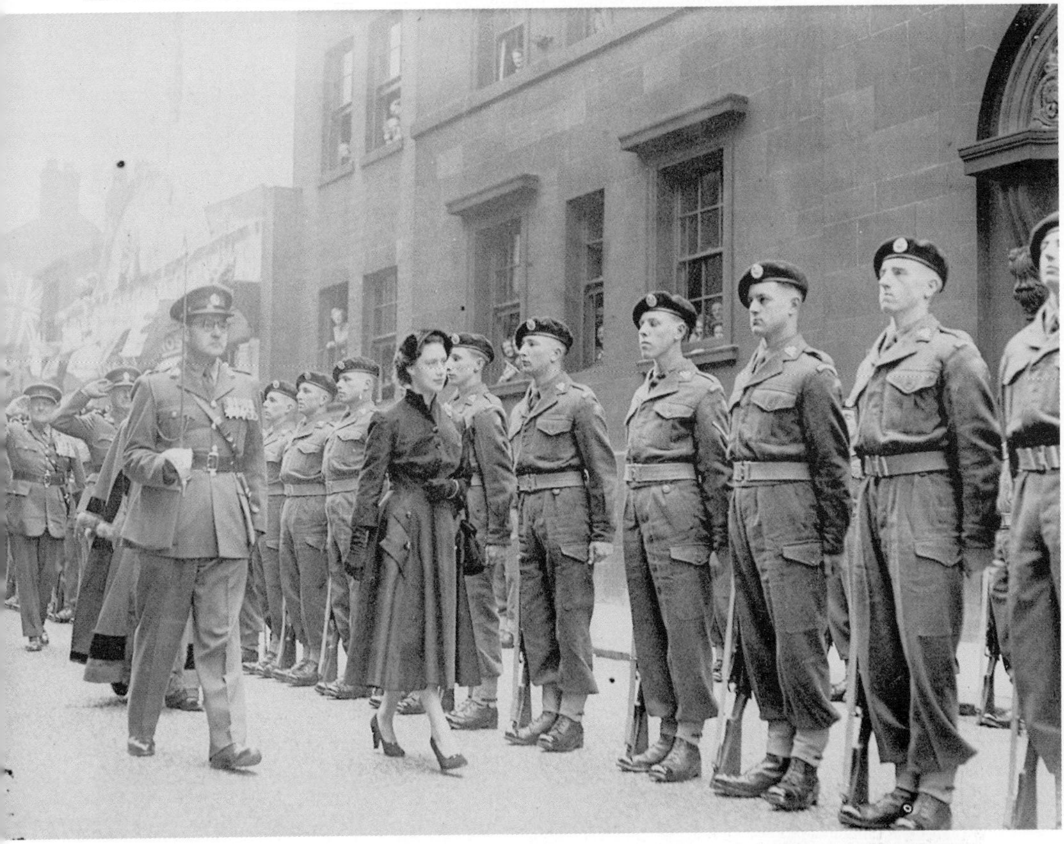

The young Princess Margaret made an official visit to Rotherham on 18 April 1953. Major J.V. Hawkins escorts the princess along Howard Street as she reviews the guard of honour supplied by the York and Lancaster Regiment and 467th Heavy Anti-aircraft Regiment. [6702]

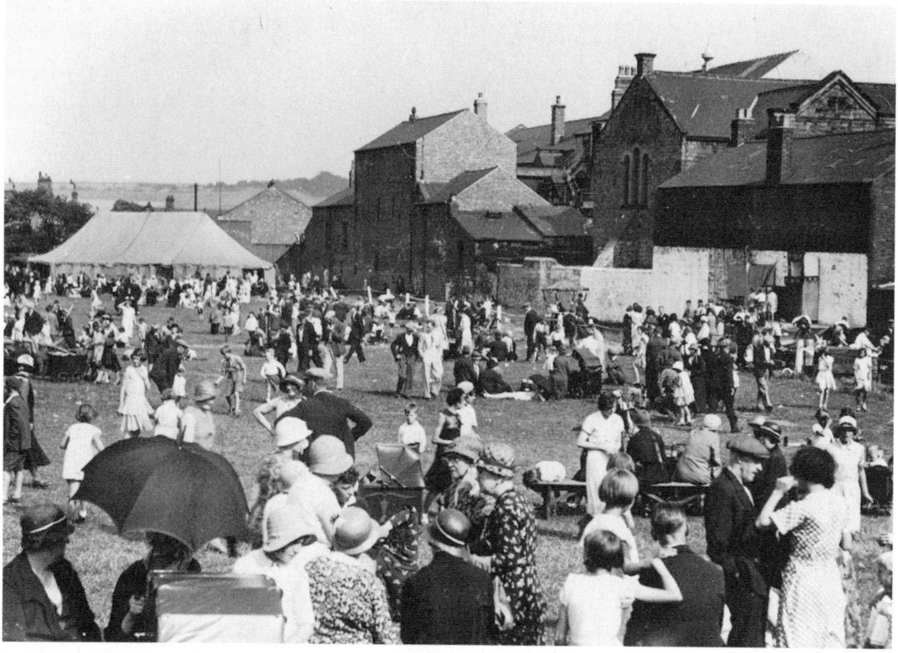

A happy crowd throng a Co-operative Gala at Kilnhurst in the 1930s. [3490]

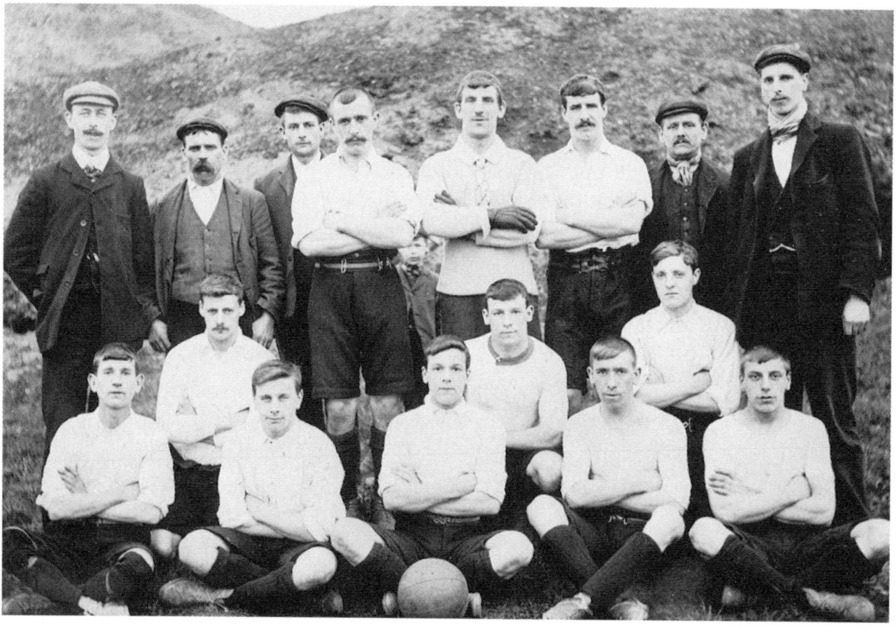

The members of the Fence football team of *c.* 1905 are unfortunately anonymous. They seem to have posed in front of the pit tip. [6658]

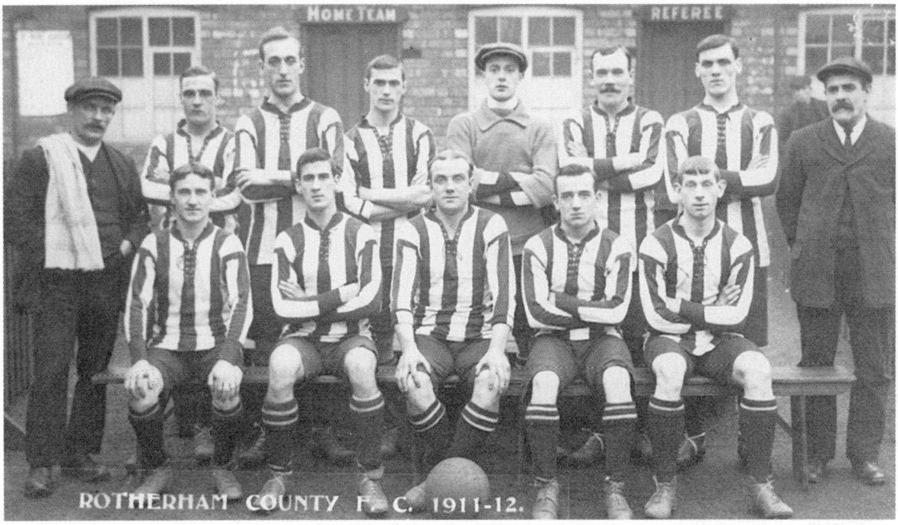

Rotherham County pose proudly at the end of the 1911/12 season, the first of three successive Midland League championships. Founded as Thornhill Rovers, the club changed its name and moved to the ground at Millmoor in 1907. It was admitted to the Second Division of the Football League in 1919, but was relegated to Division Three North in 1923. Financial problems caused an amalgamation with Rotherham Town in 1925 to form Rotherham United. [8079]

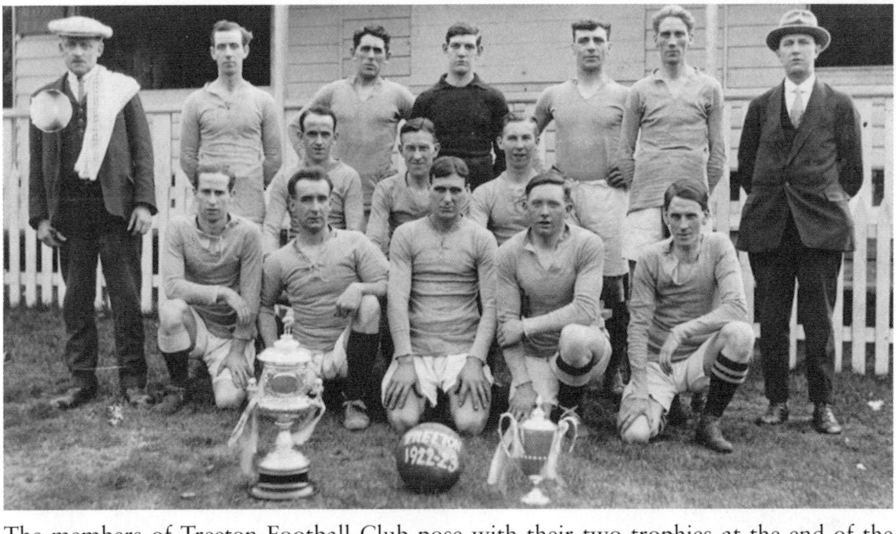

The members of Treeton Football Club pose with their two trophies at the end of the 1922/3 season. One cup is the Hatchard League champion's trophy, the other is unknown. The team members are, back row, left to right: Jack Martin, Horace Ward, Frank Pye, Harold Hopkins, Bill Lakin, ? Thompson, Sid Pashley. Middle row: Fred Smith, Jim Hampson, Eddie Hampson. Front row: Jake Westwood, Harry Rodgers, Ernest Cutts, Wilfred Johnson, Tom Rossington. [12448]

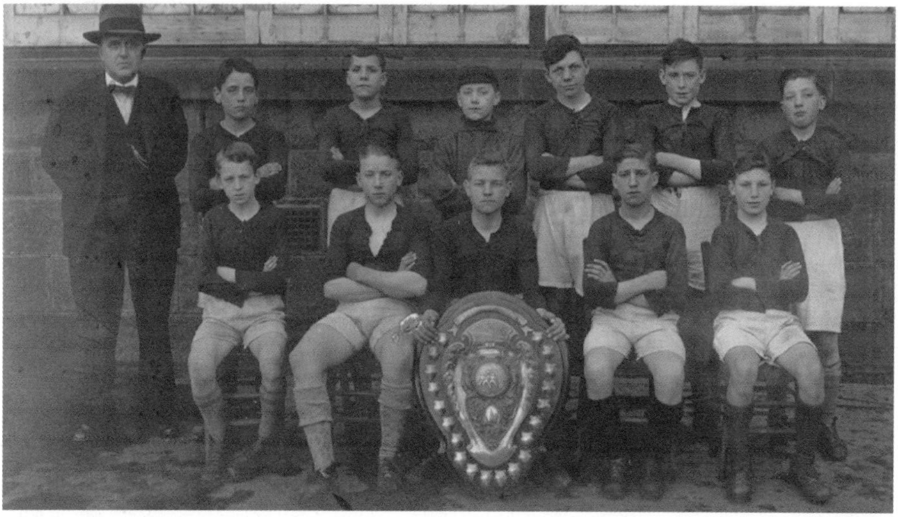

Members of the school football team at Swinton Bridge School pose proudly with the Bond Shield which they won in 1932/3. The shield had been presented by E. Bond OBE for competition between the schools in the Swinton Education area, and was first contested in 1921/2. Swinton Bridge had also won the trophy in 1925/6. [4179]

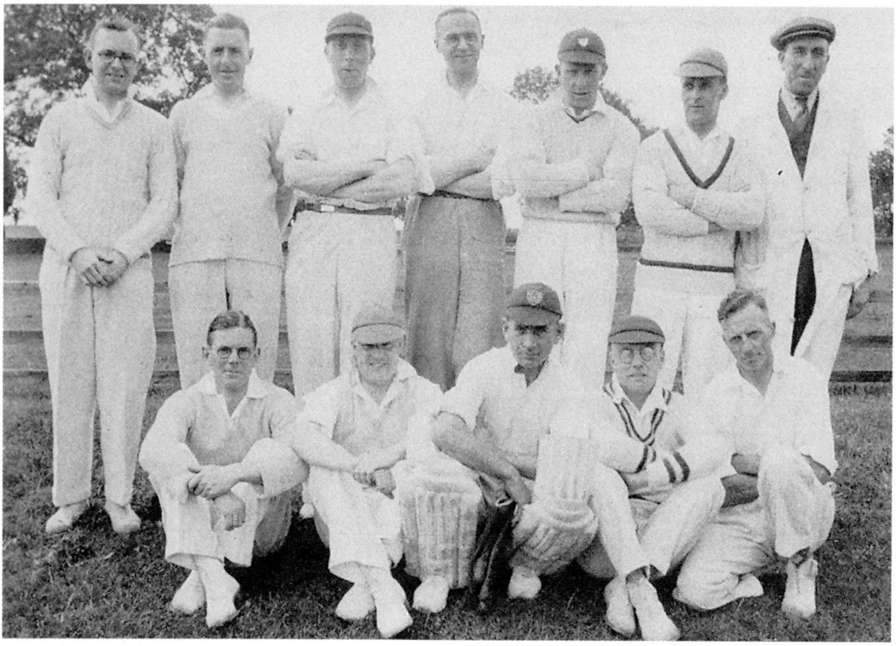

The members of the St Paul's Cricket Club, Masbrough, in August 1938. Back row, left to right: Tommy Coulthard, Wilf Taylor, Bill Appleby, Arthur Appleby, Cecil Turner, Billy Pridmore, Len Heath. Front row: Harold Taylor, Harry Tompkins, Harry Maycock, Frank Hall, Bill Ibbotson. [6657]

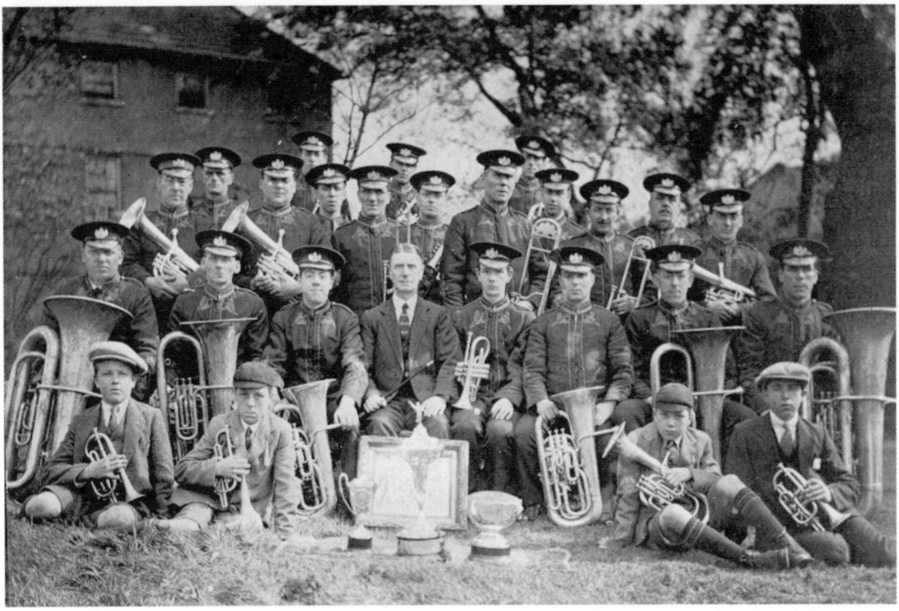

The smartly dressed members of the Rawmarsh Band pose with their trophies in the grounds of Rawmarsh Hall in 1921. Rawmarsh Baths now occupy this site. [10871]

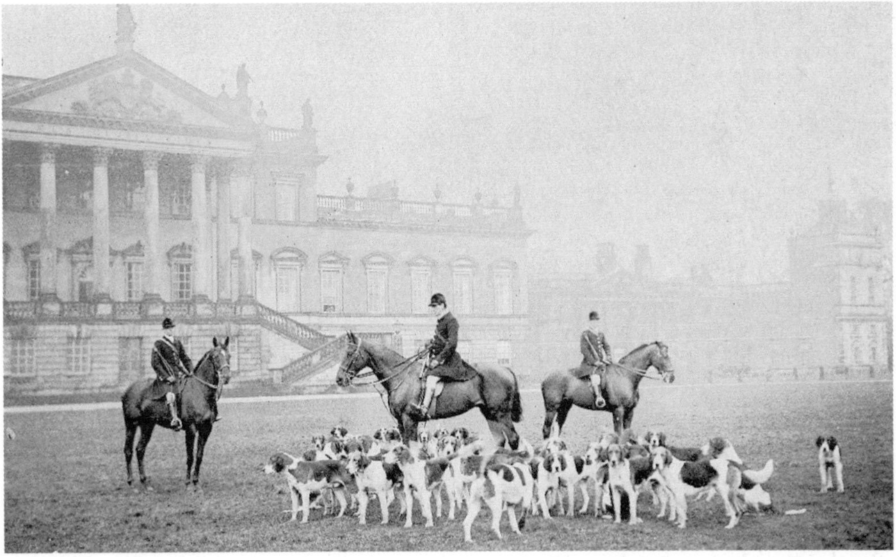

The Fitzwilliam Hunt was a common sight in the area, the hounds being kept in that part of Wentworth village known as the 'Kennels'. The pack had been founded in 1858. In January 1929, however, the Earl announced that he was disbanding the pack at the end of that season. He gave his reason as the continued industrialisation of the area, which made it increasingly difficult to hunt effectively. [272]

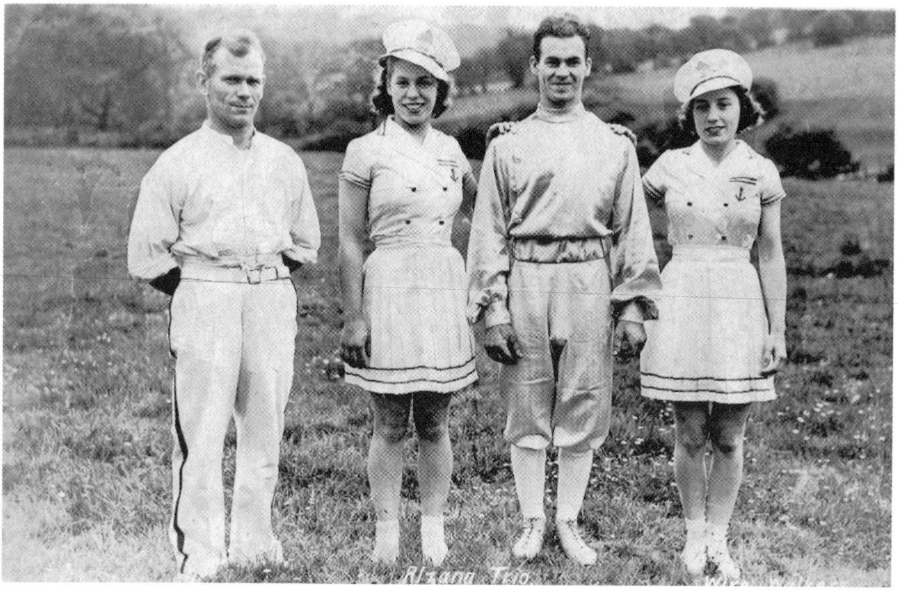

The 'Great Alzanas' consisted of Charles Davis, pictured here at the left, with his son Harold and his daughters Elsie and Hilda. Their high wire act was perfected in the front garden in Rotherham Road, Maltby. Harold's wife Minnie later joined the act. Their first public performance was a crossing of Langold Lake in 1937. They appeared at the Blackpool Tower Circus in 1946 and 1947, and then joined Barnum and Bailey in America. There they crossed Niagara and appeared in the film *The Greatest Show on Earth*. Elsie died in 1958 and Harold and Minnie settled in Las Vegas. [409]

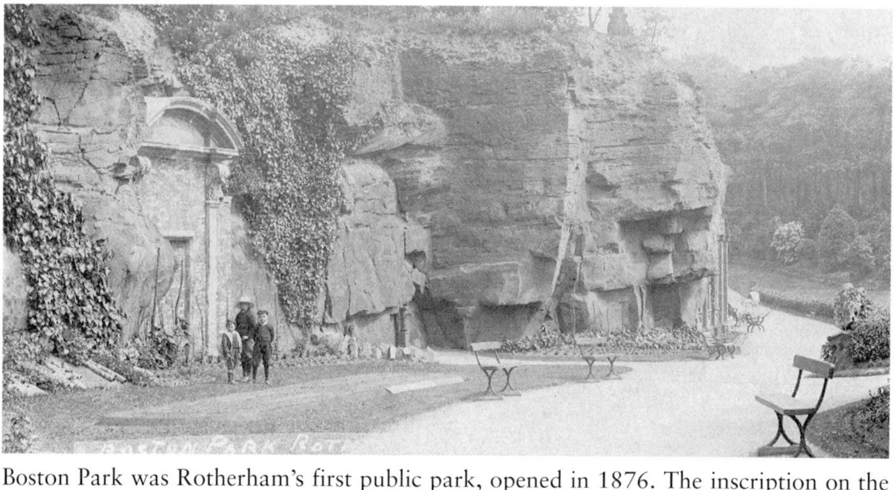

Boston Park was Rotherham's first public park, opened in 1876. The inscription on the back of this postcard, dated 1904, tells us that one of the three boys was called Bernard. They are standing by a doorway from the medieval College of Jesus that was rescued from the town centre and relocated in the park. On the top of the crag is a pinnacle removed from the parish church during restoration in 1873–5. [8661]

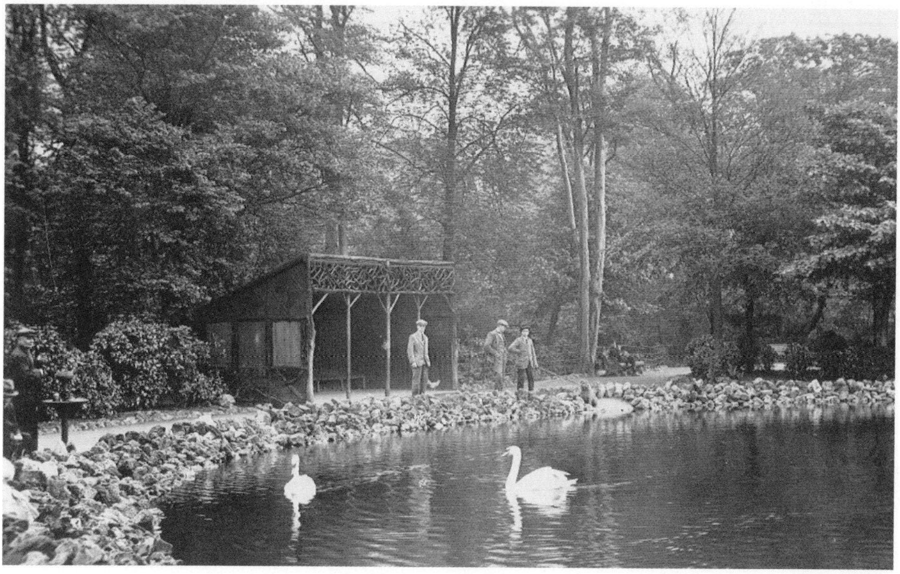

Clifton Park, Rotherham, was formed from the grounds of Clifton House which were purchased by the Corporation and opened as a public park in 1891. A small group of passers-by inspect the swans on the lake in Clifton Park in the early 1920s. Originally a fish pond, the lake was filled in during 1939 when it was felt to be unhygienic. The paddling pool and amusements now occupy the site. [4512]

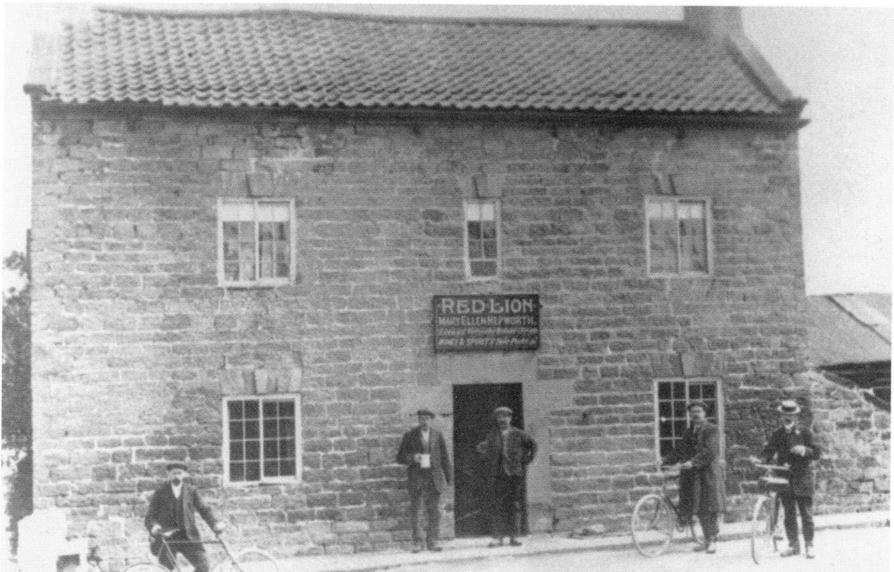

The Red Lion at Todwick was a typical, unprepossessing village pub when Mary Ellen Hepworth was licensee in about 1910. [3140]

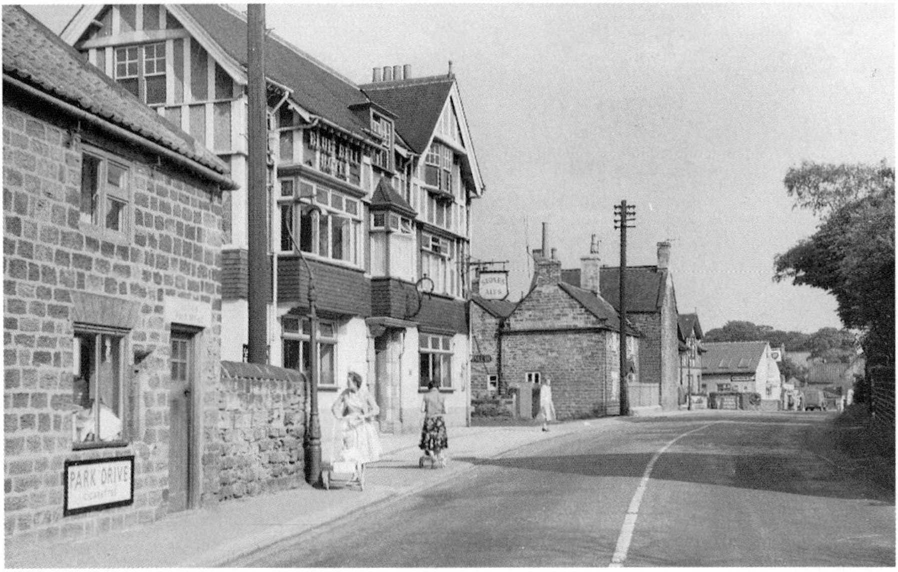

The façade of the Blue Bell in Worksop Road, Aston, dates from the early years of the present century, but the licence dates back to at least 1830, when George Staniforth combined grocery with innkeeping. [12902]

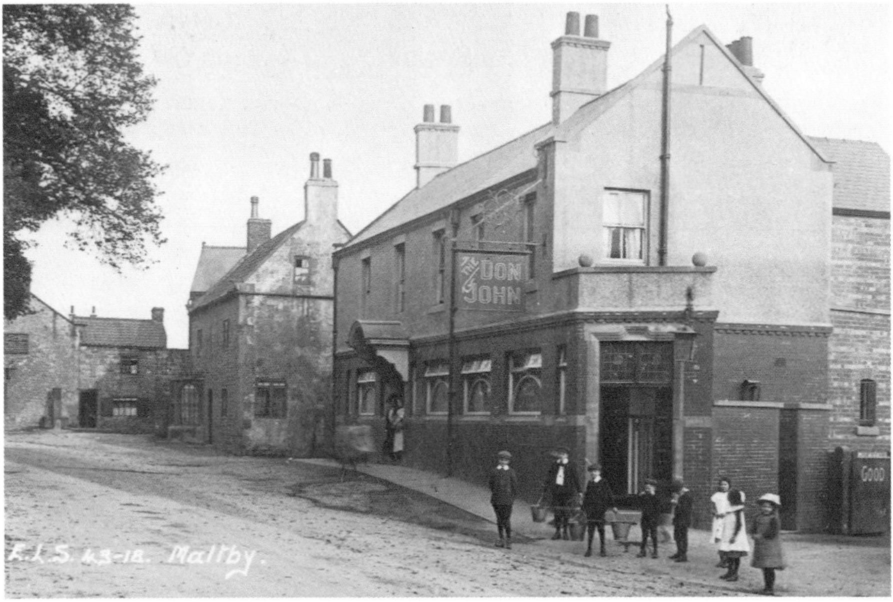

Few of the people in this photograph appear old enough to make use of the Don John on the edge of Maltby, *c.* 1910. The buckets they are carrying suggest that the children have been collecting water from the nearby wells in Blyth Road. [3538]

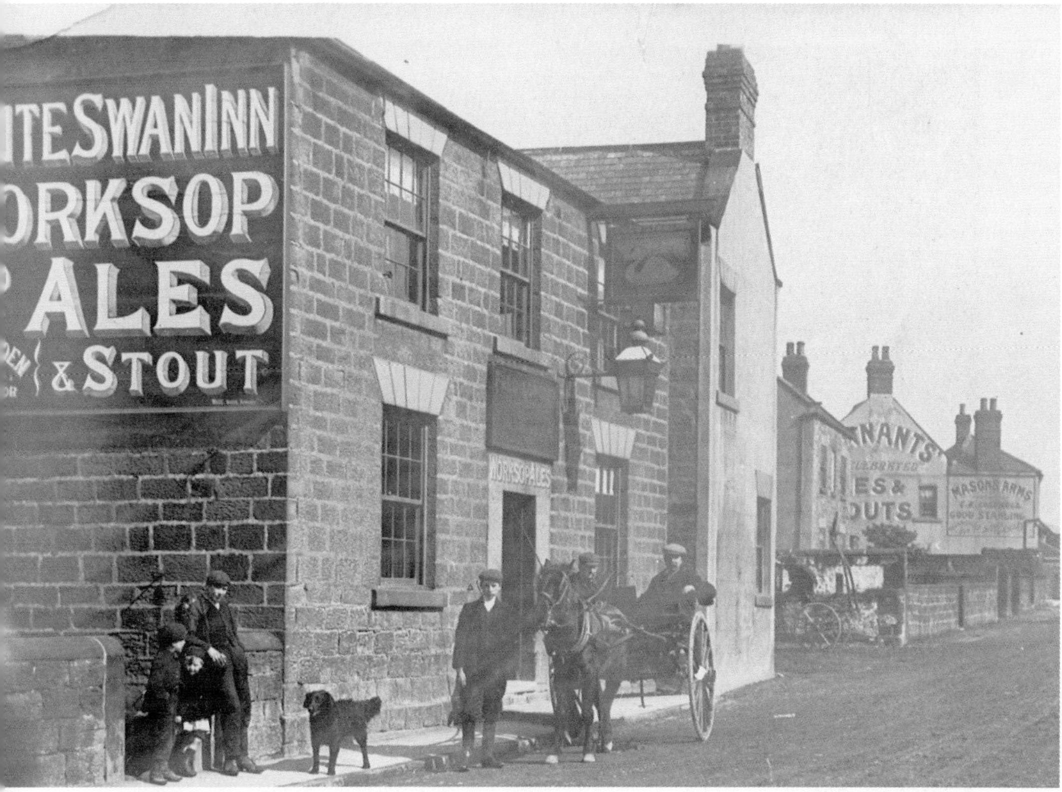

The White Swan on Bawtry Road, Wickersley, seen here during the licenseeship of Fred Longden, *c.* 1910, has now gone. The Mason's Arms in the background remains, although it no longer offers good stabling. [1963]

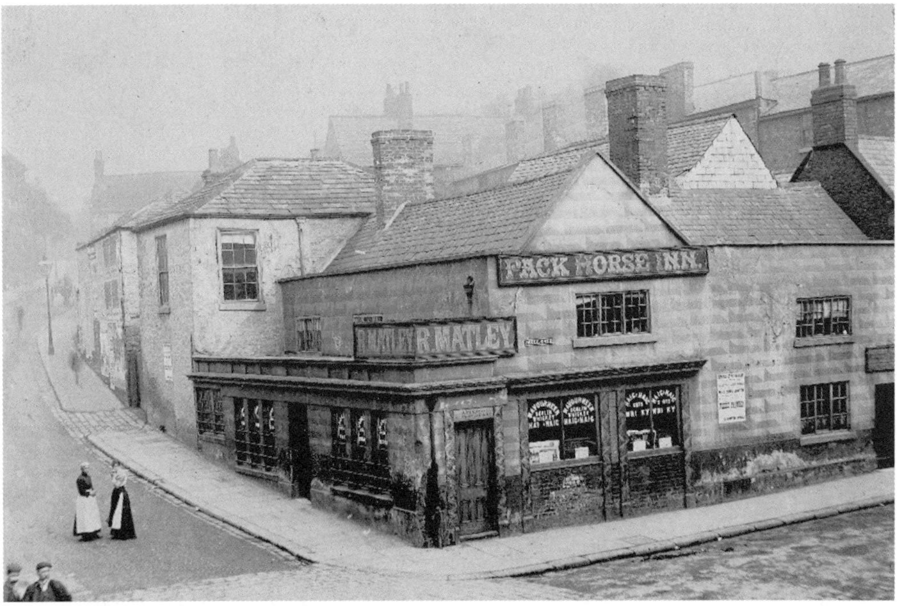

The Pack Horse Inn at the corner of Doncaster Gate and Wellgate, Rotherham, was well known until 1904. In that year the magistrates refused to renew the licence because it was notorious for after-hours drinking and gambling. The brewery's plans to replace it with a large hotel came to nothing and the Pack Horse was eventually demolished to make way for shops. The 'stonework' was actually painted on to the walls. [222]

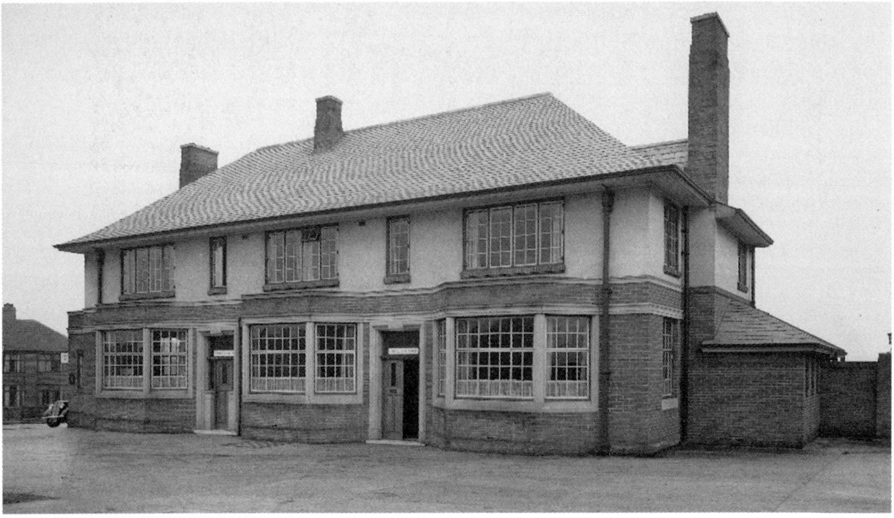

The Hind Hotel on East Bawtry Road, Rotherham is a typical 1930s roadhouse, constructed when the area was being developed for suburban housing. Opened in 1937, it was originally to be called the Edward VIII. The name was hurriedly changed when the King abdicated. [8687]

Section Six

SHOPPING

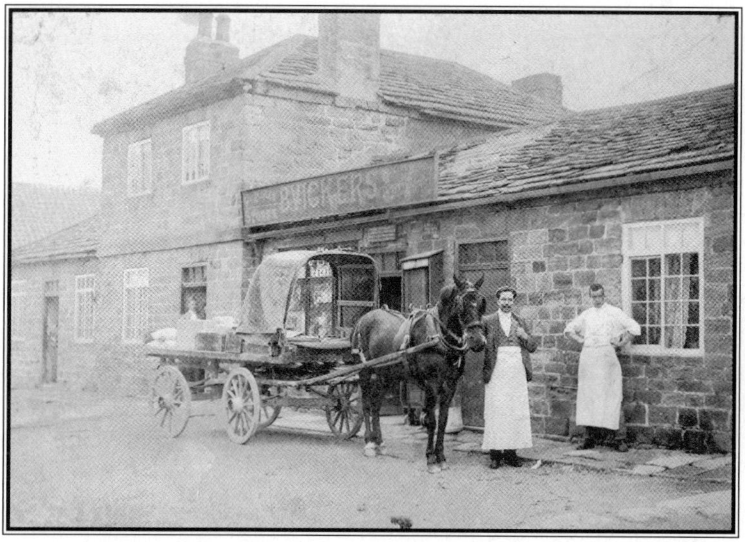

Bramham Vickers advertised his shop on Worksop Road, Aston, as the 'People's Store' and sold everything from groceries to books. The owner is standing proudly by the horse, here, in about 1905. The shop later moved across the road and is now GT News. [3764]

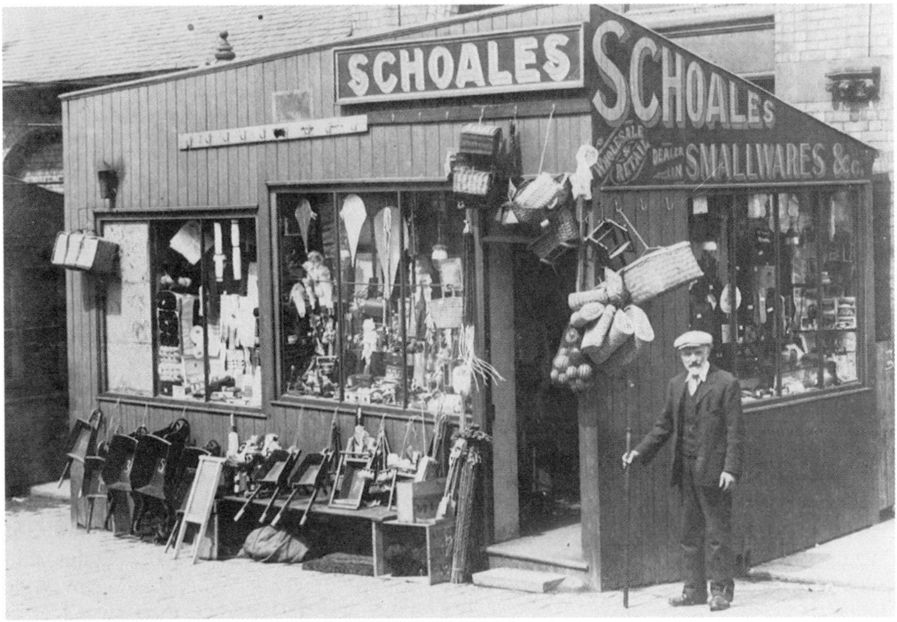

Schoales' shop, on the outside of the Market Hall at Rotherham, seems to have crammed everything under the sun into a very small area. The goods on offer range from miniature wheelbarrows and washboards to baskets. [3005]

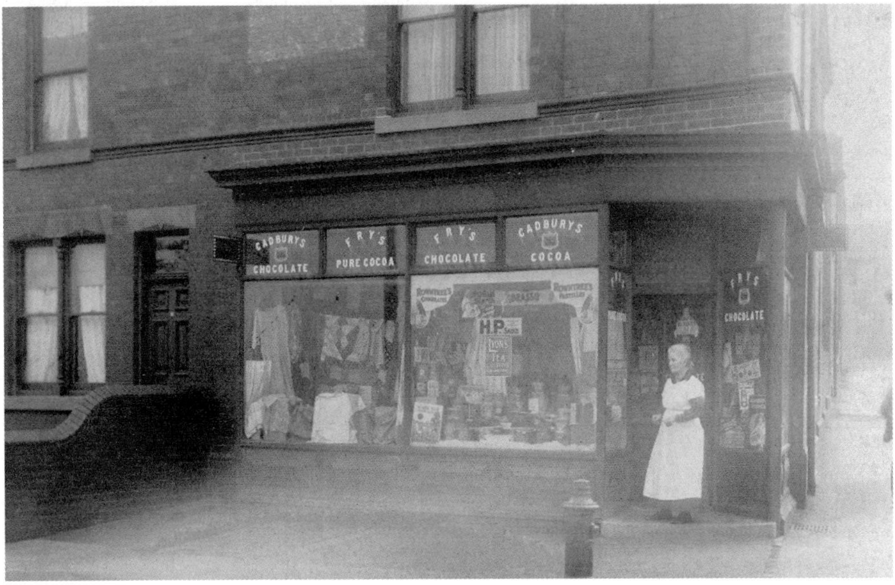

Tummey's Shop at the corner of Fitzwilliam Road and Watkin Street, Rotherham, was typical of many general stores in the outer areas of the town. Mrs Lucy Tummey ran the shop between 1916 and 1939. [4683]

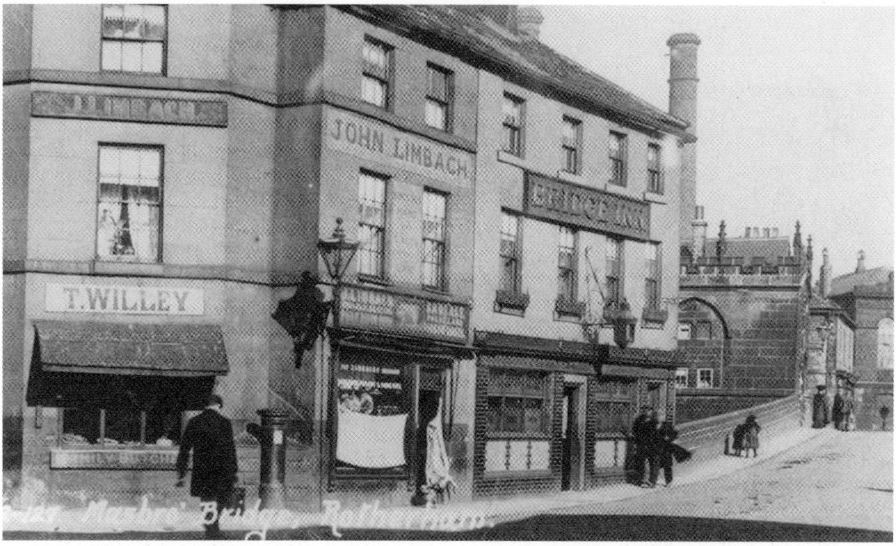

The entry into Rotherham from Masbrough passed the shops of T. Willey, butcher, and John Limbach, pork butcher, and the 18th-century Bridge Inn before passing over the medieval bridge. These properties were demolished in 1930 when the new Chantry Bridge and Bridge Inn were built. [1184]

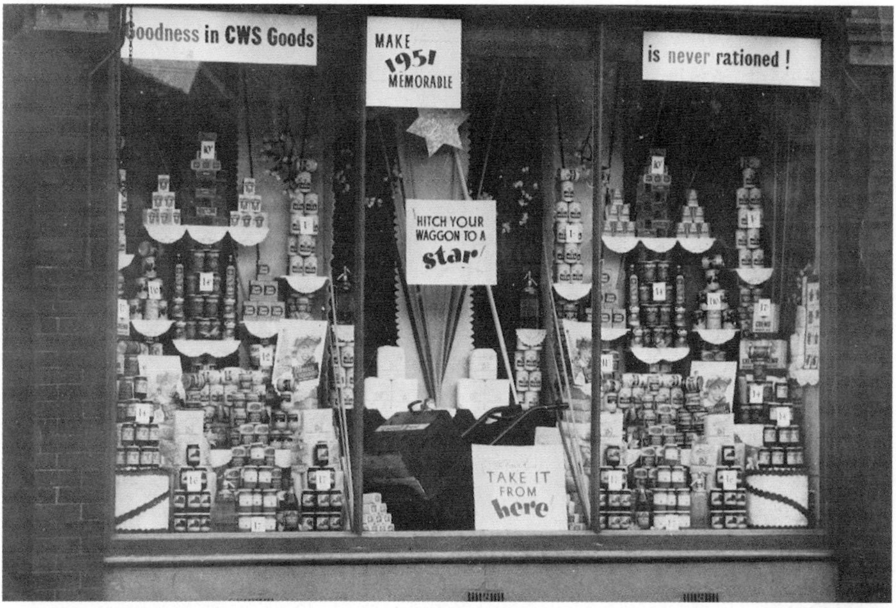

The staff of the Co-op on Rawmarsh Hill, Parkgate, were obviously proud of their 1951 window display. The reference to 'Take It From Here' is to the popular BBC radio comedy of the same name which starred Jimmy Edwards. Rationing was not yet over. [10867]

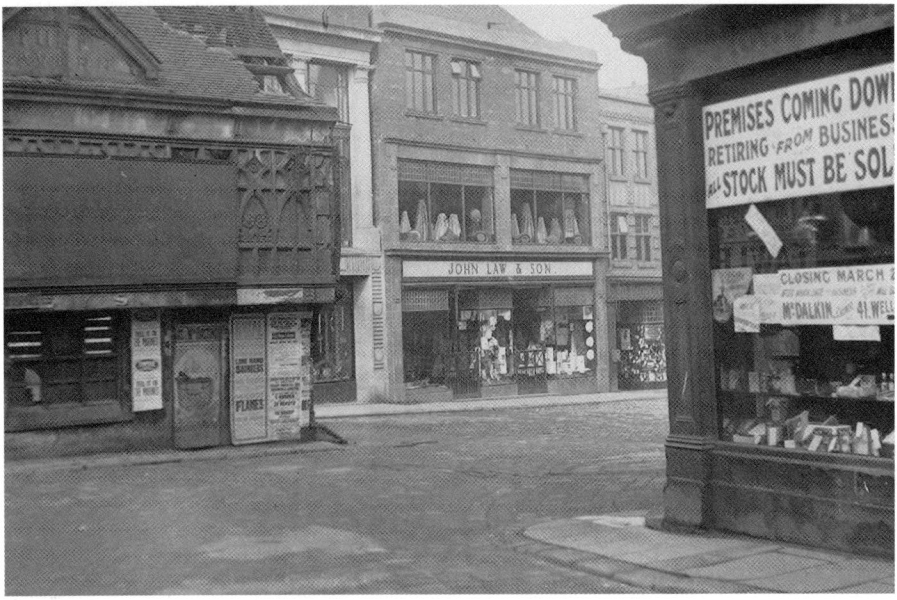

Bridgegate in Rotherham was widened in about 1928 by demolishing and rebuilding the south side. John Law's new draper's shop is newly open, with the Original Boot Co. at the right. Fawley's ironmonger's new premises are almost hidden by the timber-framed Turf Tavern. The pub had closed in 1913 and was awaiting demolition. [1134]

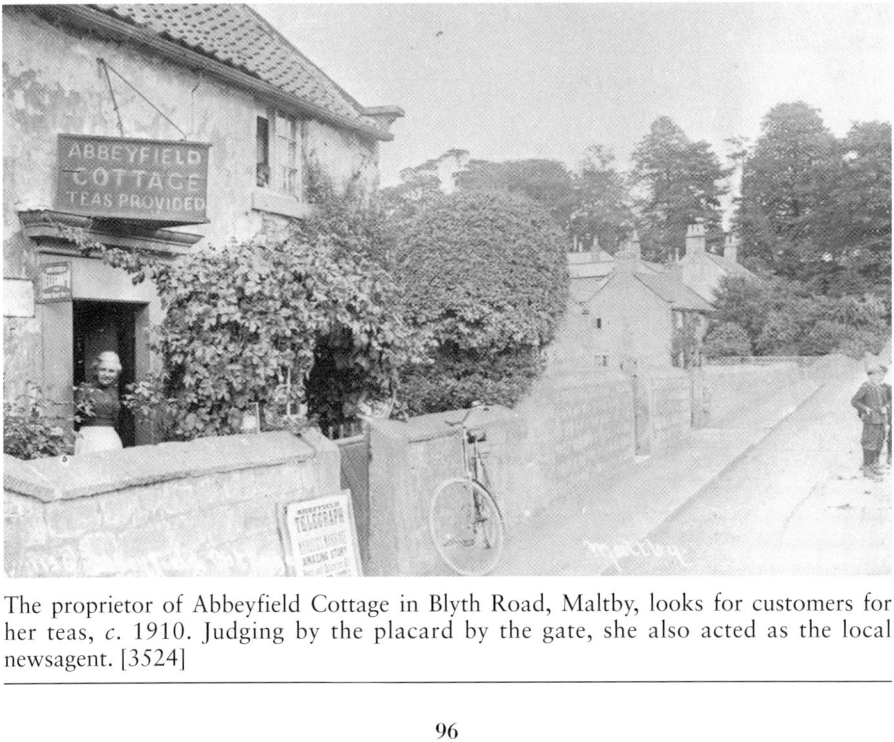

The proprietor of Abbeyfield Cottage in Blyth Road, Maltby, looks for customers for her teas, *c.* 1910. Judging by the placard by the gate, she also acted as the local newsagent. [3524]

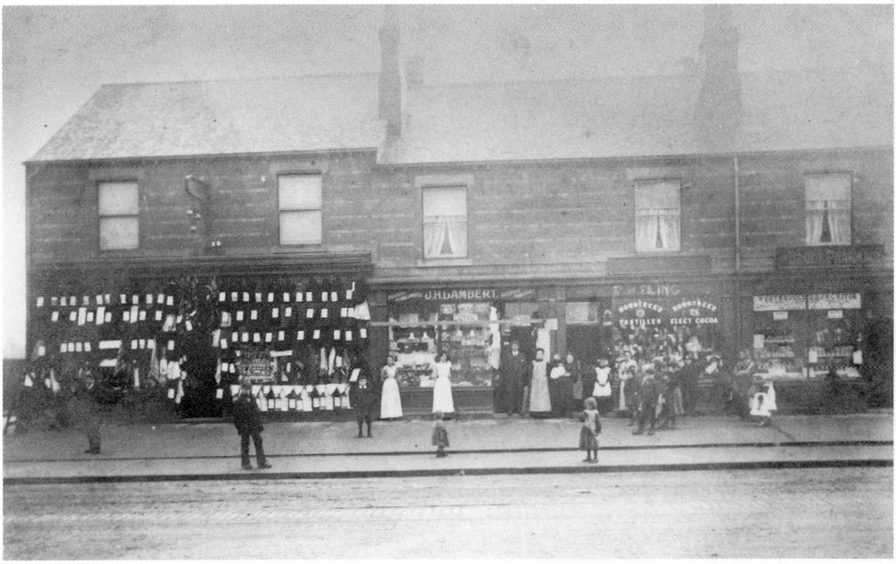

A parade of shops at Dalton Brook, *c.* 1910. At the left is J.H. Whittaker and Co., outfitter and pawnbroker, with the three brass balls above the door. The other shops are, left to right: J.H. Lambert, tobacconist, hosiery and smallwares, F.H. Eling's Brook Bakery and the Brook Pharmacy of Frederick Arthur Westbrook. [11126]

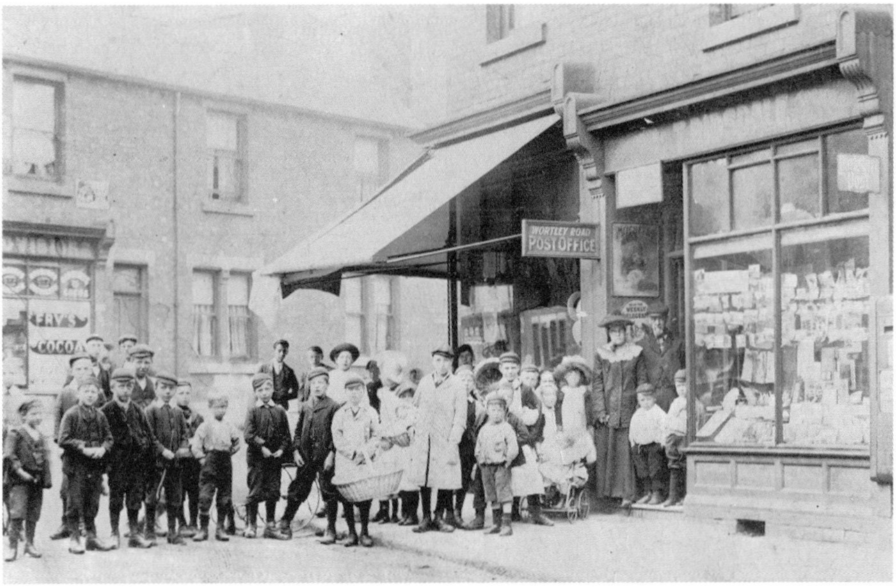

Wortley Road post office stood at the corner of Dovercourt Road at Masbrough. Mr. T. Ridsdale, the proprietor, is standing in the doorway. The boy in the centre with the basket is Joe Harper, who was to be killed at Ypres in 1915 while serving with the 2nd Battalion, York and Lancaster Regiment. [399]

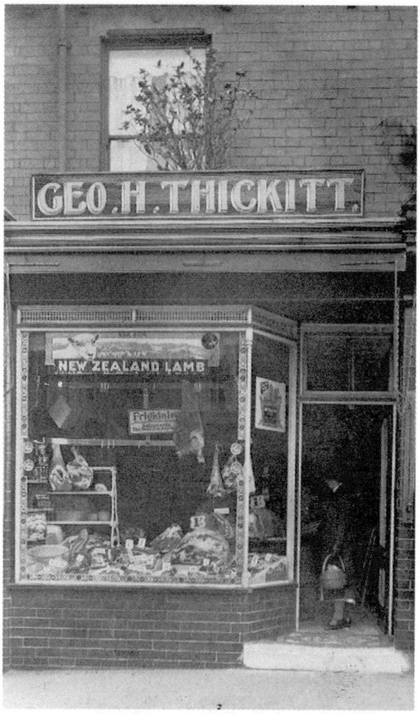

George Hugh Thickitt's butcher's shop was at 65 Laughton Road, Dinnington. 1930s prices such as 1s. a pound seem unbelievable today. The building had previously been a sweet shop run by Messrs Bailey. [14008]

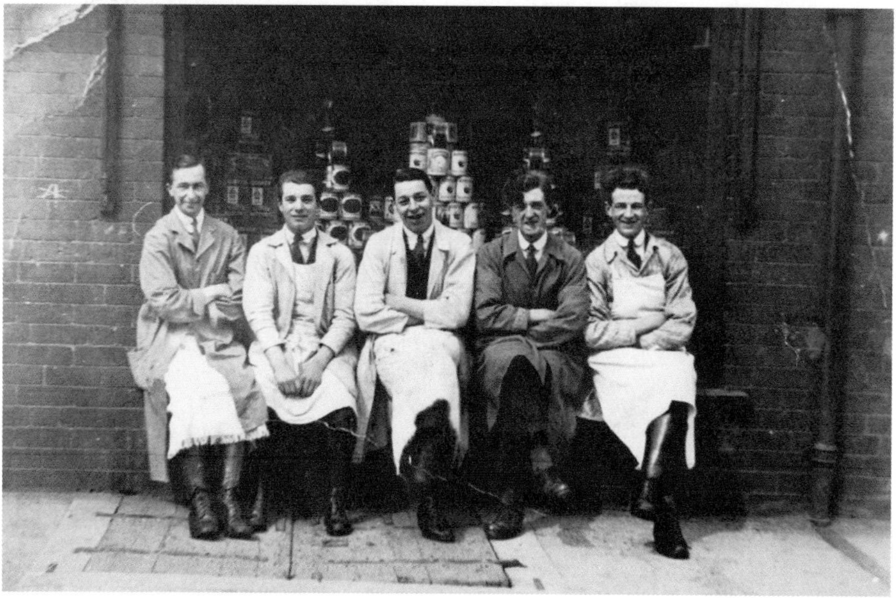

The staff of the grocery and butchery department of the Handsworth and Woodhouse Cooperative Society's Dinnington store pose outside the grocery window in New Street, *c.* 1930. The lad at the right is Albert Duckham. [4657]

Section Seven

WORKING LIFE

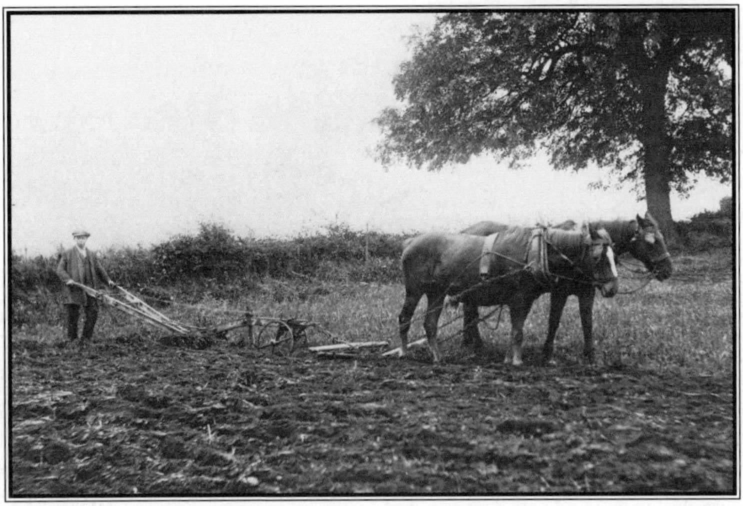

Charlie Waring ploughing at Rackford Lane, North Anston, in the 1920s. He was working for his brother-in-law Henry Presswood of Wells Farm. [524]

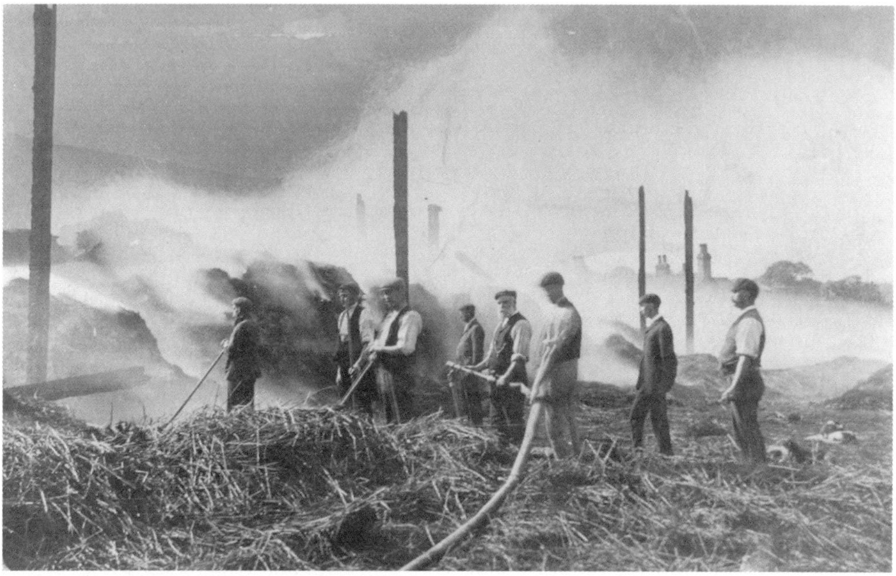

The firefighters at Yeardley's Farm, Nether Haugh, were clearly unable to save this barn when fire broke out in the years before 1914, and had to be content with damping down the burning straw. [8968]

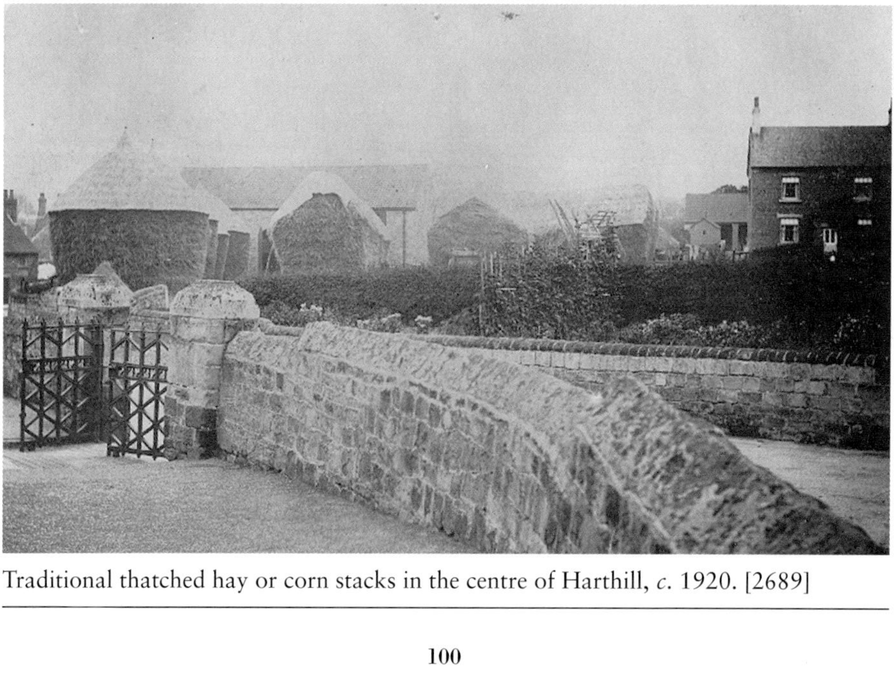

Traditional thatched hay or corn stacks in the centre of Harthill, *c.* 1920. [2689]

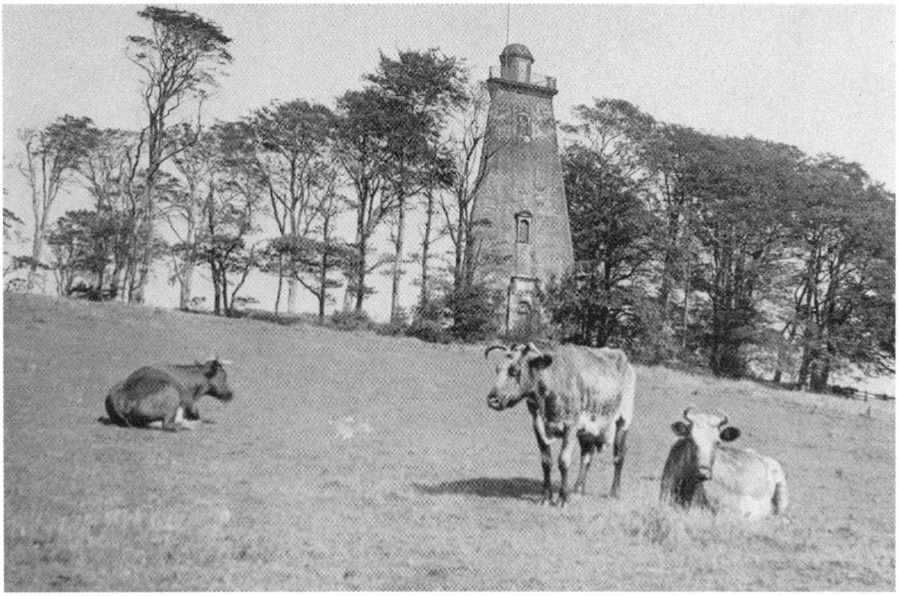

Three cows of indeterminate breed (shorthorns?) graze below Hoober Stand, *c.* 1900. The Stand was one of several follies on the Wentworth estate. It dates from 1748 and was erected by the first Marquis of Rockingham to celebrate his elevation to the marquissate and the defeat of the Jacobites. [1062]

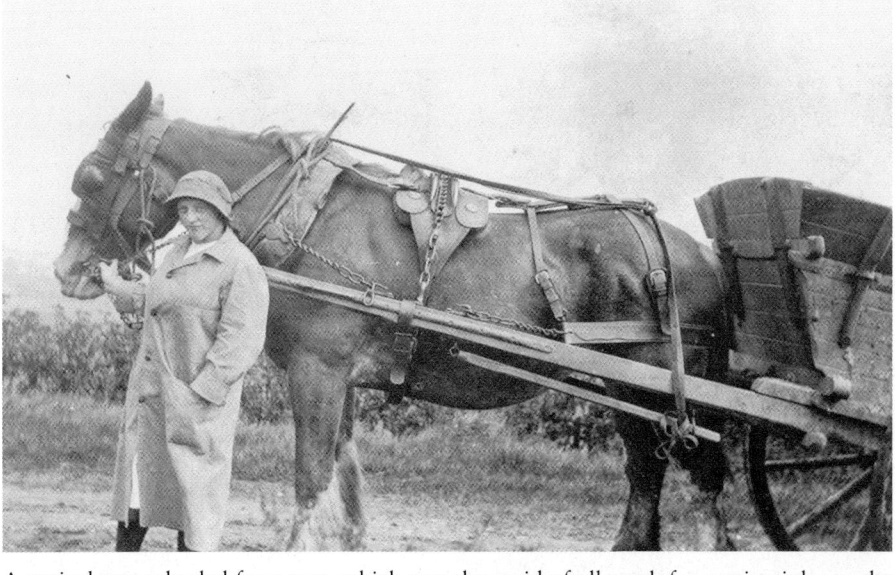

A typical two-wheeled farm cart, which was the maid of all work for carting jobs on the farm until the tractor replaced the horse. The horse is being led by Hilda Mary Smith (later Stevenson) at Kimberworth Park Farm in 1916. She is shown as a child on p. 123. [13723]

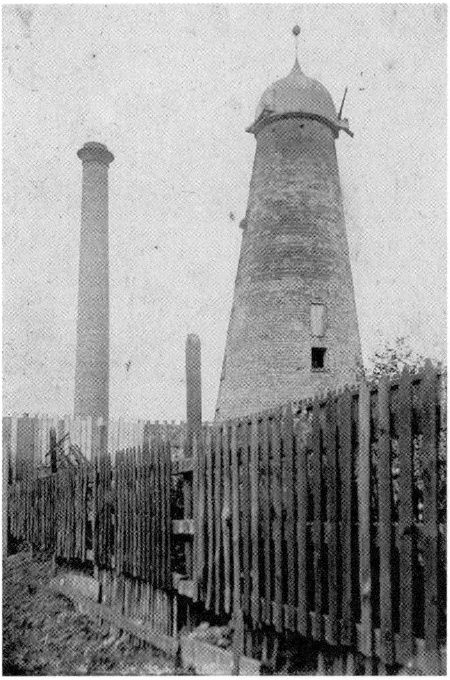

Until well into the present century almost every town and village had its own mill to grind the local corn. Dalton Brook had a windmill, but by the time this photograph was taken in the late 19th century wind power had been replaced by a steam engine, hence the chimney at the left. The mill tower seems to have been heightened at some time as the bottom is brick and the top stone. No miller is listed at Dalton in 1898 and the mill tower had gone by 1902. [8901]

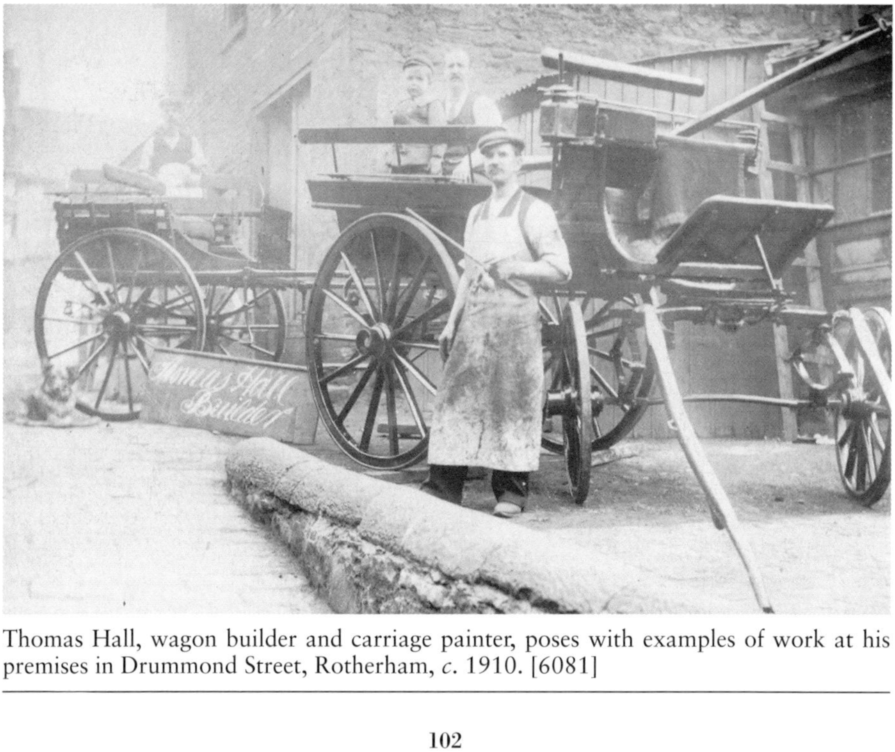

Thomas Hall, wagon builder and carriage painter, poses with examples of work at his premises in Drummond Street, Rotherham, *c.* 1910. [6081]

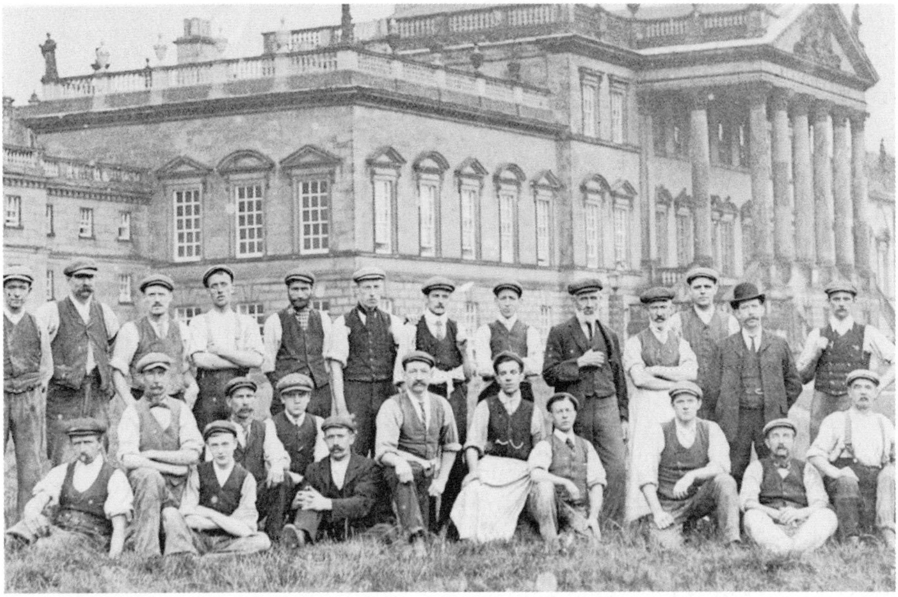

The staff of Arthur Cooper, builder, of Greasbrough, were presumably carrying out work at Wentworth Woodhouse when they were photographed in front of the house in about 1910. [277]

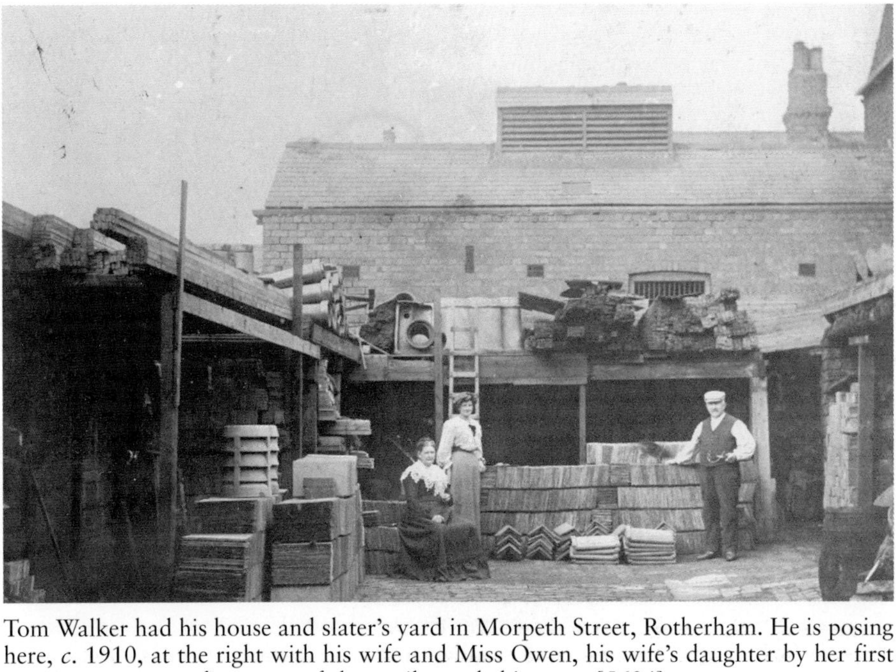

Tom Walker had his house and slater's yard in Morpeth Street, Rotherham. He is posing here, *c.* 1910, at the right with his wife and Miss Owen, his wife's daughter by her first marriage, among a fine array of slates, tiles and chimneys. [5604]

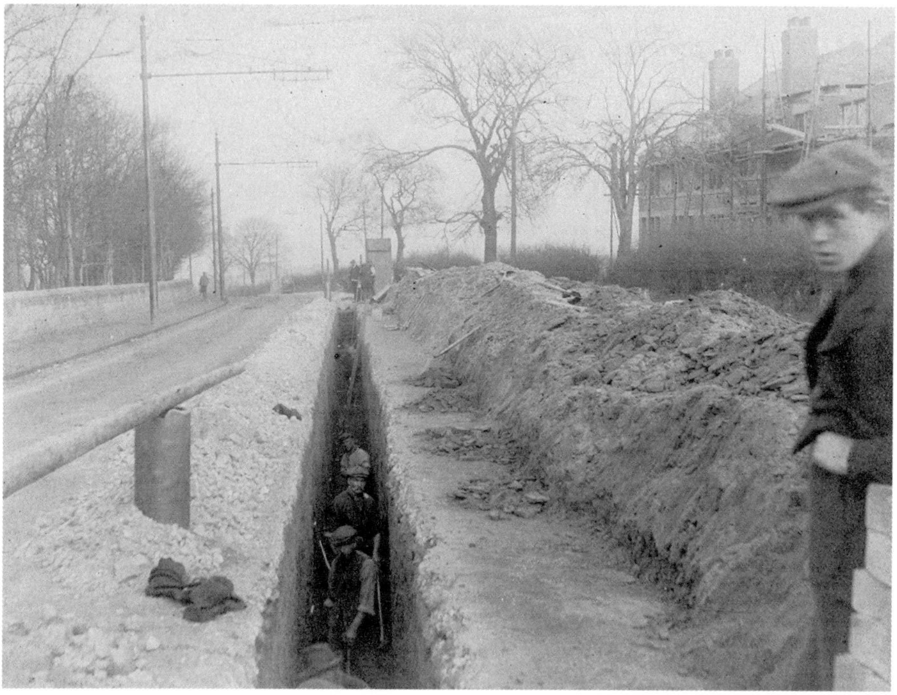

Ditch digging was a labour-intensive job in the days before the JCB. This trench for sewage pipes, some 12 ft deep, was being excavated along Bramley Hill in January 1914. Note the new houses in the course of erection at the right. [1038]

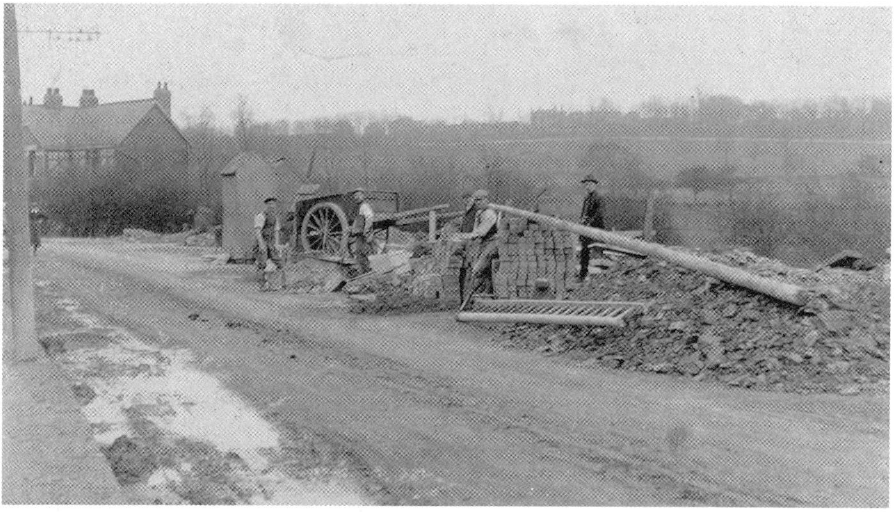

The same excavations in Rotherham Road (near Leslie Avenue) on the outskirts of Maltby in 1914. The buildings on the skyline are part of the hamlet of Hooton Levitt. [11069]

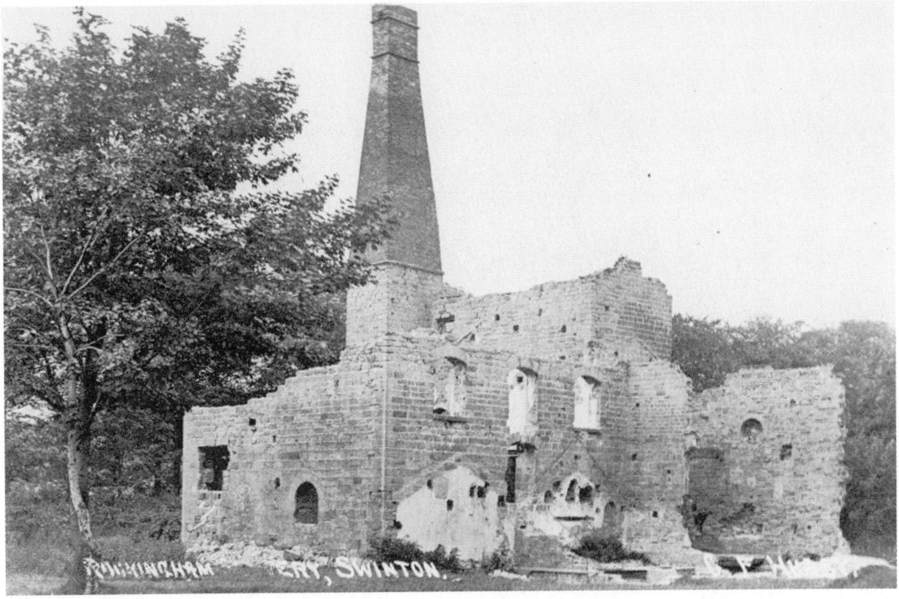

Pottery was an important local industry for several centuries. The Rockingham Works at Swinton were first established in 1745 and were taken over by the Brameld family in 1806, with financial support from Earl Fitzwilliam. High-class porcelain, which is still avidly collected, was produced until 1842. By 1900 this was all that was left of the flint mill. One bottle kiln still remains, off Blackamoor Road. [4185]

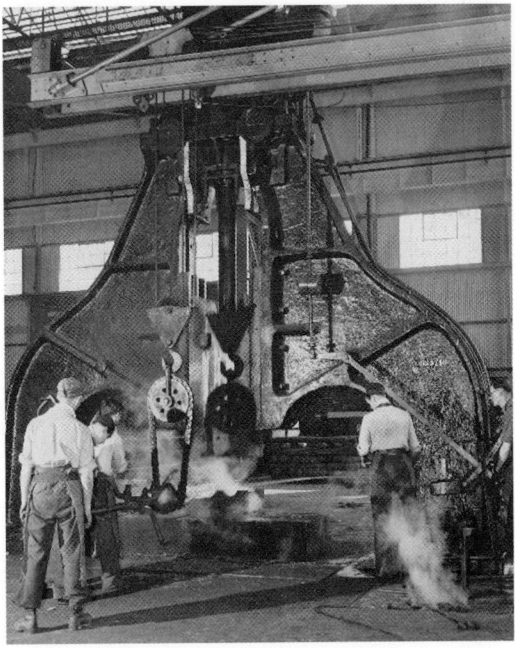

Steel, Peech and Tozer, founded at Templeborough in 1875, was the largest steelworks in the Rotherham area, with works stretching for over half a mile along Sheffield Road. A 5 ton double-action hammer forges axles in 1953. [6151]

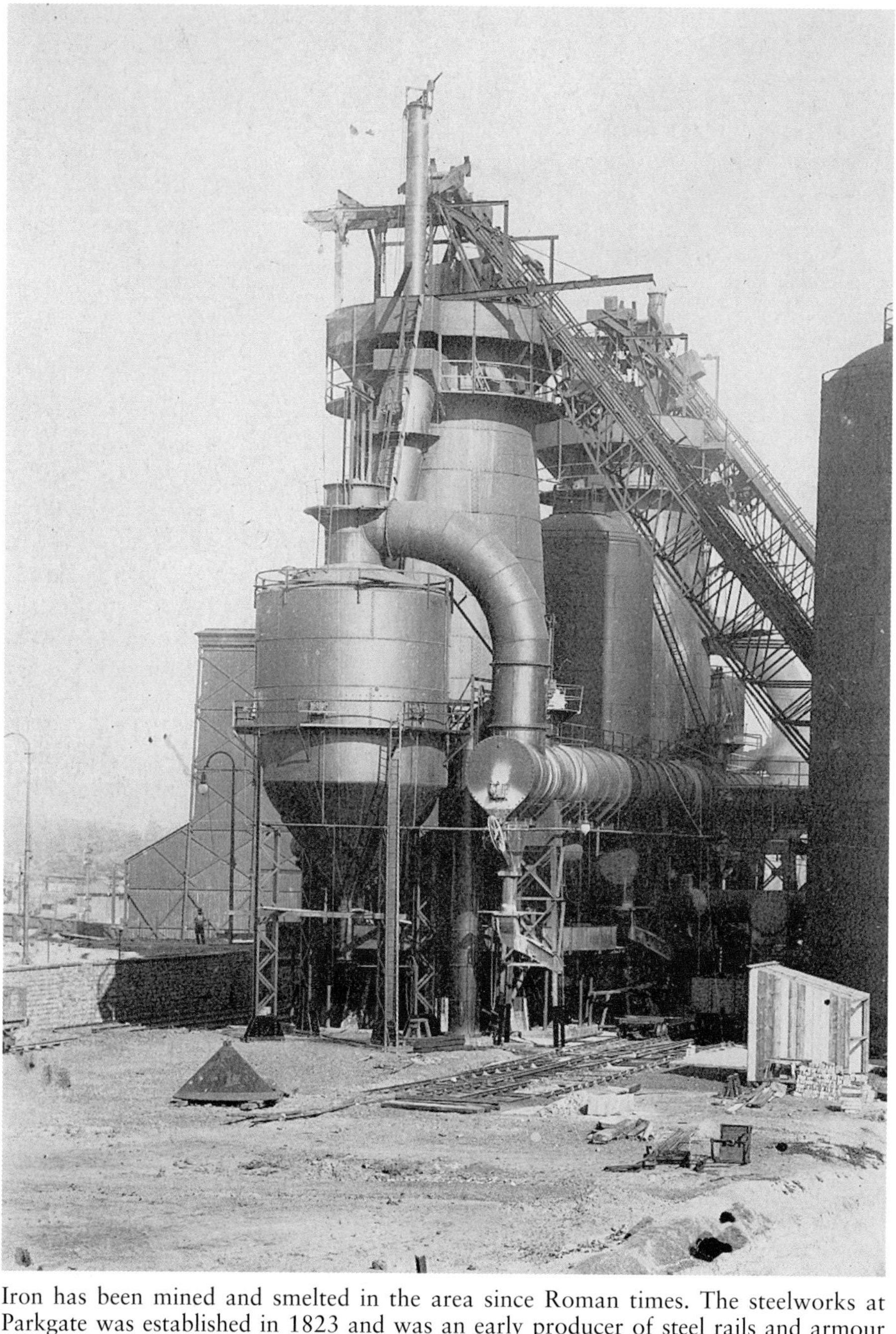

Iron has been mined and smelted in the area since Roman times. The steelworks at Parkgate was established in 1823 and was an early producer of steel rails and armour plate. New blast furnaces were erected in 1871 only to be replaced by these more modern furnaces in 1905. They were demolished in 1976. [3464]

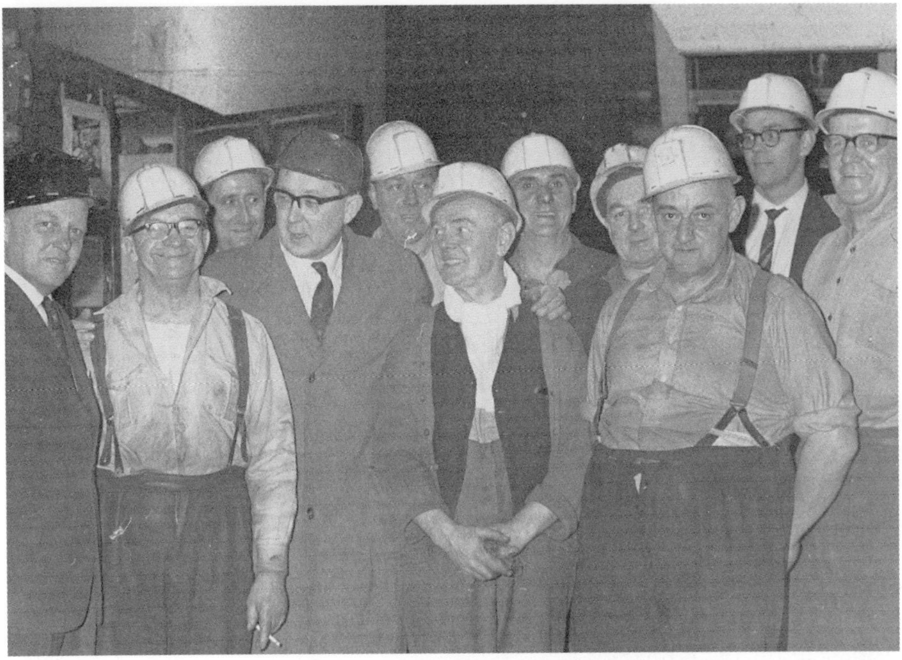

The crew of the 6,000 ton press in Steel, Peech and Tozer's wheel mill meet H. Morley, the General Manager (in the overcoat), in the 1950s. [4154]

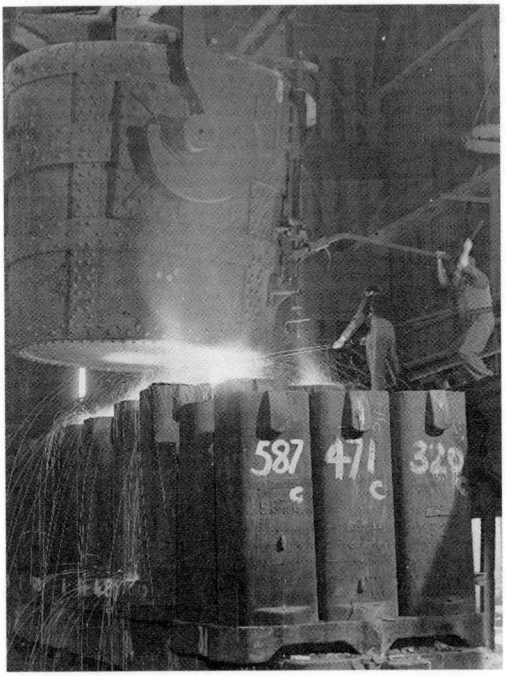

One of a series of photographs taken at Steel, Peech and Tozer in 1949–50, this view shows the contents of a 100 ton ladle of molten steel being teemed into ingot moulds in the Templeborough Melting Shop. The resulting ingots would subsequently be rolled into bars, rods and girders. [6145]

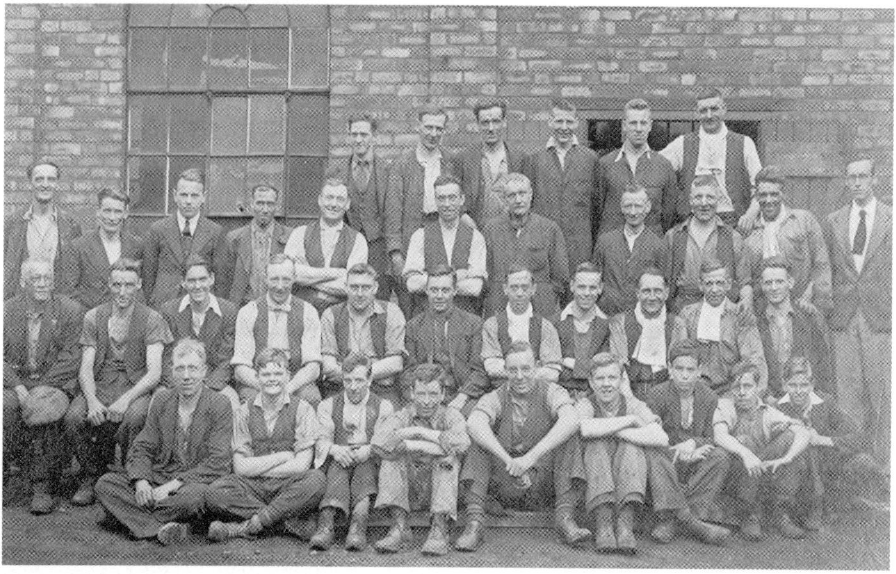

In the 19th century Rotherham became a centre for the production of wheels and axles for railways at home and abroad. The most successful of these companies was John Baker and Bessemer Ltd, with works in Rotherham and Kilnhurst. This group of wheel forge men were photographed in September 1935. Standing at the extreme right is Henry Baker, grandson of the company's founder. [3495]

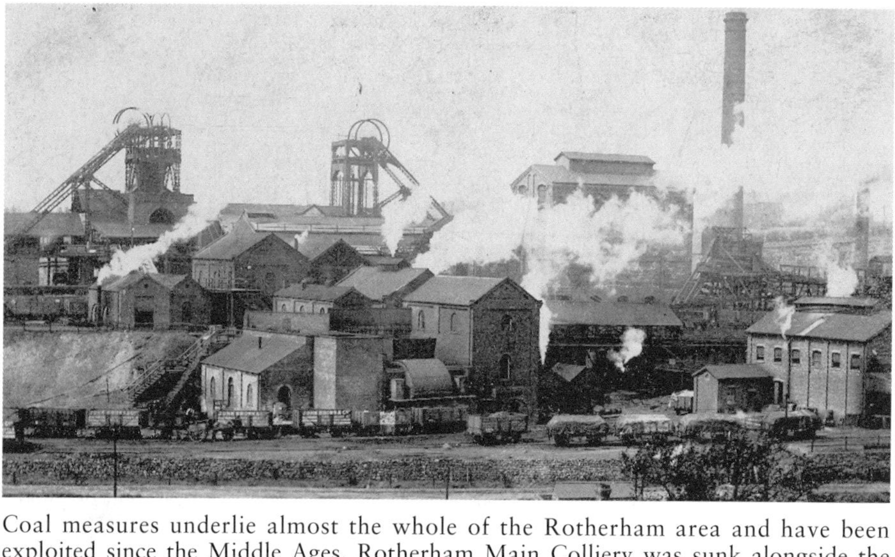

Coal measures underlie almost the whole of the Rotherham area and have been exploited since the Middle Ages. Rotherham Main Colliery was sunk alongside the River Rother at Canklow by the Sheffield steelmaker John Brown and Co. in 1890. Houses for the workers were built nearby and the company supported a school for their children. The colliery closed in 1954 and roadworks have recently obliterated the last of the buildings. [13547]

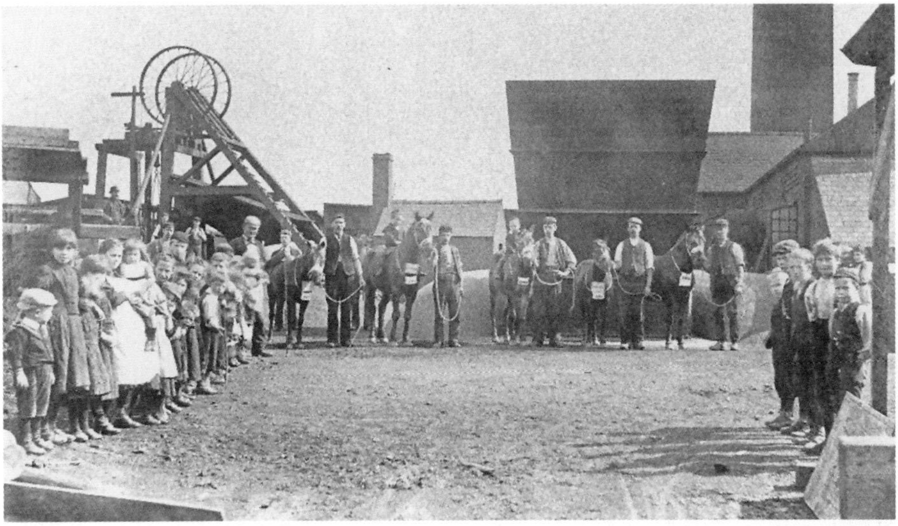

A parade of pit ponies has attracted a good crowd of children at Waleswood Colliery. The temporary nature of the headgear at the left suggests that the photograph was taken when sinking operations were taking place, possibly in about 1902 when the shaft was being extended to reach the Flockton seam. [3224]

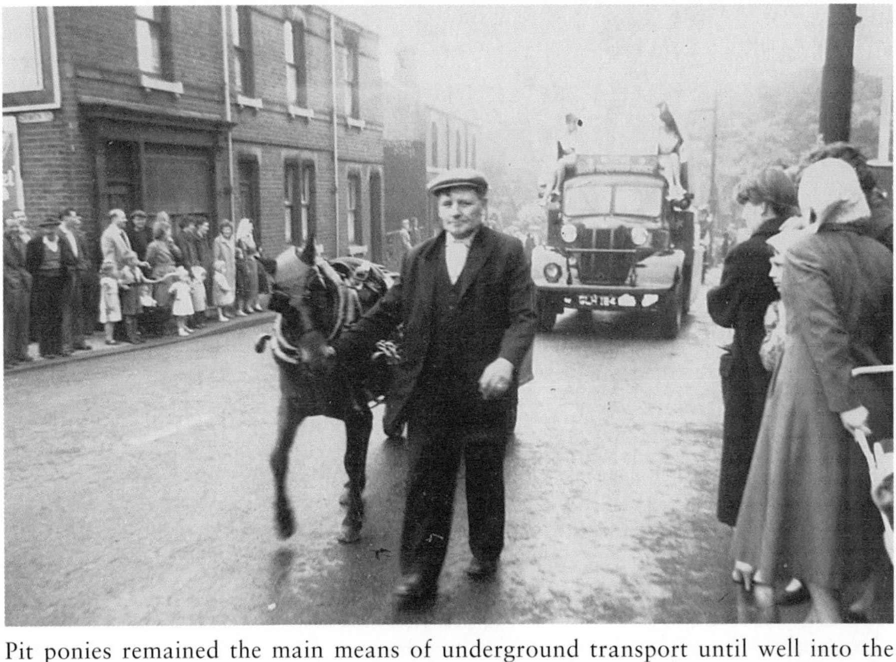

Pit ponies remained the main means of underground transport until well into the present century, but were steadily ousted by mechanical means of transport. This is the last working pit pony in the Rotherham area being paraded through Rawmarsh High Street, probably *c.* 1960. [12803]

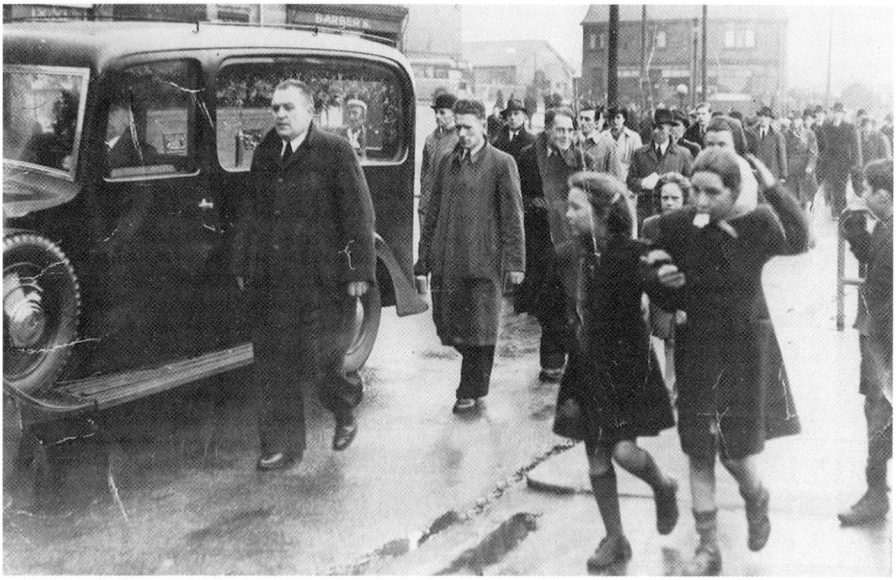

The mining of coal has always exacted a price in human lives. In an underground explosion at Maltby Colliery in 1923, 27 men were killed while trying to contain an underground fire. Although the rescue teams spent 19 days underground, only one body was recovered. One further, unidentified, body was discovered in 1947. The funeral cortège is seen here passing through the centre of the town. [3715]

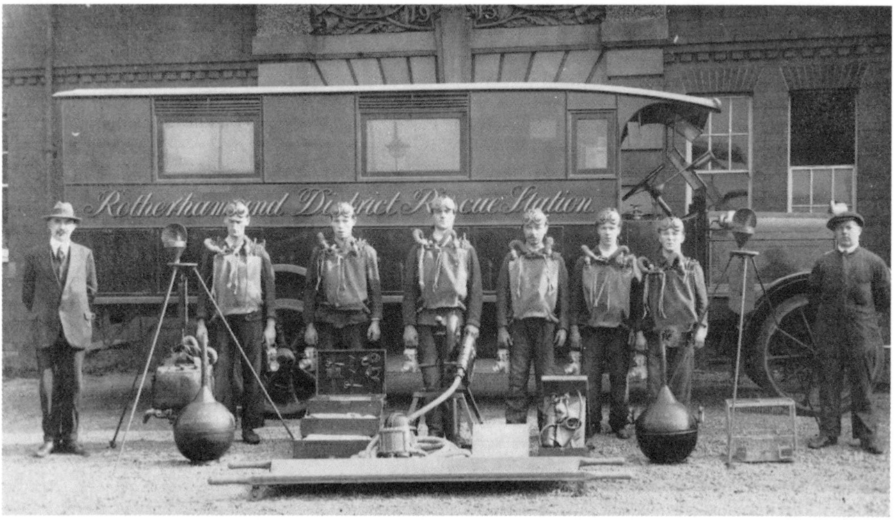

With explosions and roof falls an ever-present danger, the various volunteer mines rescue teams were an important part of the workforce. These are the members of the Maltby Colliery rescue team photographed at the Rotherham and District Rescue Station in the early 1920s. The second man from the right is Arthur Bailey, and on his right is Joseph Brierley. [4374]

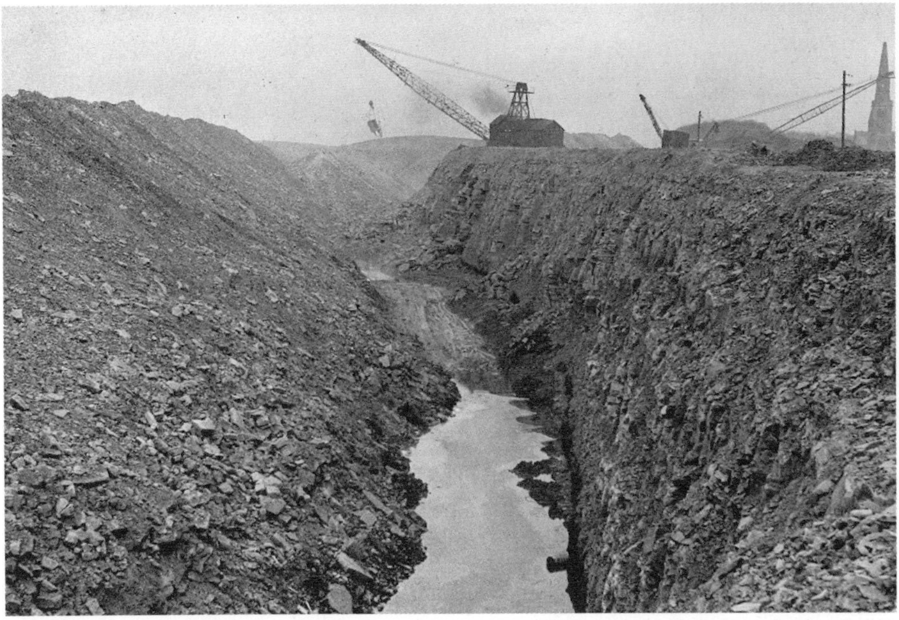

In June 1942 tractors, scrapers and excavators moved into the fields around Wentworth and began several years of opencast mining around the house and village. By July 1944 5,000,000 tons of overburden had been removed and 750,000 tons of coal mined. This view of 1946 shows how close the drag-line excavators came to the parish church. Mining continued into the early 1950s, but restoration was such that it is now almost impossible to see where the excavators worked. [391]

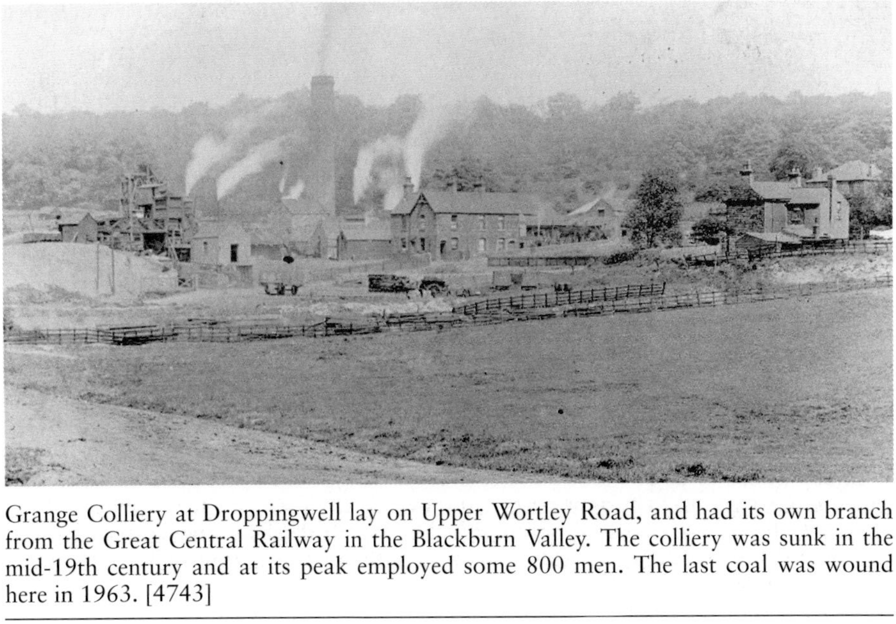

Grange Colliery at Droppingwell lay on Upper Wortley Road, and had its own branch from the Great Central Railway in the Blackburn Valley. The colliery was sunk in the mid-19th century and at its peak employed some 800 men. The last coal was wound here in 1963. [4743]

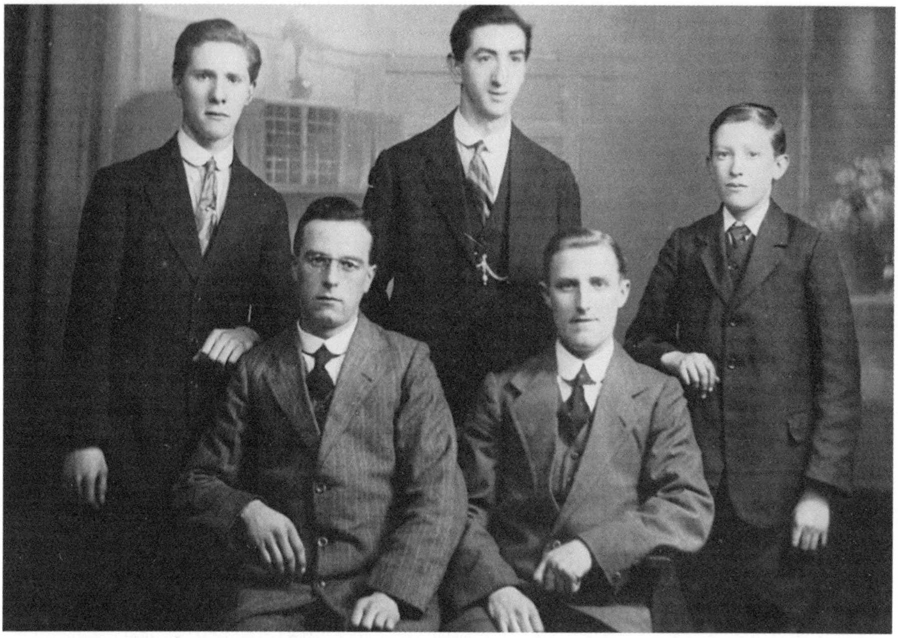

The office staff at Grange Colliery. Back row, left to right: A.E. Walsh (organist at Kimberworth church), C. Clark, J. Jenkinson. Front row: C.B. Cooper, A. Portman (uncle to the actor Eric Portman). [4941]

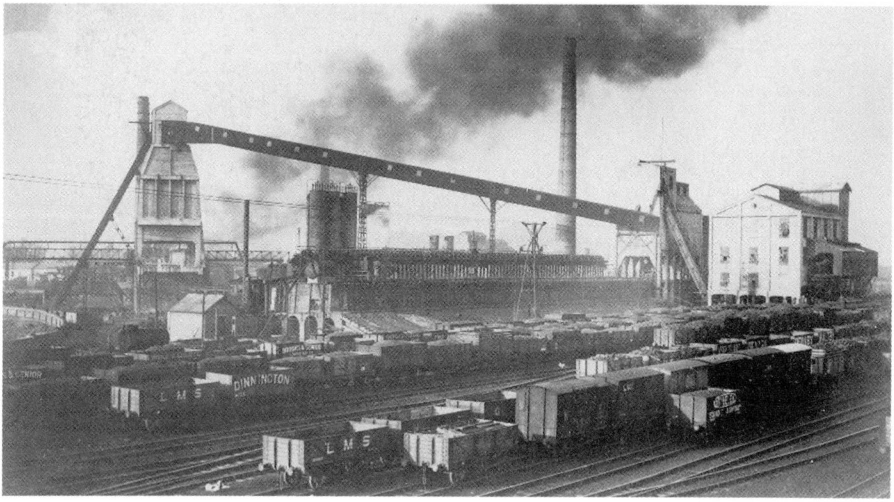

Where there is coal you will find coal by-products. The South Yorkshire Coke and Chemical Works at Parkgate was founded in 1919, and produced blast furnace coke, sulphate of ammonia, benzol, road tar, naphthalene, etc. When it was photographed in 1936, it was claimed to be the most modern plant in the country. The works closed in 1975 when the owners, the National Carbonising Co., found that they could not compete with the NCB's price for coke. [3462]

Section Eight

PEOPLE

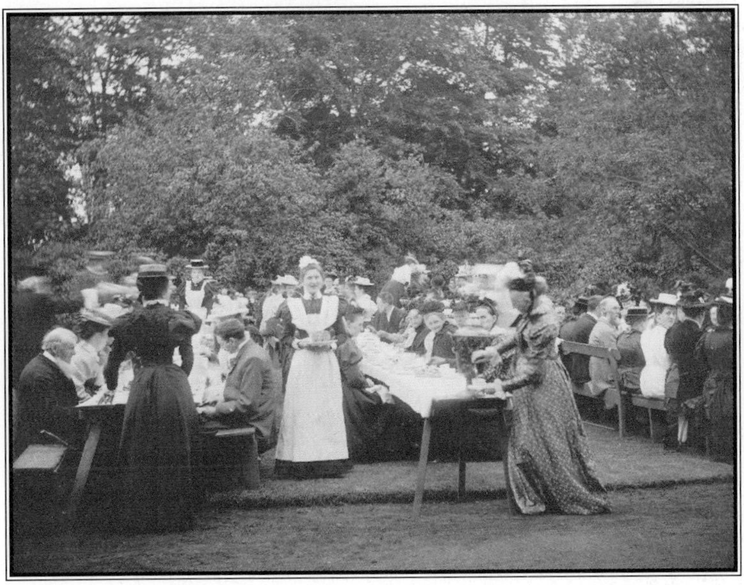

An alfresco wedding reception at Aston followed the marriage of Florence Agnes, daughter of the rector, the Rev. R.J. Haynes, to Robert Laurie Walsh of Sheffield on 7 July 1898. [5950]

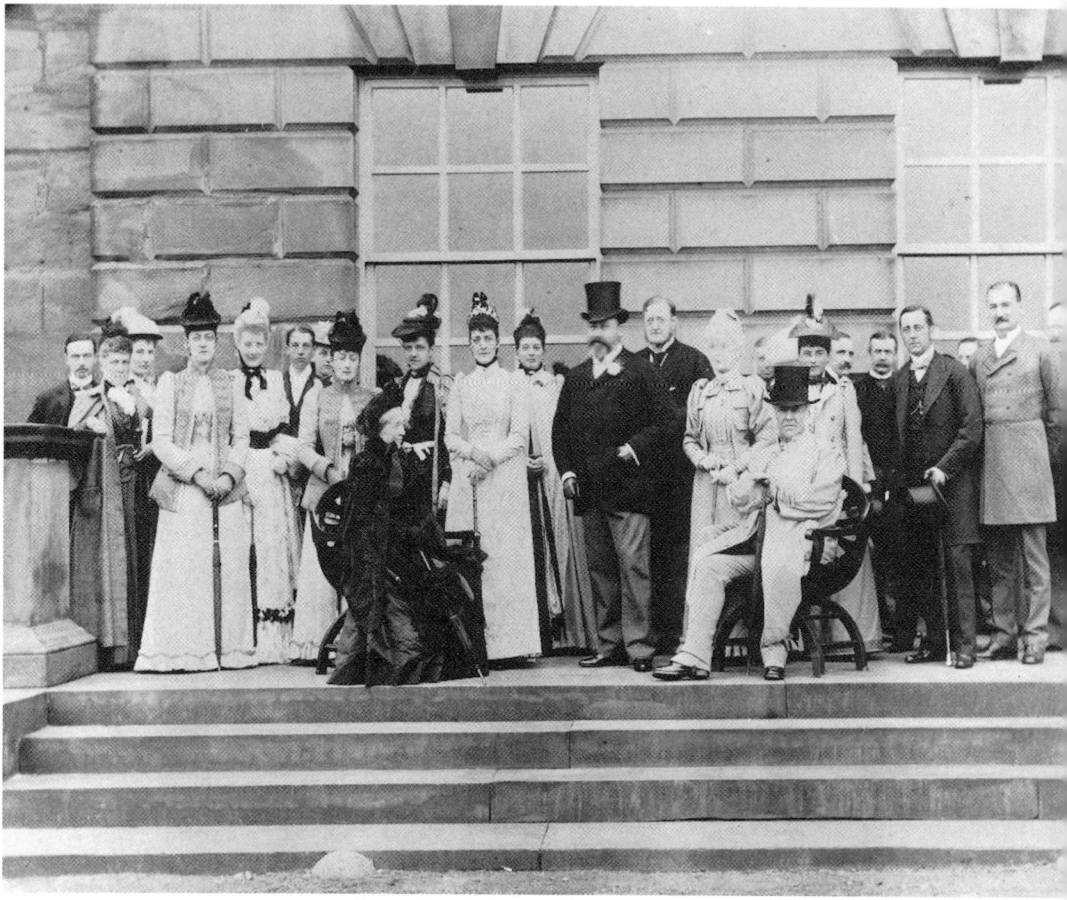

In 1891 the Prince of Wales (later Edward VII) and Princess Alexandra visited Wentworth Woodhouse, having travelled by train via Doncaster to the Manchester, Sheffield & Lincolnshire Railway station at Parkgate. On the last day of their stay they came to Rotherham to perform the official opening ceremony of Clifton Park. The Prince and his wife are standing in the centre of this group, with the Earl and Countess Fitzwilliam seated at the front. The party included the Prince's daughters Victoria and Maud (later Queen of Norway), the Earl of Scarbrough and the Duke and Duchess of Buccleuch. [285]

Sir Charles Stoddart (1839–1913) was company secretary of the Park Gate Iron and Steel Co. Ltd, and served as Mayor of Rotherham four times. He was Lieutenant-Colonel and commandant of the 2nd Volunteer Battalion of the York and Lancaster Regiment. The regard in which he was held by the people of Rotherham was proved by the crowds that turned out for his funeral on 28 May 1913. The gun carriage shown here was supplied by the West Riding Artillery from Wentworth. Over 1,200 employees from Parkgate followed the cortège from the parish church to the cemetery. [930]

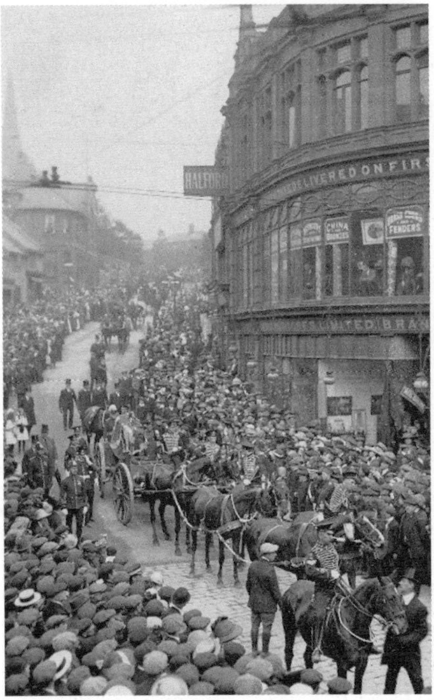

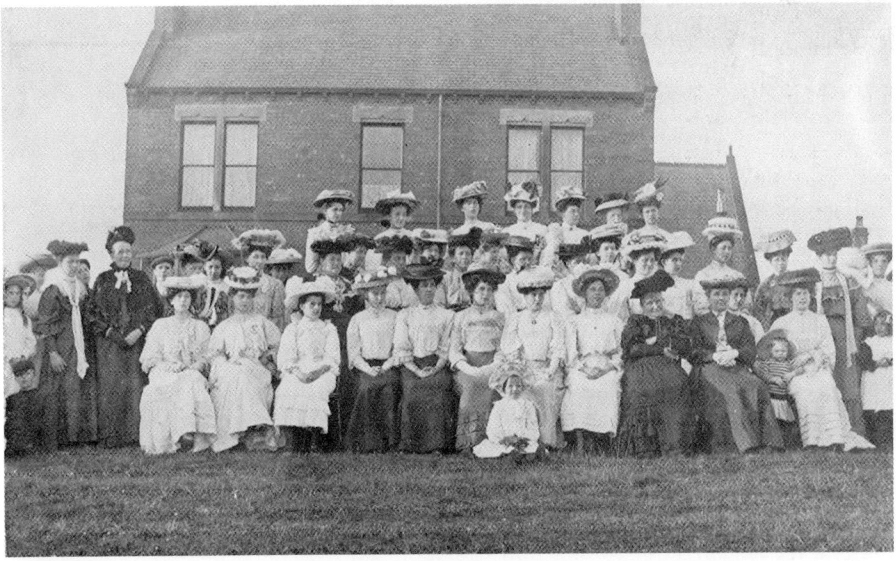

A fine array of hats was worn by ladies of all ages at this Mission Fete at Treeton, *c.* 1905. [3094]

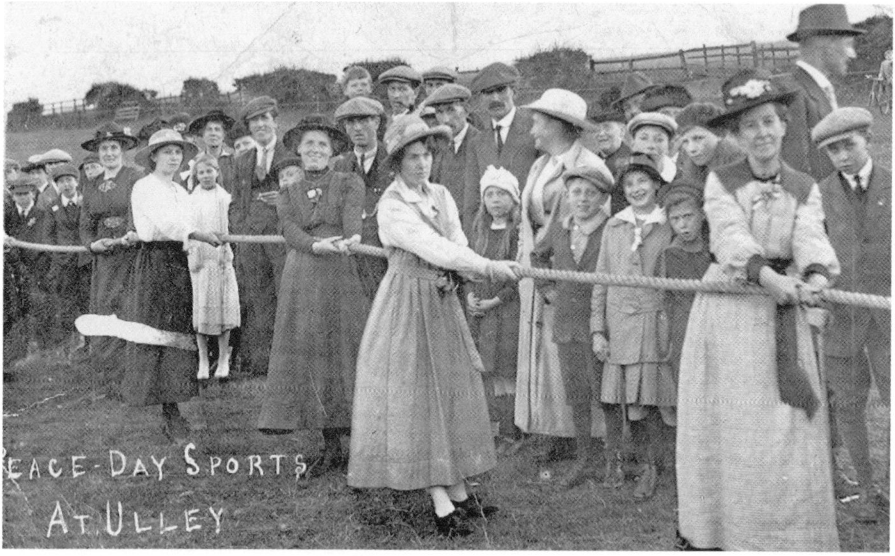

Most local towns and villages held celebrations to mark the signing of the Treaty of Versailles on 28 June 1919, which brought a formal end to the First World War. At Ulley the event was marked by a Peace Sports Day on 19 July. These ladies hardly look dressed to be part of a tug-of-war team. [3209]

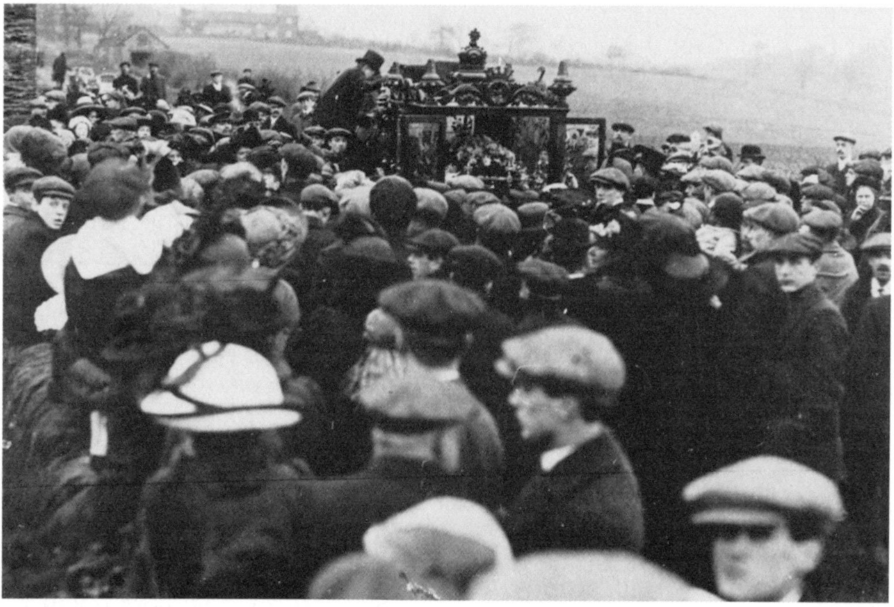

Crowds gather at Kimberworth Park outside Abdy Farm, Rockingham, on 20 November 1912 for the funeral of the cousins Amy Collinson and Frances Nicholson, who had been found murdered near Amy's home on 15 November. Walter Sykes was arrested and executed for the murder, but there are strong reasons to doubt his guilt. [5353]

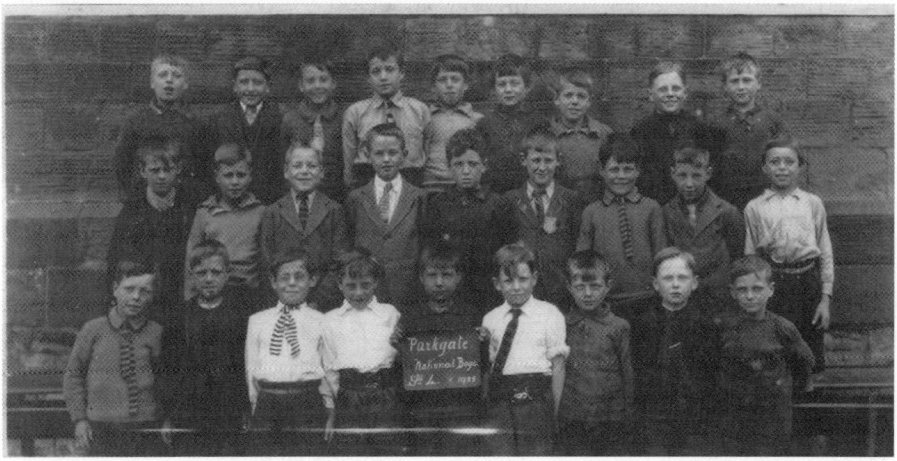

The members of Standard 4, Parkgate National Boys' School, pose proudly for the camera, 1925. [3460]

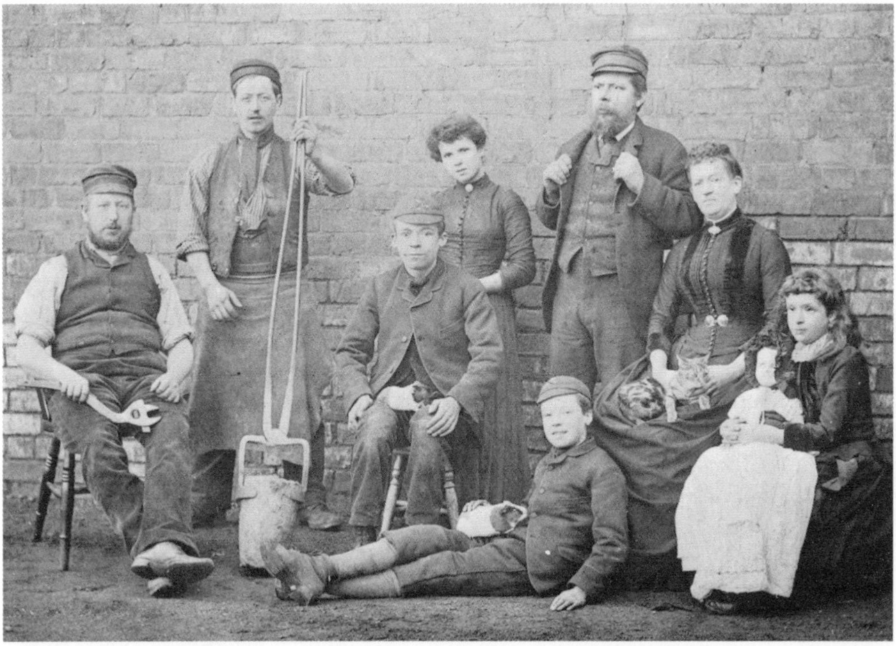

An anonymous Rotherham family (possibly the Mortes) in an early photograph, *c.* 1900. Most of them seem to have brought their favourite possessions: a doll, the family cat, two guinea pigs, a spanner and a crucible. [876]

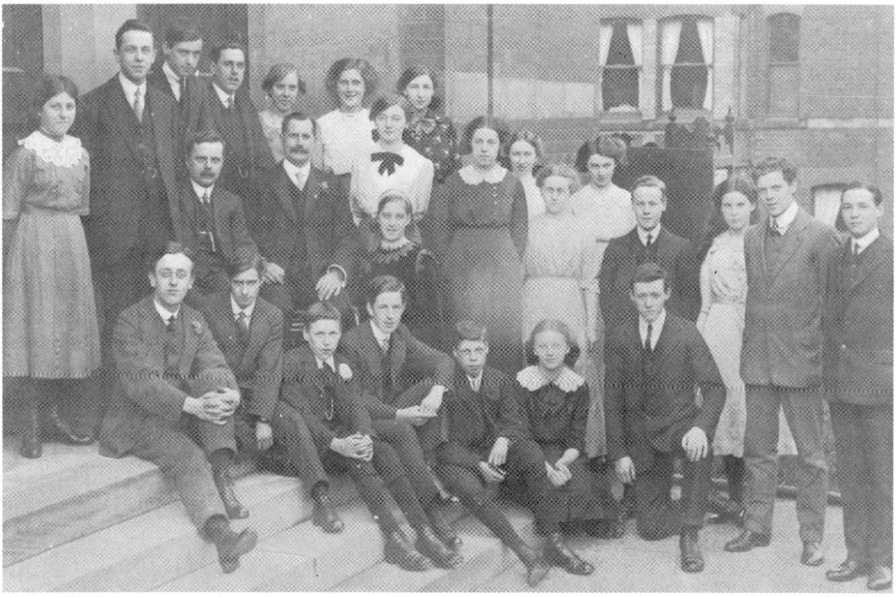

The Christian Endeavour Society outside Gerard Road Wesleyan Chapel, *c.* 1912. Two of the young men seen here, Leslie Morte (second from the left) and Sam Oates (second from the right) joined the 2nd Battalion, York and Lancaster Regiment in the First World War. Second Lieutenant Oates later transferred to the Royal Engineers and was killed in action in 1917. [4407]

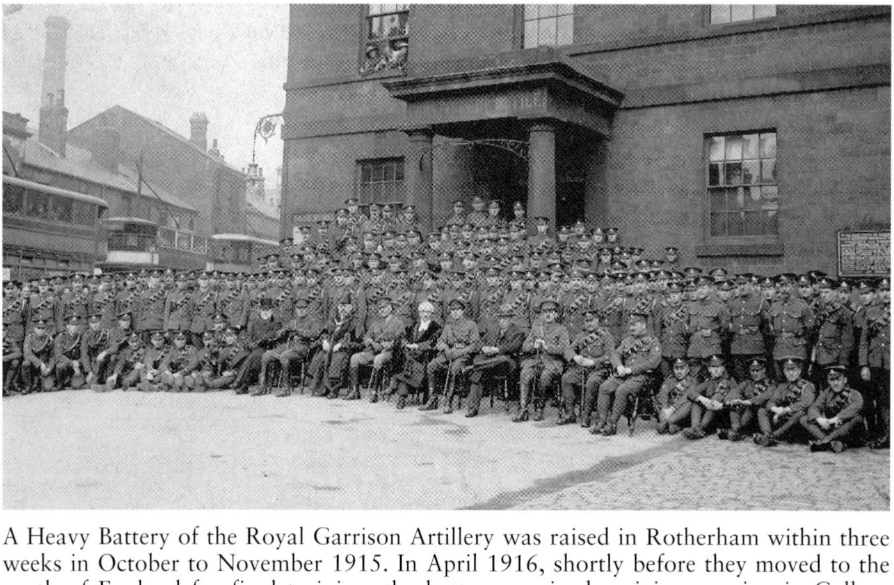

A Heavy Battery of the Royal Garrison Artillery was raised in Rotherham within three weeks in October to November 1915. In April 1916, shortly before they moved to the south of England for final training, the battery received a civic reception in College Square. Former Mayor P. Bancroft Coward, the Mayor, T.W. Grundy, and the Town Clerk, Charles des Forges, are seated in the centre of the front row. [3179]

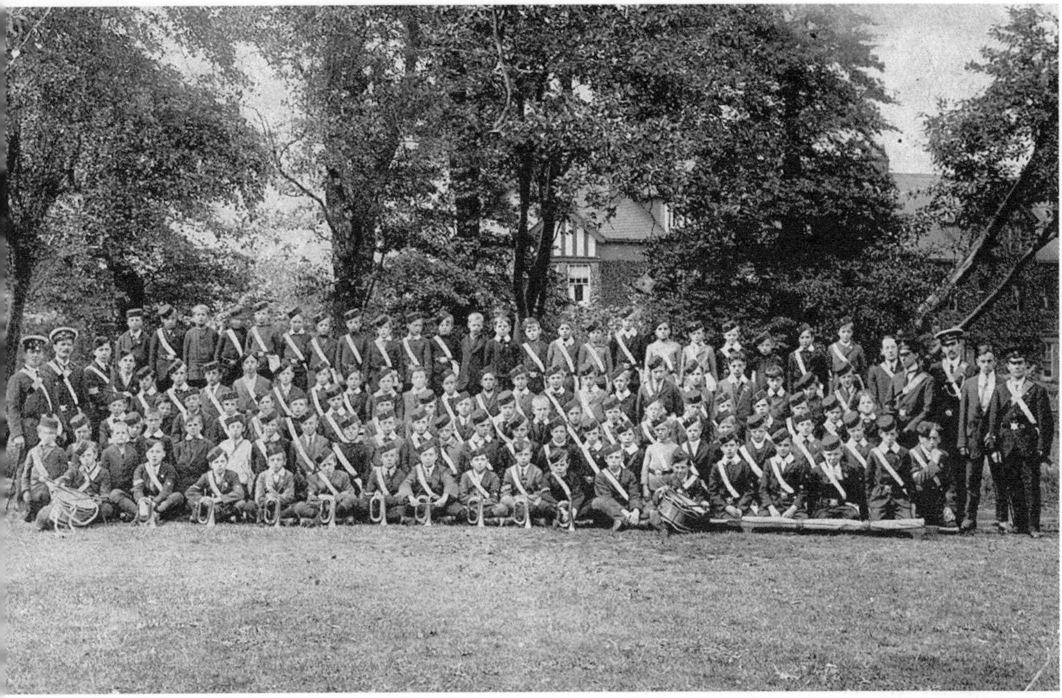

The Rotherham and District Battalion of the Boys' Brigade was formed in 1918. The various companies were attached to churches and chapels. This group, photographed in Clifton Park in about 1927, was made up from Eastwood Primitive Methodist Chapel No. 2 Company and 'Hastings Own' Masbrough Independent Chapel No. 3 Company. [8081]

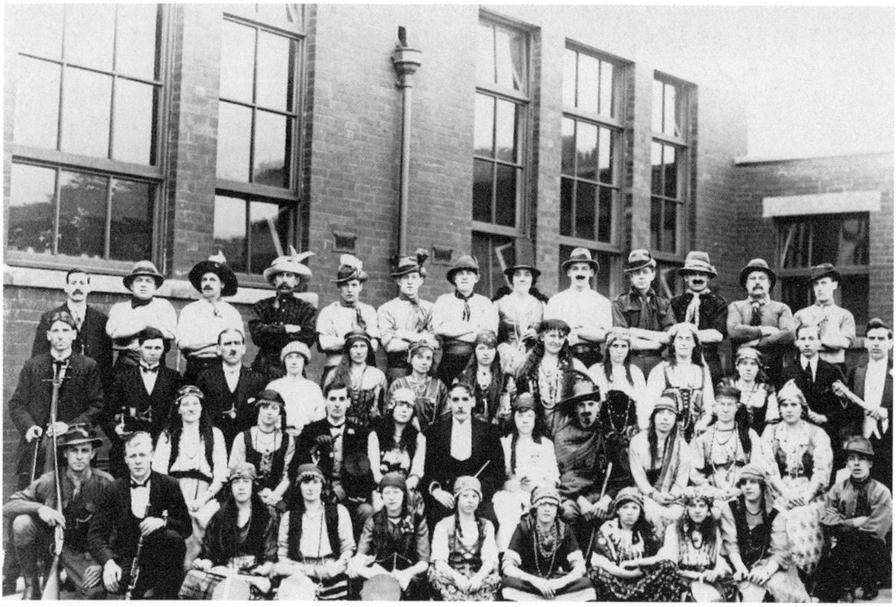

Members of the Dinnington Harmonic Society dressed for their Gypsy Carnival in 1922. [4638]

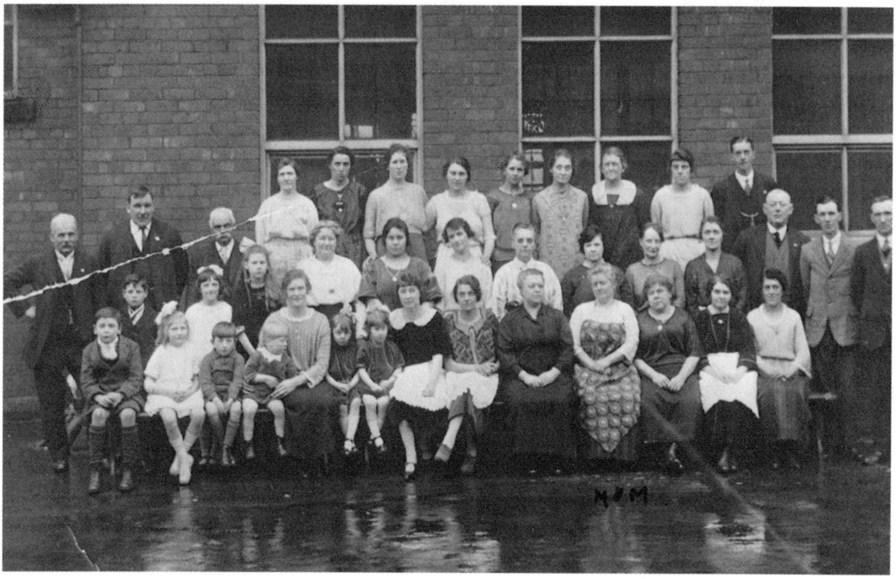

Good Friday Teas were a regular event at Brinsworth in the 1920s. Organised by the wives of ASLEF members based at the Canklow Locomotive Depot, the teas were held at Brinsworth School. [4447]

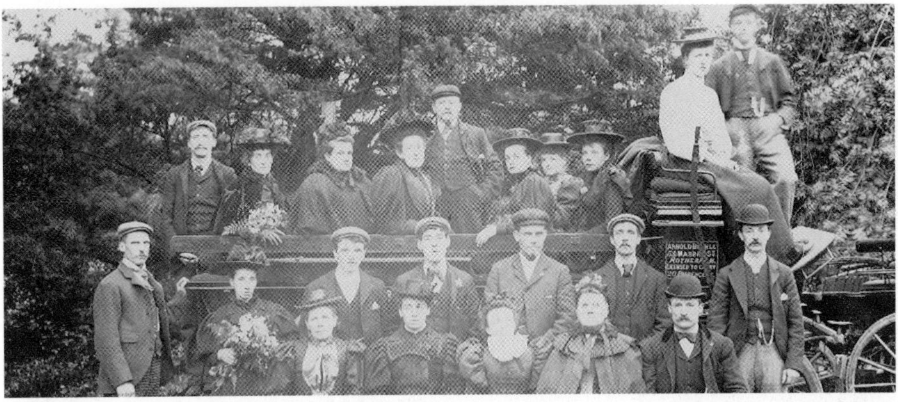

In the days before the internal combustion engine, outings were confined to places that could be reached by railway or horse power. The wagonette owned by Arnold Bunkle, of Masbrough Street, Rotherham, was licensed for 20 passengers, although there are 22 people in this view. The venue is probably Roche Abbey, *c.* 1900. Mr Bunkle himself is standing at the extreme right. [5106]

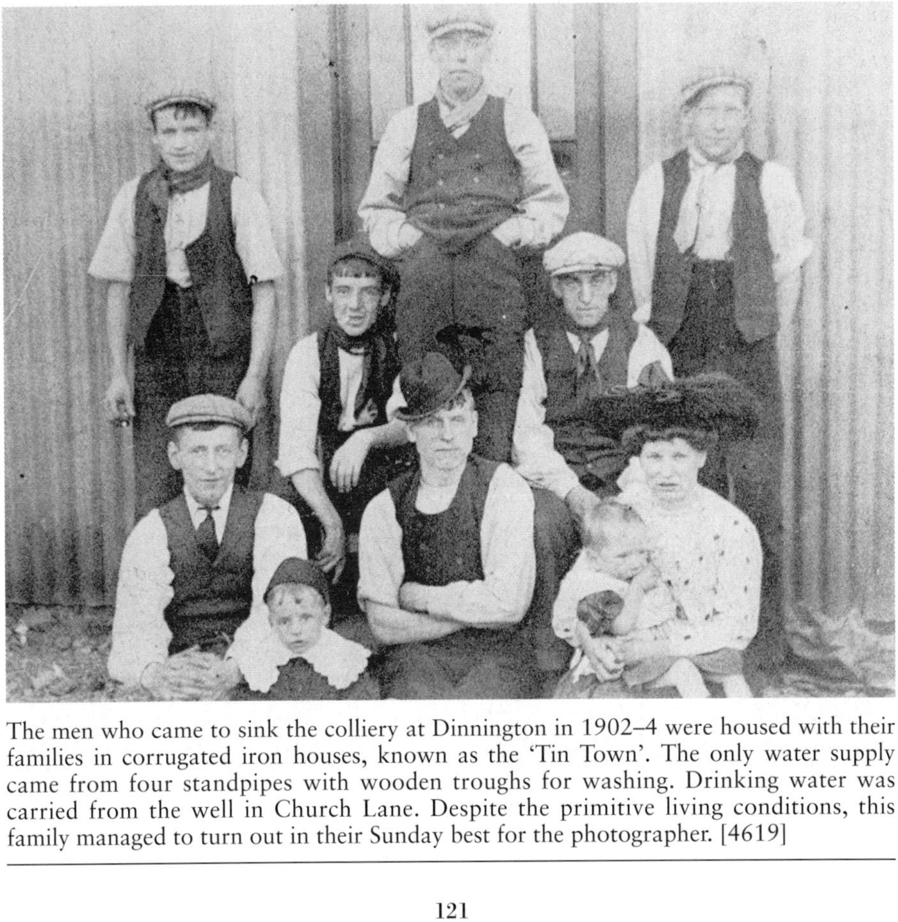

The men who came to sink the colliery at Dinnington in 1902–4 were housed with their families in corrugated iron houses, known as the 'Tin Town'. The only water supply came from four standpipes with wooden troughs for washing. Drinking water was carried from the well in Church Lane. Despite the primitive living conditions, this family managed to turn out in their Sunday best for the photographer. [4619]

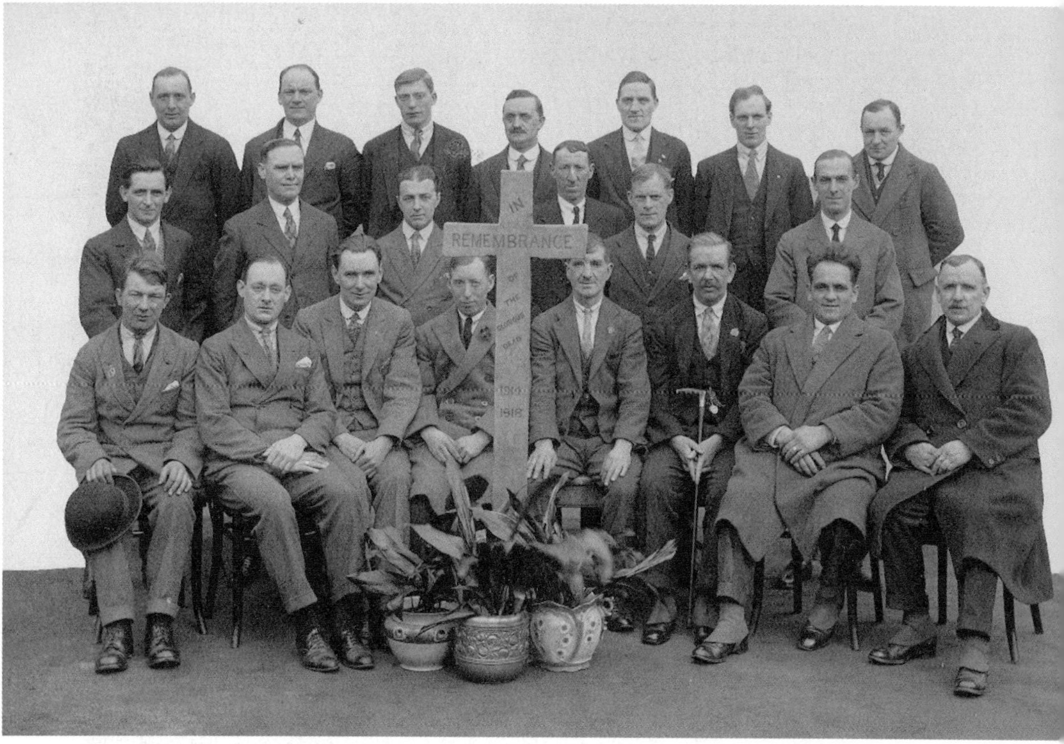

The concrete war memorial cross pictured here was secretly erected overnight near Rawmarsh church in July 1926. The British Legion members who erected it were protesting at the length of time it was taking for an official war memorial to be erected. The War Memorial Committee had identified a site near the Baths, but the official memorial was eventually unveiled in June 1928 on the site of its unofficial predecessor. [8021]

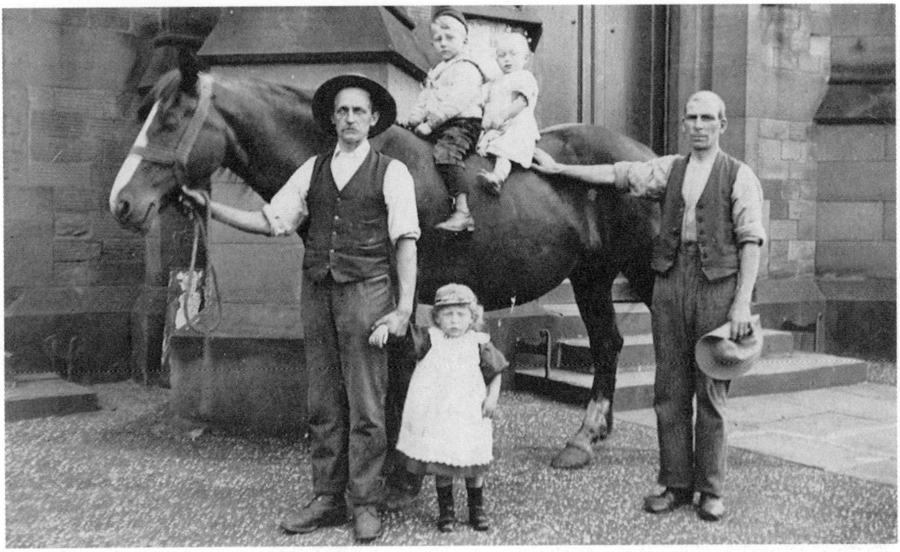

Photographed outside Greasbrough church in 1902, Herbert Smith holds the head of the horse in one hand and his daughter Hilda Mary (later Mrs Stevenson) in the other. His sons George and Herbert are on the horse's back and his brother Fred, verger at the church, brings up the rear. Herbert was the son of George Smith, builder, and died in December 1902, aged 41. [13678]

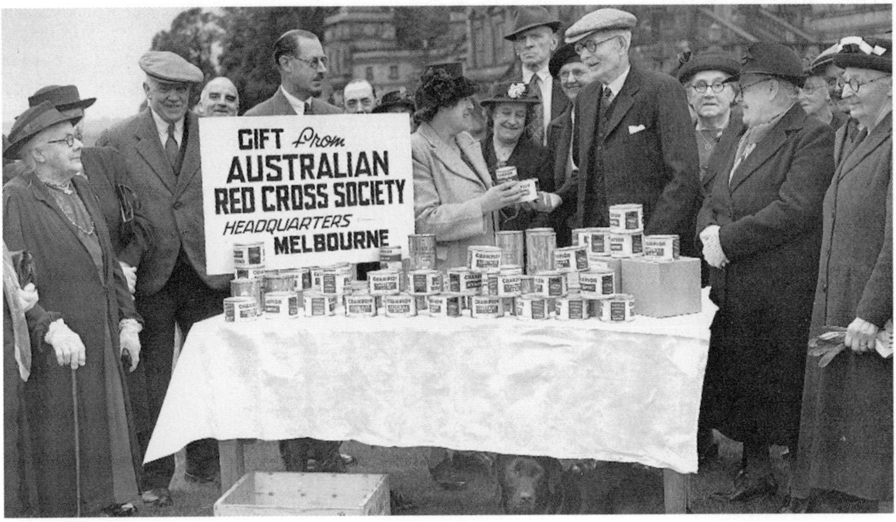

Food rationing remained in force for some time after the Second World War. Several Commonwealth countries, including Australia, sent food to help the mother country. In June 1949 part of a shipment from the Australian Red Cross was distributed to 25 old people at Wentworth. Councillor Mrs Blewitton hands a share to 91-year-old Mr B. Moorhouse of Snowdrop Farm, Wentworth's oldest inhabitant. Col. J.W.B. Landon, agent to Earl Fitzwilliam, stands on her right. [382]

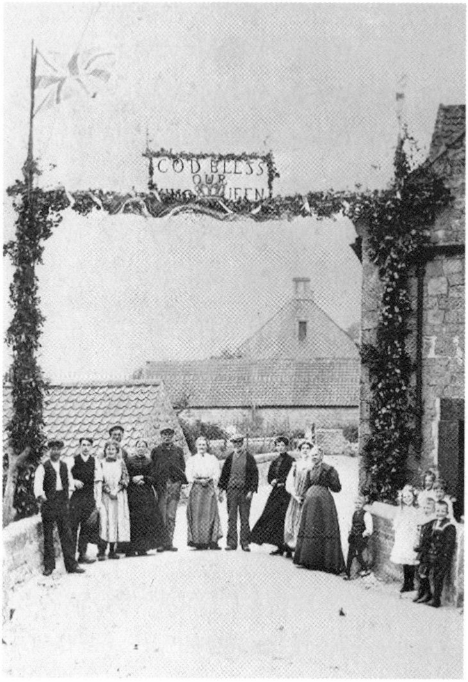

This arch at North Anston was probably erected to celebrate the coronation of George V in 1911. [560]

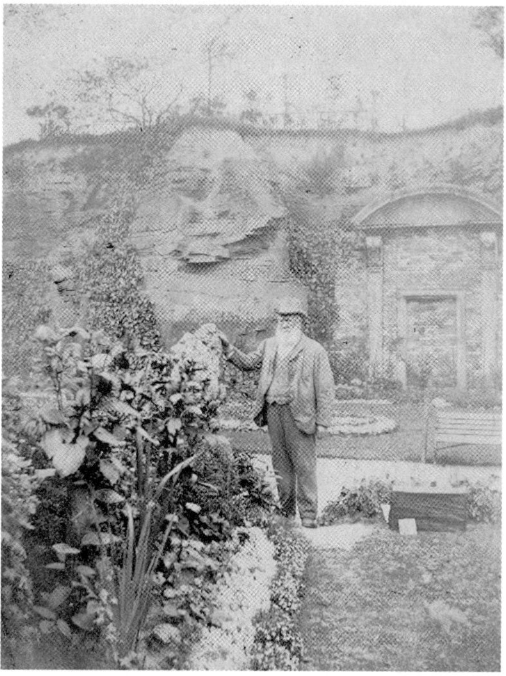

Henry Albiston was the head gardener to Rotherham Corporation and was responsible for laying out Boston Park in 1876 and Clifton Park in 1891. He is seen here in the 1890s with one of his flower beds in Boston Park. [775]

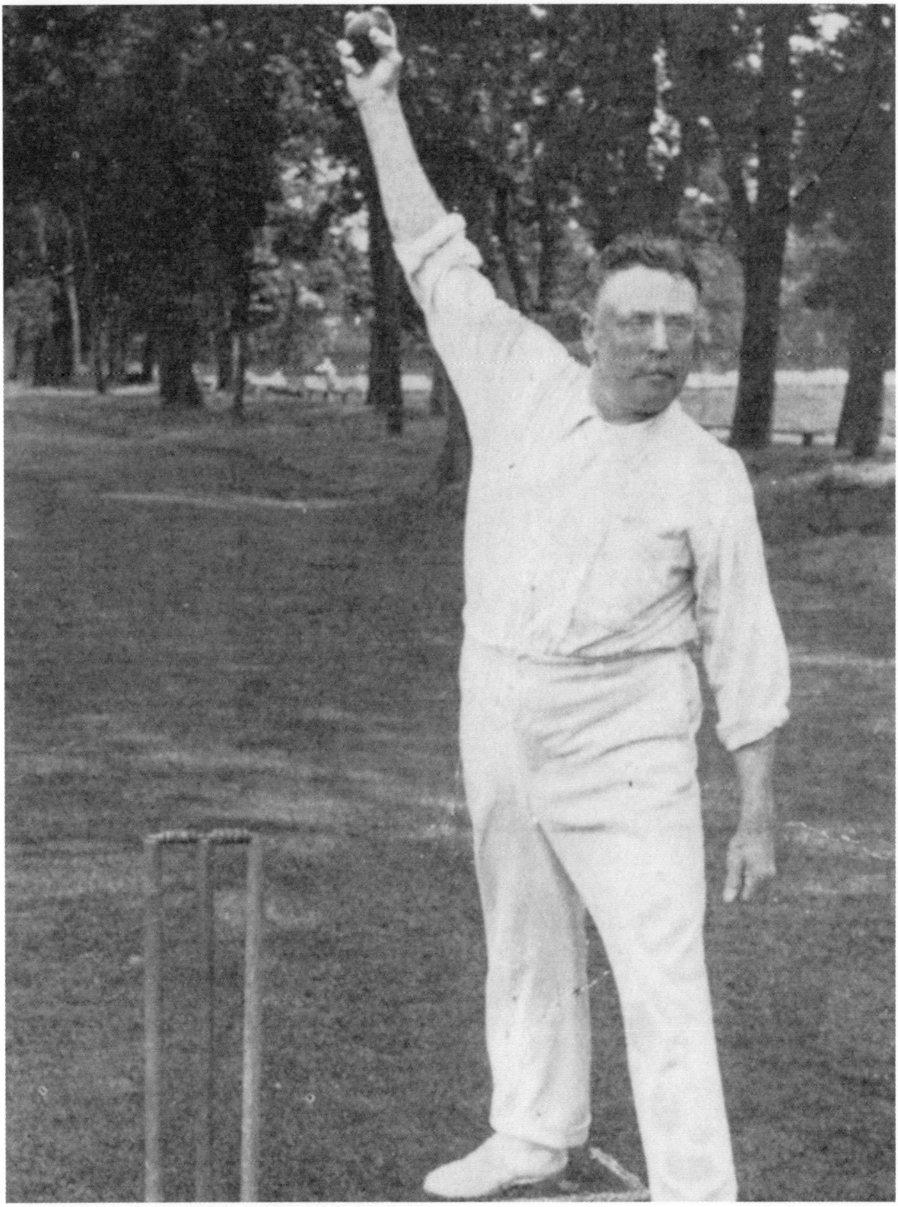

John Thomas Rawlin (1857–1924) was born at Greasbrough. A fast-medium bowler and useful batsman, he played only five games in five years for Yorkshire. A move to Lords in 1887 brought more success. In a ten-year career with Middlesex he twice took eight wickets in an innings against his home county, toured Australia in 1887/8 and played three times for the Players v. the Gentlemen. With the money earned in his benefit year, he built Middlesex House at Greasbrough. His son, Eric R. Rawlin, played for Yorkshire between 1927 and 1936. [921]

Acknowledgements

The photographs that have been used in this book have all been drawn from the Illustrations Collection of the Archives and Local Studies Section of Rotherham Central Library, Walker Place, Rotherham S65 IJH. The collection contains over 15,000 photographs documenting life in all areas of Rotherham Metropolitan Borough from the 1850s to the 1990s. The numbers in square brackets at the end of each caption are the Archives and Local Studies Section's reference numbers.

Thanks are due to the many members of the public, too numerous to mention individually, who have donated original photographs to the Illustrations Collection or have allowed their originals to be copied. Without them this book would not have been possible.

Thanks are also due to the Archives and Local Studies Section staff for their help in identifying and dating many of the photographs.

BRITAIN IN OLD PHOTOGRAPHS

ALDERNEY

Alderney: A Second Selection, *B Bonnard*

BEDFORDSHIRE

Bedfordshire at Work, *N Lutt*

BERKSHIRE

Maidenhead, *M Hayles & D Hedges*
Around Maidenhead, *M Hayles & B Hedges*
Reading, *P Southerton*
Reading: A Second Selection, *P Southerton*
Sandhurst and Crowthorne, *K Dancy*
Around Slough, *J Hunter & K Hunter*
Around Thatcham, *P Allen*
Around Windsor, *B Hedges*

BUCKINGHAMSHIRE

Buckingham and District, *R Cook*
High Wycombe, *R Goodearl*
Around Stony Stratford, *A Lambert*

CHESHIRE

Cheshire Railways, *M Hitches*
Chester, *S Nichols*

CLWYD

Clwyd Railways, *M Hitches*

CLYDESDALE

Clydesdale, *Lesmahagow Parish Historical Association*

CORNWALL

Cornish Coast, *T Bowden*
Falmouth, *P Gilson*
Lower Fal, *P Gilson*
Around Padstow, *M McCarthy*
Around Penzance, *J Holmes*
Penzance and Newlyn, *J Holmes*
Around Truro, *A Lyne*
Upper Fal, *P Gilson*

CUMBERLAND

Cockermouth and District, *J Bernard Bradbury*
Keswick and the Central Lakes, *J Marsh*
Around Penrith, *F Boyd*
Around Whitehaven, *H Fancy*

DERBYSHIRE

Derby, *D Buxton*
Around Matlock, *D Barton*

DEVON

Colyton and Seaton, *T Gosling*
Dawlish and Teignmouth, *G Gosling*
Devon Aerodromes, *K Saunders*
Exeter, *P Thomas*
Exmouth and Budleigh Salterton, *T Gosling*
From Haldon to Mid-Dartmoor, *T Hall*
Honiton and the Otter Valley, *J Yallop*
Around Kingsbridge, *K Tanner*
Around Seaton and Sidmouth, *T Gosling*
Seaton, Axminster and Lyme Regis, *T Gosling*

DORSET

Around Blandford Forum, *B Cox*
Bournemouth, *M Colman*
Bridport and the Bride Valley, *J Burrell & S Humphries*
Dorchester, *T Gosling*
Around Gillingham, *P Crocker*

DURHAM

Darlington, *G Flynn*
Darlington: A Second Selection, *G Flynn*
Durham People, *M Richardson*
Houghton-le-Spring and Hetton-le-Hole, *K Richardson*
Houghton-le-Spring and Hetton-le-Hole: A Second Selection, *K Richardson*
Sunderland, *S Miller & B Bell*
Teesdale, *D Coggins*
Teesdale: A Second Selection, *P Raine*
Weardale, *J Crosby*
Weardale: A Second Selection, *J Crosby*

DYFED

Aberystwyth and North Ceredigion, *Dyfed Cultural Services Dept*
Haverfordwest, *Dyfed Cultural Services Dept*
Upper Tywi Valley, *Dyfed Cultural Services Dept*

ESSEX

Around Grays, *B Evans*

GLOUCESTERSHIRE

Along the Avon from Stratford to Tewkesbury, *J Jeremiah*
Cheltenham: A Second Selection, *R Whiting*
Cheltenham at War, *P Gill*
Cirencester, *J Welsford*
Around Cirencester, *E Cuss & P Griffiths*
Forest, The, *D Mullin*
Gloucester, *J Voyce*
Around Gloucester, *A Sutton*
Gloucester: From the Walwin Collection, *J Voyce*
North Cotswolds, *D Viner*
Severn Vale, *A Sutton*
Stonehouse to Painswick, *A Sutton*
Stroud and the Five Valleys, *S Gardiner & L Padin*
Stroud and the Five Valleys: A Second Selection, *S Gardiner & L Padin*
Stroud's Golden Valley, *S Gardiner & L Padin*
Stroudwater and Thames & Severn Canals, *E Cuss & S Gardiner*
Stroudwater and Thames & Severn Canals: A Second Selection, *E Cuss & S Gardiner*
Tewkesbury and the Vale of Gloucester, *C Hilton*
Thornbury to Berkeley, *J Hudson*
Uley, Dursley and Cam, *A Sutton*
Wotton-under-Edge to Chipping Sodbury, *A Sutton*

GWYNEDD

Anglesey, *M Hitches*
Gwynedd Railways, *M Hitches*
Around Llandudno, *M Hitches*
Vale of Conwy, *M Hitches*

HAMPSHIRE

Gosport, *J Sadden*
Portsmouth, *P Rogers & D Francis*

HEREFORDSHIRE

Herefordshire, *A Sandford*

HERTFORDSHIRE

Barnet, *I Norrie*
Hitchin, *A Fleck*
St Albans, *S Mullins*
Stevenage, *M Appleton*

ISLE OF MAN

The Tourist Trophy, *B Snelling*

ISLE OF WIGHT

Newport, *D Parr*
Around Ryde, *D Parr*

JERSEY

Jersey: A Third Selection, *R Lemprière*

KENT

Bexley, *M Scott*
Broadstairs and St Peter's, *J Whyman*
Bromley, Keston and Hayes, *M Scott*
Canterbury: A Second Selection, *D Butler*
Chatham and Gillingham, *P MacDougall*
Chatham Dockyard, *P MacDougall*
Deal, *J Broady*
Early Broadstairs and St Peter's, *B Wootton*
East Kent at War, *D Collyer*
Eltham, *J Kennett*
Folkestone: A Second Selection, *A Taylor & E Rooney*
Goudhurst to Tenterden, *A Guilmant*
Gravesend, *R Hiscock*
Around Gravesham, *R Hiscock & D Grierson*
Herne Bay, *J Hawkins*
Lympne Airport, *D Collyer*
Maidstone, *I Hales*
Margate, *R Clements*
RAF Hawkinge, *R Humphreys*
RAF Manston, *RAF Manston History Club*
RAF Manston: A Second Selection, *RAF Manston History Club*
Ramsgate and Thanet Life, *D Perkins*
Romney Marsh, *E Carpenter*
Sandwich, *C Wanostrocht*
Around Tonbridge, *C Bell*
Tunbridge Wells, *M Rowlands & I Beavis*
Tunbridge Wells: A Second Selection, *M Rowlands & I Beavis*
Around Whitstable, *C Court*
Wingham, Adisham and Littlebourne, *M Crane*

LANCASHIRE

Around Barrow-in-Furness, *J Garbutt & J Marsh*
Blackpool, *C Rothwell*
Bury, *J Hudson*
Chorley and District, *J Smith*
Fleetwood, *C Rothwell*
Heywood, *J Hudson*
Around Kirkham, *C Rothwell*
Lancashire North of the Sands, *J Garbutt & J Marsh*
Around Lancaster, *S Ashworth*
Lytham St Anne's, *C Rothwell*
North Fylde, *C Rothwell*
Radcliffe, *J Hudson*
Rossendale, *B Moore & N Dunnachie*

LEICESTERSHIRE

Around Ashby-de-la-Zouch, *K Hillier*
Charnwood Forest, *I Keil, W Humphrey & D Wix*
Leicester, *D Burton*
Leicester: A Second Selection, *D Burton*
Melton Mowbray, *T Hickman*
Around Melton Mowbray, *T Hickman*
River Soar, *D Wix, P Shacklock & I Keil*
Rutland, *T Clough*
Vale of Belvoir, *T Hickman*
Around the Welland Valley, *S Mastoris*

LINCOLNSHIRE

Grimsby, *J Tierney*
Around Grimsby, *J Tierney*
Grimsby Docks, *J Tierney*
Lincoln, *D Cuppleditch*

Scunthorpe, *D Taylor*
Skegness, *W Kime*
Around Skegness, *W Kime*

LONDON

Balham and Tooting, *P Loobey*
Crystal Palace, Penge & Anerley, *M Scott*
Greenwich and Woolwich, *K Clark*
Hackney: A Second Selection, *D Mander*
Lewisham and Deptford, *J Coulter*
Lewisham and Deptford: A Second Selection, *J Coulter*
Streatham, *P Loobey*
Around Whetstone and North Finchley, *J Heathfield*
Woolwich, *B Evans*

MONMOUTHSHIRE

Chepstow and the River Wye, *A Rainsbury*
Monmouth and the River Wye, *Monmouth Museum*

NORFOLK

Great Yarmouth, *M Teun*
Norwich, *M Colman*
Wymondham and Attleborough, *P Yaxley*

NORTHAMPTONSHIRE

Around Stony Stratford, *A Lambert*

NOTTINGHAMSHIRE

Arnold and Bestwood, *M Spick*
Arnold and Bestwood: A Second Selection, *M Spick*
Changing Face of Nottingham, *G Oldfield*
Mansfield, *Old Mansfield Society*
Around Newark, *T Warner*
Nottingham: 1944–1974, *D Whitworth*
Sherwood Forest, *D Ottewell*
Victorian Nottingham, *M Payne*

OXFORDSHIRE

Around Abingdon, *P Horn*
Banburyshire, *M Barnett & S Gosling*
Burford, *A Jewell*
Around Didcot and the Hagbournes, *B Lingham*
Garsington, *M Gunther*
Around Henley-on-Thames, *S Ellis*
Oxford: The University, *J Rhodes*
Thame to Watlington, *N Hood*
Around Wallingford, *D Beasley*
Witney, *T Worley*
Around Witney, *C Mitchell*
Witney District, *T Worley*
Around Woodstock, *J Bond*

POWYS

Brecon, *Brecknock Museum*
Welshpool, *E Bredsdorff*

SHROPSHIRE

Shrewsbury, *D Trumper*
Whitchurch to Market Drayton, *M Morris*

SOMERSET

Bath, *J Hudson*
Bridgwater and the River Parrett, *R Fitzhugh*
Bristol, *D Moorcroft & N Campbell-Sharp*
Changing Face of Keynsham,
B Lowe & M Whitehead
Chard and Ilminster, *G Gosling & F Huddy*
Crewkerne and the Ham Stone Villages,
G Gosling & F Huddy
Around Keynsham and Saltford, *B Lowe & T Brown*
Midsomer Norton and Radstock, *C Howell*
Somerton, Ilchester and Langport, *G Gosling & F Huddy*
Taunton, *N Chipchase*
Around Taunton, *N Chipchase*
Wells, *C Howell*
Weston-Super-Mare, *S Poole*
Around Weston-Super-Mare, *S Poole*
West Somerset Villages, *K Houghton & L Thomas*

STAFFORDSHIRE

Aldridge, *J Farrow*
Bilston, *E Rees*
Black Country Transport: Aviation, *A Brew*
Around Burton upon Trent, *G Sowerby & R Farman*
Bushbury, *A Chatwin, M Mills & E Rees*
Around Cannock, *M Mills & S Belcher*
Around Leek, *R Poole*
Lichfield, *H Clayton & K Simmons*
Around Pattingham and Wombourne, *M Griffiths, P Leigh & M Mills*
Around Rugeley, *T Randall & J Anslow*
Smethwick, *J Maddison*
Stafford, *J Anslow & T Randall*
Around Stafford, *J Anslow & T Randall*
Stoke-on-Trent, *I Lawley*
Around Tamworth, *R Sulima*
Around Tettenhall and Codsall, *M Mills*
Tipton, Wednesbury and Darlaston, *R Pearson*
Walsall, *D Gilbert & M Lewis*
Wednesbury, *I Bott*
West Bromwich, *R Pearson*

SUFFOLK

Ipswich: A Second Selection, *D Kindred*
Around Ipswich, *D Kindred*
Around Mildenhall, *C Dring*
Southwold to Aldeburgh, *H Phelps*
Around Woodbridge, *H Phelps*

SURREY

Cheam and Belmont, *P Berry*
Croydon, *S Bligh*
Dorking and District, *K Harding*
Around Dorking, *A Jackson*
Around Epsom, *P Berry*
Farnham: A Second Selection, *J Parratt*
Around Haslemere and Hindhead, *T Winter & G Collyer*
Richmond, *Richmond Local History Society*
Sutton, *P Berry*

SUSSEX

Arundel and the Arun Valley, *J Godfrey*
Bishopstone and Seaford, *P Pople & P Berry*
Brighton and Hove, *J Middleton*
Brighton and Hove: A Second Selection, *J Middleton*
Around Crawley, *M Goldsmith*
Hastings, *P Haines*
Hastings: A Second Selection, *P Haines*
Around Haywards Heath, *J Middleton*
Around Heathfield, *A Gillet & B Russell*
Around Heathfield: A Second Selection,
A Gillet & B Russell
High Weald, *B Harwood*
High Weald: A Second Selection, *B Harwood*
Horsham and District, *T Wales*
Lewes, *J Middleton*
RAF Tangmere, *A Saunders*
Around Rye, *A Dickinson*
Around Worthing, *S White*

WARWICKSHIRE

Along the Avon from Stratford to Tewkesbury, *J Jeremiah*
Bedworth, *J Burton*
Coventry, *D McGrory*
Around Coventry, *D McGrory*
Nuneaton, *S Clews & S Vaughan*
Around Royal Leamington Spa, *J Cameron*
Around Royal Leamington Spa: A Second Selection,
J Cameron
Around Warwick, *R Booth*

WESTMORLAND

Eden Valley, *J Marsh*
Kendal, *M & P Duff*
South Westmorland Villages, *J Marsh*
Westmorland Lakes, *J Marsh*

WILTSHIRE

Around Amesbury, *P Daniels*
Chippenham and Lacock, *A Wilson & M Wilson*
Around Corsham and Box, *A Wilson & M Wilson*
Around Devizes, *D Buxton*
Around Highworth, *G Tanner*
Around Highworth and Faringdon, *G Tanner*
Around Malmesbury, *A Wilson*
Marlborough: A Second Selection, *P Colman*
Around Melksham,
Melksham and District Historical Association
Nadder Valley, *R. Sawyer*
Salisbury, *P Saunders*
Salisbury: A Second Selection, *P Daniels*
Salisbury: A Third Selection, *P Daniels*
Around Salisbury, *P Daniels*
Swindon: A Third Selection, *The Swindon Society*
Swindon: A Fourth Selection, *The Swindon Society*
Trowbridge, *M Marshman*
Around Wilton, *P Daniels*
Around Wootton Bassett, Cricklade and Purton, *T Sharp*

WORCESTERSHIRE

Evesham to Bredon, *F Archer*
Around Malvern, *K Smith*
Around Pershore, *M Dowty*
Redditch and the Needle District, *R Saunders*
Redditch: A Second Selection, *R Saunders*
Around Tenbury Wells, *D Green*
Worcester, *M Dowty*
Around Worcester, *R Jones*
Worcester in a Day, *M Dowty*
Worcestershire at Work, *R Jones*

YORKSHIRE

Huddersfield: A Second Selection, *H Wheeler*
Huddersfield: A Third Selection, *H Wheeler*
Leeds Road and Rail, *R Vickers*
Pontefract, *R van Riel*
Scarborough, *D Coggins*
Scarborough's War Years, *R Percy*
Skipton and the Dales, *Friends of the Craven Museum*
Around Skipton-in-Craven, *Friends of the Craven Museum*
Yorkshire Wolds, *I & M Sumner*